William Anderson Smith

Loch Creran

Notes from the West Highlands

William Anderson Smith

Loch Creran
Notes from the West Highlands

ISBN/EAN: 9783744662017

Printed in Europe, USA, Canada, Australia, Japan

Cover: Foto ©ninafisch / pixelio.de

More available books at **www.hansebooks.com**

LOCH CRERAN.

LOCH CRERAN:

Notes from the West Highlands.

BY

W. ANDERSON SMITH.

ALEXANDER GARDNER,
PAISLEY; AND 12 PATERNOSTER ROW, LONDON.
1887.

PREFACE.

This continuation of Natural History Sketches appeals to kindred lovers of Nature, and especially to the friends and readers of "Benderloch."

Rhugarbh, Ledaig, N.B.,
    Feb., 1887.

LOCH CRERAN.

JUNE, 1881.

THE whole country has been looking so gay of late, in the full blaze of the wonderful sunlight we are blessed with, that on sea and shore alike we have an *embarras de richesses* of beauty, as well as of life and growth. Two men were for hours hard at work endeavouring to clear a small portion of sea-bottom from the abundant growth of marine annuals, and found the task too hard for them even in a long spring tide. Such an enormous growth partially explains the teeming life of the littoral in the summer time. Now is the time when the few in our district with leisure, and love of that un-Scottish fish, skate, can enjoy an hour's skate-spearing when our flat friends come inshore from the deeper waters, to deposit their strange eggs among the tangle in shallow water. Yesterday one man speared seven in a very short time on a small portion of sea bottom. To-day we found the breeze too rough, and the bottom consequently too much obscured to be able to make use of the iron, so we floated rapidly over the tangle fronds, casting unavailing glances into the general breadth of shaded blacks and browns. The whole bottom was completely obscured by a most unusually prolific growth; even a great stretch, that we had flattered ourselves had been made barren of algæ but a month or two ago, showed scarce a yard of bottom.

What harm can mussels do to oysters! indeed. Just come round this way; and we take our incredulous friend to the few hundred molluscs lately thrown from the boat at random on the foreshore. On the gravel, of late, a deposit of young mussels has been rapidly maturing, and upon these the large oysters from deeper water had accidentally been thrown. We lift one after another to find the byssus of the mussel firmly attached, and gradually extending over the shells, which are closed for a time at low water. A very few days and a good few of these strong oysters with powerfully developed muscles would have been most effectually choked by the numerous tenacious cords of the mussel having closed the shell too firmly to permit the "spring" of the oyster to expand and open it. What would they not have done to a bed of small, delicate-shelled oysters in a similar position? It is impossible to estimate the injury done in this way to an oyster bed by a shell fish which grows to a certain maturity with great rapidity. There is a large bank of mussels of a certain size at the mouth of the river Awe that are said to die down every autumn when they reach a certain stage; so that those about an inch or so in length must be but six months old. At this age an oyster is a delicate helpless creature, while these mussels are capable of forming a bank of such a mass, and so tied together, that nothing has a chance upon it but themselves.

The young barnacles already cover every possible vantage ground in countless thousands; shells, wattling, stones—all are alive with the sharp-edged mischiefs. It is interesting to note how the various classes of shells intermingle, the young of one class seating themselves on the backs of another, and the young of the other returning the compliment—all in the most indiscriminate manner. Great masses of ascidians constantly appear in the dredge, as well as the eggs of cuttle fish in groups. Amid a mass of tangle attachments we found an egg of the Rough Hound, which we tossed into the "live" bucket, thinking to keep it and bring it out. On re-examining it we found several young shells on the back of the egg, of an interesting character, and to obtain these we resolved to destroy the egg. Carefully cutting it open, the occupant was found to be fully formed, and placed in water it immediately uncoiled, and showed signs of life. The eyes were shut like a young puppy's, and it continued breathing through its mouth steadily, as if its gills were not sufficient to supply it. Its vitality was low, apparently, so we determined to keep it "in good sperrits," like the Polar potentate, and removed it from the water with this object. It now displayed great energy, and struggled most desperately against the proposed change. The little fish was the picture of the full-grown dog-fish, and the title of *Roussette* was even more strongly applicable to the prettily-spotted youngster than to the various full-grown specimens we have captured.

This week we dissected a number of skate, speared on their spawning ground near at hand. Two of them had just been on the point of depositing their handbarrow-like eggs, whose horns were protruding. Another had an egg in process, the tough coating having been already formed, while all had masses of eggs on each side, scarcely discernible from those of hens ere the shells are formed. It would be interesting to ascertain whether they lay an egg daily, as in the case of fowls, and over what period their spawning time extends? The resemblance of the egg masses to those of domestic fowls, and the regular attendance of the fish every morning at the "cairn" in the sea, surrounded with tangle and comparatively shallow, would lead one to expect a daily egg-laying until the proper quantity was disposed of. These fish were mostly fed upon shell fish. Various hermit crabs, some Porcellanidae, one or two gapers or Myae, and a good many cockles seemed to comprise the greater portion of their contents. That they should have been able to withdraw the well-sunk shells of the gapers from their secure position in the clay of the loch's bottom, we did not expect; but the strong syphon tube of this shellfish is frequently well protruded, and what is stiff soil at low water is no doubt a much softer material when covered by the sea. At anyrate, shell-fish was the main dish at their feast. Nor did we see a fragment of fish proper in the stomachs of any of them.

The tide was low, and we were out at the utmost verge with our assistants, busily engaged, when one of them pointed to the "fish ripple" on the surface of the advancing tide, and declared the shoal to be one of young herring about seven inches long. This appeared to us unlikely, so as we had been walking in well over our knickerbockers after flounders, we turned stork or heron for the nonce, and walking into the sea stood stock still for some time, until the sea should bring its living burden towards us. Long we watched, and watched in vain; for although the creatures occasionally played near by, and appeared of small dimensions, we could not get a proper glance to say positively they were *not* herring. At length, when the water had crept further up our limbs than we had calculated, a splash and ripple behind us told of a portion of the shoal having passed. Carefully changing front, we "herded" the shoal towards the shore, and managed to direct them towards a stream that enters the little bay, and whose waters were now sufficiently brackish before the rising tide. Everything had gone gaily hitherto, and a fine shoal of many hundred fish had been ushered into a manageable position; but on shouting for our assistant on shore to bring a hand net, our instructions were misunderstood by the Gaelic-speaking individual addressed, and only a "graip" was the result of a prolonged absence at our boat-house. But no time was to be lost in a second visit, and with a rush we drove a miserable fragment of the shoal into a corner, and captured them with our hands. There they darted about in the little water courses like flashes of living silver, and as they came out of the water and glanced in the sunlight, we thought no more beautiful creatures ever danced over the land or through the water. Alas for the eventualities to which investigation is subject! The delicate beauties were sent to the cottage, where they reached the kitchen, and, before a specimen could be secured for more careful examination, they were actually all "gutted" by our extra-careful domestic! They proved to be sand smelts (*atherina*).

From some fathoms we bring up the spawn of the various nudibranchs, with almost all the inhabitants of the littoral, too, represented, although these are commonly deposited and matured in shallow water. The dredge in some localities comes up actually over-weighted with great pudding-looking ascidians, that must be spread thickly over the bottom of the sea. To the more tough-skinned of these many young of various creatures, oysters, serpulæ, barnacles, and various zoophytes are found affixed, and everything seems to be a parasite on everything else. It is quite remarkable how often crabs of the less active class—such as the long-legged spider-crabs—are found quite covered with a growth of sponge, not only impeding their movements, but gradually eating into their flesh. The old-fashioned belief in the good health of wild animals of all kinds will not stand the light of inquiry. Scarce a skate-fish but has a parasitic worm near the edge of its mouth, safely housed out of reach of the unwilling owner.

On shore the sound of guns in continuous rapid succession tells of a different class of sport to what we are commonly accustomed in a country where our grouse demand a good wholesome tramp. Only the determination to have rook pies, and plenty of them, and the necessity, for the peace of the dwelling as well as the satisfaction of the neighbourhood, to make a clearance among the congregation of blackcoats discussing a case of heresy in high quarters, could account for such objects of slaughter. For a week past disconsolate youngsters, who have failed in their first examination, and tumbled to the foot of the tree in place of flapping among the branches, have been observable day by day. Beautiful creatures they are, too, and not unequal to using their beaks with severity. The farmers, however, find rooks just too plentiful, and so a riddance is made at the only time when a rook is considered a desirable adjunct to our cuisine. Properly to make a rook pie, the breasts alone of the youngsters should be used, and these should be steeped in milk previously, in order to remove the strong taste of the natural bird. To our mind they should be skinned, not plucked.

As we wander down the avenue under the noble beeches, and look up at the rookery and its occupants, a strange effect is produced by the young beech leaves. Each one of these, although but lately introduced into the wooded world, is perforated by numberless minute holes, evidently having already paid the penalty of being young and tender, like the rooks about them, and been perforated by some leaf-eating insect. In vain we search them with our lens, however, as all we note is the brown edging of the perforations, probably the result of dead tissues, as in the autumnal tints. When we note that scores of magnificent trees were thus perforated as to the leaves, and each leaf drilled with numerous holes, the sudden influx of enemies must have been very great. We fear those trees thus attacked will not carry their foliage far through the summer. The horse chestnuts are this year the finest objects in the woods. Not only for number but for individual excellence the flowers are notable, as they crowd the trees to the topmost boughs. But why speak of one tree when every tree and bush is this season hanging with bloom. The white thorns are hiding leaves and wood alike; the holly, that last year was almost barren, is now strewing the pathways with its delicate white stars in myriads; the rowan is over-weighted with blossom, and must be actually crushed with fruit should it come to maturity. Even the perforated beeches are hanging rich with blossom, and never saw I promise yet of such a coming fruit season.

Now, we might look for that nest for a week without seeing it; and yet, now that we know it, our eyes can scarcely be kept from it, and it seems an absolute impossibility that we could have passed it day by day, only one yard off the public highway, fully open and exposed, and only trusting to the strange peculiarity of colouring on the eggs. Beautifully mottled and blotched, and of fair size, yet the eye fails to observe them amid the half-dry herbage. Why such a careful and shy bird as the sandpiper should have been induced to select a location within a yard of a frequented road, and place its nest and eggs not under a tuft or overshadowed, but open and exposed, seems unaccountable, except on the supposition that it has been successful in a similar situation before. "A bird has a nest every year in that fork!" says a voice; "there are birds in it already this year;" so to the bifurcated tree we turn, to find, where the two stems part company, a deep cleft about four feet from the ground. Peering in, we find the birds have flown, leaving nothing behind but an addled egg; so that once again the shrewd selection of this location has successfully introduced another brood to a world that admires and protects successful shrewdness. The egg looked like that of the blue-tit, a bird smart enough for anything, but the original colouring had not been improved by the domestic arrangements of the little family.

We have had very hard frost of nights, and now there is wailing in Benderloch, for although most of our fruits are now sufficiently advanced to resist any such truculent assault in June, yet the potatoes have caught it most assuredly. "Half the potato crop gone," says one lugubriously, but we know this is most likely a great exaggeration, as the wind was blowing smartly in the mornings, and blew the frost off the leaves ere the sun got strong. We understand that in sheltered quarters the plants caught it, however, and a neighbour, who had a number of shaws among his well-brairded grain, where they were protected from the wind, found them all black, while those in the drills close by escaped.

Traversing the wood on a still day, we lately met quite

a large flight of downs, sailing along at all elevations and with considerable speed, shewing there must have been a current of air imperceptible to the senses. They were the plumed seeds of the dandelion emigrating to new locations, where they would have more elbow-room than among their parents. A most determined plant is the dandelion, and gardeners especially wage unequal war with it. Yet the plant is one that is appreciated for its virtues, not only by the schoolboy, who collects it for his tame rabbits, but by more important members of the community. Were it not that it grows so well and universally, and is so readily obtainable, no doubt it would be more highly valued as a table vegetable than it is with us. The leaves make capital *greens* when young and fresh. Then, how many now-a-days drink dandelion coffee without appreciating the fact that they may as well make it as buy it. A friend has recently informed us that he finds the home-made article somewhat more bitter, but certainly more useful, than the purchased. All that is required is to dry the roots and grind them up, when the infusion becomes a beverage that is pleasing to many, and of great service to that section of our animal economy of which so little is yet known—the liver. We should like to know more about the liver, and would advise any medical student, who takes up the subject for the benefit of the multitude generally, and returned Indians especially, to go in the first instance where they can get plenty of sound livers to examine! Why are the sharks, the rays, and the gadidæ all so well provided with oil-filled livers? The vast importance of the liver apparently in those fishes, where they occupy such a large proportion of their "room," and monopolise so much of their fighting weight, is a useful subject for consideration and analogical examination.

Frequently, too, they are diseased, for it is an old-fashioned idea to suppose that wild animals, and fish especially, are free from the ills that flesh is heir to. Many hundreds of livers have we seen in various states of disease, and skates have been found floating on the surface of the water in such a condition from over-production of oily liver that they could not descend, from the floating power of the *buoy* they had been cursed with.

We were walking down to the gate with a friend when a fine, bold-looking bird, with a splendid flight, a forked-tail of swallow-like proportions, and a general hawk-like look about the head and eye, sailed past us within a very few yards and disappeared. It was quite unfamiliar to us, and proved to be our first close introduction to Richardson's skua (*Lestris Richardsonii*), the sea hawk, of which and its congenors we hear so many tales. This predatory gull is a very handsome bird, with a fine carriage, and nothing of the sneak in his appearance at any rate. We are given to understand that one or two have been shot in this district in recent times; but it is not a common bird by any means anywhere, although more abundant in the northern portion of the kingdom.

She did it quite coolly and with pre-arranged dexterity; that at least was perfectly apparent! Given a wire fence with too few wires, a well-cropped field on the one side and a well-grown crop on the other, and the necessary stimulus to intelligence and exertion was supplied. So the cow deliberately walked up to the fence, and went through it like a human being. First she slipped her head neatly between the two wires, then she got her fore legs over, and drew her hind legs one by one after her, all in the most systematic manner. There were a lot of companions with her, but not one followed or attempted to follow her. She was alone in her successful foray. We were much struck with this fact, as the animal in all likelihood had observed and imitated some human being thus crossing the fence; and it is remarkable that so very frequently one animal alone of a group develops, or owns, an intelligence so much superior to its class or companions. We appreciated and enjoyed the story of the farmer at the trial of hunters, who scornfully declared to the owner of a horse that "he had a coo that wad jump better." He freely offered to bet on his "coo," and was most anxious for a friend to take charge of the "twenty" he was open to back her for. "Hud yer tongue," observed a friend quietly, "hoo wull ye git yer coo to jump?" With a quiet nudge of his elbow and a knowing wink, he whispered, "putt her on the wrang side o' a field o' neeps." He had evidently had his trials with that cow ere he discovered and acknowledged her powers!

The alder trees all over the country here are covered with a white blight, similar to the one that attacked the larch trees last season. In this case, no doubt from the character of the food, the insect seems to be a much larger creature that emerges from amid the white fluff at the roots of the leaves. The larches seem to be free this year as yet, but we have seen that both the beech and the alder have their turn of supporting an insect plague. The whole appearance of these trees is affected by the myriads of creatures whose cottony surrounding whitens the foliage.

An enthusiastic neighbour recently went over the face of the Falcon's Cliff on the Black Island, and abstracted from the peregrine's nest three young birds. One was killed in the ascent, but the other two are thriving vigorously. On the same occasion a nest of sheldrake's eggs, near hatching, were obtained, and the question of how to keep them warm until the young men reached home was cleverly solved by setting the young falcons on them. In this way the eggs were successfully carried, and next day the young sheldrakes made their appearance. As this splendid duck readily accommodates itself to domestication, no doubt they will prove a handsome addition to the surroundings of the mansion house. The peregrine falcon has built upon the same cliff from time immemorial, and we question if ever its nest was robbed in a similar manner. A boat's anchor and chain were carried to the top of the cliff, and the anchor having been made secure, the chain was thrown over the rock, and down this the ingenious robbers descended to a point of vantage. We have seen the parent falcons frequenting the neighbouring shores in an unsettled condition since, and we suspect they are fixing upon another site for a home on the mainland, where a fine cliff presents some distinct advantage, although nearer a multitude of enemies than the late location.

We are actually being dried up, a very remarkable circumstance in our showery west, and water is by no means readily obtainable even by the wandering poultry. We lately observed a cow making most intelligent efforts to reach the water at the bottom of a covered well; this she had uncovered, but whether she was ultimately successful in her quest we could not wait to see. A duck was standing on the stone edge of a rivulet, out of which it was drinking the water quite nine inches below it. The manner in which the bird balanced itself on the edge of the stone, while it reached down for a billful of water, swinging back, throwing up its head, and letting it trickle down its throat, was most amusing. A duck is a heavy bird at the best, and its legs are set so far back that the whole weight is in front, and how it could support its "too, too solid flesh," hanging thus head downward, was difficult to conceive. Its feet must be much more muscular than at first sight appears. We never saw even an awkward duck in a more awkward position.

Year after year at a certain time come to our ears the monotonous sound of the cuckoo's note, and immediately thereafter follows the almost equally monotonous story of its eggs and its ways, with numberless disquisitions thereanent. Two years ago we noted the presence of a young cuckoo in a nest near at hand, that had managed to oust its foster brethren in orthodox fashion, and reigned supreme. We were very near permitting a similar murderous proceeding on our other side, but determined in place thereof to purloin the egg of the marauder. The last egg of a cuckoo we purloined was from the nest of a hedge-sparrow, where it is not so strange that a cuckoo could deposit it; but in this instance the egg was in the nest of a tit-lark or meadow pipit (*anthus pratensis*)—which is not properly a lark, but a pipit— and how the cuckoo could deposit it there *naturally* we could not conceive. The nest was most skilfully concealed in a small cavity under a piece of bank on the hill, most thoroughly protected from any ordinary eye, and with such a small entrance that we do not believe a cuckoo could have laid it there. The egg is very little larger than that of the meadow pipit, and little different in shade, so we took two of the pipit's five eggs and the one of the cuckoo, to show the proper appearance thereof as it lay in its place among the others. But we did not quite anticipate the result. After blowing one of the pipit's eggs so as to ascertain the condition of the rest, we found it considerably advanced; and, consequently turned to the egg of the cuckoo with great care, so as to secure it uninjured. This was more than we managed, from a most unexpected cause. *The young bird was much more completely formed in the egg of the cuckoo than in that of the pipit*, and the result was somewhat disastrous. Is the young bird really more rapidly matured in the egg of the cuckoo than in that of the pipit? Does it hatch sooner, or remain longer inside in a mature state, gaining strength for the coming attack on its foster brethren? We cannot answer these questions; all we know is that the two eggs of the tit-lark were much less mature than that of the cuckoo, and to all appearance would be longer of hatching. We should be glad to learn if any one has made a similar observation, or if the young cuckoo has been observed at any time to be hatched before the other occupants of the nest? There is so much that is strange in this bird that we should not be at all surprised to find that it matures in the egg more rapidly, so as to be more certainly a match for its co-occupants. Our discovery of the advanced condition of the cuckoo's egg was based on no previous theory, but a sudden and unexpected surprise. We have no doubt the cuckoo deposited the egg in this pipit's nest with its bill, as they are said to do, otherwise we cannot conceive how it got there.

JULY, 1881.

We have had broken, uncertain weather, but suddenly yesterday the roads were converted into streams, the streams into torrents, and every trickling hill runlet into bounding cascades. The wind shifted from quarter to quarter, and "herded" the clouds between Ben Breck and Ben Lora, until we had got the full benefit of the storm. The very fields were in streams, and many a grey mare's tail hung from the faces of the hills, until the enormous rainfall had got somewhat away. What a funny figure you cut, my young friend, with your best bonnet as a bustle under your ulster, and a Tam o' Shanter replacing it above your black eyes, as Dugald good-naturedly carried you on his sturdy shoulders across the pond made by the flooded stream, whose waters were racing across his potato field and through his growing oats in a dozen abounding streams! We had our laugh notwithstanding, and you were not so wholly taken up with your soaking feet and bedraggled petticoats that you could not enjoy the gay sides of Ben Lora, with the white spirits of Ossian fleeting through the green. How could any one anticipate or make preparation for such a six hours' visitation, unless he had seen the genius of the rain working under pressure? We sympathised with the stranger who came to a hilly region in the north and commenced bridging the streams across the road on his new lands. An old native passing by remarked quietly, "Wait till the inspector comes 'roond," and, shaking his head doubtfully, passed on. No inspector came, however, and month after month passed away, and all seemed well. At last a night of rain, such as yestereven, came upon them, and in the early morning a knock at the door, when answered, revealed the old man, who simply said, "The inspector's been roond," and passed on once more. On proceeding along the road, across which the streams were running little beyond their normal volume, the new proprietor found that the inspector from the hills had strewn his bridges among the neighbouring fields, the work not having been to his mind! It is scarcely credible the rapidity with which the streams swell with us; and the deep descents having hurled the drops from their dripping faces, with one sudden movement apparently, return at once to their customary tranquil, jog-trot existence. In a couple of hours an impassible torrent was a moderate stream.

A few years ago the sea-swallows fixed upon the little half-islet in front of the cottages as a suitable place for nesting, and built their nests as usual just beyond high water of the big March spring-tides. It so happened that two years in succession the July tides were higher, and on account of heavy gales more destructive, than usual, and overpassed the March marks, so that the nests were unhappily overwhelmed. There was room for them somewhat higher up on the islet, but the beautiful birds seem to have decided that the locality was unlucky, and so we this year miss entirely their graceful forms from the view in front. They did not return for several years. They nest on one particular islet at the entrance to our loch, and on the islets on Loch Etive.

The question we have raised as to the cuckoo, seems to us a very interesting one, and deserving of a little more attention; so we will state the problem more definitely in order that the subject be investigated by other observers. A few days ago we had another cuckoo's egg brought us by a young friend and dexterous bird-nester, who had taken it from the nest of a skylark, in which were three eggs of the owner. This egg proved to be quite fresh, and the chances are that it would be hatched along with the eggs of the lark, and the youngster would be obliged to thrust his companions out. In the case of the egg formerly noted, the cuckoo would have been hatched first, and would then have tumbled the eggs of the titlark out of the nest to make room for itself, thus explaining the many instances in which the eggs of the owners of nests in which young cuckoos are found lie about the nest outside. It has been stated, seemingly, that the cuckoo has the power of carrying its eggs in its body for some days, until a favourable opportunity occurs to drop them into a secure resting place, so that it might be partially vivified before being deposited, and thus explain its forward state compared with the foster-parent's own. The point to be settled is, whether this has been done, or whether it really matures more rapidly than other small birds? The former supposition seems the more probable, seeing that the young cuckoo has to be prepared, and is really found prepared, for either emergency. Thus it can either jostle out the foster-brethren, or throw out the unhatched eggs —unless this latter proceeding is the work of the parent cuckoo when it finds its egg near the point of hatching, an unlikely event, as the foster parents would not submit to this, unless the young "giant" were there to monopolise their affection and attention.

We were plodding along in the steady downfall, endeavouring to draw amusement from the sloppy surroundings, and, seeing we were in for a thorough soaking, seeking to make the best of it. As we arrived at the long road across the moss the path became a series of rivulets crossing and intersecting the road in all directions. Suddenly we found ourselves making awkward movements to avoid stamping on living creatures, all ready to escape from us if they could, but so numerous we really could scarcely allow them to escape. Some distance was covered ere we could really realise the fact that the whole road was alive with young frogs, so very minute that they could only have divested themselves of their tadpole tails that very day, and yet in active multitudes. They had started apparently on their first terrestrial excursion, and had taken advantage of the aqueous condition of the road to break the transition from the one element to the other, and not put too heavy a strain all at once on their breathing apparatus. We do not recollect seeing such a multitude so very minute; and well for them that the feathered tribes had all been forced to take shelter, else, had they been caught in such an unprotected position, few would have lived to tell the story of their first experience "on the road." What a joy they would have proved to our ducklings had they been within range!

"Donald has been at his drains, and cleared out the one that leads into the sea at the little bay," we say, as we traverse the boggy land. On reaching it we prepared to help our companion across, and, standing astride of the cutting, are perforce obliged to look down at the clear running runlet beneath us. What is that ascending the drain, with the motion of a butter fish, and something of the appearance? At first we supposed it to be an eel, then that a gunnel fish had been making an effort to acclimatise itself and had entered the fresh water stream. But the prompt glance of our lady companion settled the question, and she at once declared it to be a leech. Now, we have seen scores of leeches in a small, sluggish burn, but, strange to say, we had never before seen a leech on the way up or down a running water, so that it was with much interest we possessed ourselves of a creature that has suffered sadly from the progress of medical science, and is going into limbo with Dr. Sangrado. Not that our capture was a black leech—it was only a goodly specimen of the horse-leech—dark brown, with dark black bands or markings up the back. We had never heard before of a horse-leech in the district; but here it gave unmistakable evidence of its activity. Strange, we had always seen them curled up in the ungainly position of a slug, and never by any chance had we noticed them on the move, as we had found our prisoner. Placed in a dish in the window, in water, we forgot it, and set about our ordinary avocations, determined to seek a leisure hour in which to be better acquainted with its habits. It at first affixed itself with its broad foot to the bottom of the dish, and then scoured around for food of any description. In this it was unsuccessful, as the water was pure and its armed mouth under "government control." The amount of attention bestowed upon a matter of that character is not always in unison with the real necessities of the case; so Mr. Leech, whose relatives had long been such aristocratic individuals, determined to set about a tour of exploration for the purpose of supplying its outrageous appetite.

Where is the leech? suddenly became the cry, as the chance of its escape suggested itself. The chances were in favour of its having attached itself to some stationery limb, or sought out such at any rate; but a diligent examination soon disclosed the sluggish-looking creature under our feet beneath the table. Leeches not uncommonly set out from a pond or ditch, and traverse some distance in search of insects, not always a profitable journey, as in the raid of our capture across the carpet. But the adventures of the poor creature were not yet over, as some one with a dim recollection of the ways of our youth, covered the jelly can with flannel, without any idea whatever of the necessary perforations, through which the water could be aerated. The result in the morning was a dead leech, whose teeth remained unexamined, and whose life had fallen a sacrifice to ignorance and want of care.

William led the way to a little door with a quiet smile the other day, and we followed and entered into the small apartment, without any idea of our friends' object. Not until we entered the little place did we appreciate the occupants. For, squatting on a small bundle of straw in a corner, was a splendid specimen of a young golden eagle, little more than a month old, and yet with the making of a magnificent bird. Near by on a hamper, and within the same, three young hawks were disporting themselves, and seeking to act as if that point of the world, at least, was theirs to do what they liked with. One of the three had wandered in its youthful egotism into the immediate proximity of the eagle, only to have one great foot extended, which catching the bold youngster in its grasp, soon drew a quantity of blood from its torn side and wing. The great stretch of wing, while the fluff had not yet disappeared from the plumage of the eagle, the huge and evidently prematurely completed foot, and its asserting its claim to lord it over all minor birds of prey, were noticeable features. The bird was taken from the face of a cliff in Kingairloch, by a young man who went over the edge of the cliff for some 16 feet—one of the eaglets falling out of the nest and perishing on the rocks below. Six lambs had at least been consumed, as the legs of that number were found, along with half a hare, in the nest, so it was easy to understand that while the gamekeeper was desirous of encouraging the noble birds, the farmer was quite as anxious to have the nest destroyed. A thrill of pleasure passed through us as we all looked at the beautiful young giant among birds, and king of the grouse lands, and willingly would we have taken it with us but for the feeding part of the programme, no slight consideration. So we were content perforce to have one of the kestrils, and our hands have been quite sore with the onslaughts it has made upon them both with teeth and claws. The latter are the most amusing parts to watch, as the most instinctive movement in the bird is that of endeavouring to clutch at everything in the way, and strike with fearless determination at any supposed antagonist. This action is most powerfully characteristic, and in such a young creature is most amusing. It has no idea of fear whatever, and very little intelligence apparently, as it does not normally distinguish between friend and antagonist, nor even between those actions that are kindly and those that are questionable.

We were amused with the gambols of a seal on our way to Appin, as if it had a leaf of tangle in its mouth, with which it apparently enjoyed itself gambolling recklessly around. The people in the vicinity declare this to be no unusual action with him, and that he frequently comes up when in a rollicking mood and disports himself thus, tangle in teeth?

The sheldrakes, recently hatched and apparently doing well, were set upon a few days after their advent by two tame gulls, with their strong beaks, and the whole lot killed.

Later we heard strange tales of his Royal Highness, and desire to know the truth. So we turn the key of the door softly, and enter with our companion. There the kingly prisoner lay on his bundle of straw, or rather half crouched with his back towards us, as he turned his head lazily, and gave the feeble childish cry that is all that emanates from the tribe. He stretches his wings helplessly as if to deprecate handling, for does not the lady who claims his majesty's allegiance draw them out to exhibit their splendid proportions, as if the golden eagle were a pet turkey fattening for Christmas! His demeanour is simply careless and indifferent, and the attitude not noble, so we muster courage to demand an account of his late gay and lively comrades in captivity, the two young kestrels from his own native Kingairloch cliffs. What answer can he give, indeed?—are not the wing feathers all that remain of the bonny birds that have gone to build up the frame of this King of the Cannibal Islands. No doubt as "falcons" they approached and claimed kinship, and showed a clear record of a life of rapine and reiving on the part of their ancestors to the flood; but although "corbies will no' pick out corbies' een," a golden eagle in captivity, in place of sympathising with his associates, has not hesitated to devour a brace of kestrels, with rabbit lying alongside!

Well for you, my little beauty, that we removed you from the claws of the spoiler, or you would doubtless have shared the fate of your brothers. Our kestrel is becoming an interesting pet, and no longer attacks those it knows with beak and claw. With a little coaxing it will step upon our hand, and loves to be talked to and taken notice of. We removed it from the kitchen, where it had free quarters, to a roomy cage against the wall outside; but it did not get sufficient company there, and pined sadly, so it had to be taken in again by the sympathetic servant girl, who has taken a strange fancy for the bold handsome bird, and with whom it is much more familiar than with anyone else. The peculiar telescopic movement, up and down, of the head, seems an instinctive action when it is very watchful; but when quite at rest the head is sunk down upon the bosom as in other birds.

The peregrine falcons recently captured in the vicinity were balls of fluff when first secured, but are now very handsome birds in fine plumage—male and female—the latter much the larger, as is commonly the case among the raptores. They have not been sufficiently familiarised with their owners, however, and are not interesting pets in consequence; while their continual "squeaking" is enough to split one's head. The worst of the raptores, when thus kept in confinement, is the strong and disagreeable effluvia they emit.

We were recently amusing ourselves watching the small black-headed gulls following the steamer in Loch Linnhe, only less interesting and graceful than the sea-swallows. One single herring-gull appeared among them; but had not long been engaged in the same avocation of diving behind the steamer, when it became enraged at one of the blackheads, and followed it with great pertinacity across and across the loch, the smaller bird escaping by constantly "jinking" its pursuer as it pounced upon it. The other blackheads meantime continued careless and unobservant, but at length one of them seemed to consider the "persecuting" stage had been reached, and set off full flight to help the pursued. This it did just as a school boy would, by running across and across the course of a bully chasing a little boy, the larger bird continuing most pertinaciously until the steady persistence of the new comer forced it to desist most unwillingly. It must have been extremely aggravated at the bird it first followed, as it never made the smallest effort to touch the interloper. Probably the little miscreant had removed, by greater quickness, a titbit it had marked for its own.

Passing the poet's garden we learned of a nest and eggs of a character not well known in the district. Through the rustic gates and along the strawberry beds, now richly furnished, and aggravatingly extensive for the most strong-minded to traverse, we pass, until at length, amid the heavily-laden gooseberry bushes, we come to a halt. Upon one of these, a foot from the ground, the nest is placed, made of dried grass and with fine greenish speckled eggs, most of the marking being in a circle at the larger end. Our first instinct is to say a "nettle creeper," from our boyish recollections; but the eggs are not quite the same. The description of the bird is that of a whitethroat, however, and such we have ourselves seen about the neighbourhood. On more careful consideration, we find it is the nest of the lesser whitethroat (*Curruca Sylviella*), the nest of which resembles that of *C. Cinerea* in being made of hay or very dry grass, from which we understand it derives its name of haychat, under which it is known in some southern counties. The eggs in this nest are quite cold and clearly deserted, and as another similar has been built near by, from which a brood was safely hatched, we all conclude the same pair had removed thither—a predacious cat that had haunted this corner having alarmed the parental breast. The sympathetic gardener evidently has considerable misgivings as we remove the deserted nest and eggs, but had he seen us endeavouring to preserve the said eggs next morning he would have felt amply satisfied. Not only were the eggs full of young birds, but they were rotten into the bargain, and it required a powerful return of our boyish enthusiasm to enable us to finish our task. The whole weight of the nest and five eggs was a fraction over one half ounce.

While exhibiting this nest and desiring local information, we found few who were acquainted with either nest or eggs; but a friend in our own neighbourhood took us scrambling over a hedge, and through tangled vegetation heavy with rain drops, to a large fuschia bush. Here an empty nest was clearly of the same character, but from its extra size it seemed to us to belong to the whitethroat itself—*C. Cinerea*, a much more common bird than the lesser, and well-known to many school-boys as the nettle-creeper, from frequenting beds of nettles. In a lengthened bird-nesting experience we do not recollect to have met the nest of this bird, the lesser whitethroat, before.

There must surely be fish in plenty in Loch Linnhe, for the whales have been active of late. One went ashore at the bay near Dunstaffnage, and was killed most ignobly by means of pitchforks; and another coolly went away with the bag net for salmon from Kingairlochside, the net being discovered some four or five miles off, with four or five grilse and a salmon in it. Had it been loose it might have strangled Mr. Whale, but being fixed it enabled the animal to tear it clear away, and split it up. Clearly it was not after salmon, a fish even the bottle-nose does not apparently hanker after in the presence of herring, if, indeed, they could eat them at all, which is more than questionable. They must have been led astray by some shoal of herring which passed through the large-meshed net.

See the bird of the hawk tribe hovering over the highest point of the island there, and occasionally stooping, but hitherto unsuccessfully! It is apparently a kestral from its movements, and we watch it as it scarcely moves a wing while we thread the long passage and cross the loch—nothing but an occasional flutter all the time. Gently, now, for the tide is low; and we run the keel on the rough gravel beach. What a rush of dancing petticoats through the heath of the island as the crowberries and blaeberries attract the eyes of the young, and the saffron butterflies, which are to-day the prevailing species, skip away before the advancing cap. On our last visit the little blue butterfly was the most common, but now it has been replaced, although the blue is still common on the neighbouring Lismore. We hear the grasshoppers chirping, and see the "old men" leaping among the heath for the first time this season; for they "love the merry, merry sunshine," and do not seemingly make their appearance at all in the muggy weather we have experienced. We want a young black-backed gull, and notice is given accordingly; but the minds of all are distracted by the many novelties and beauties. A great group of seals are lying on an outlying rock, looking like grey lichen, as the sun has dried them; they plunge into the water of the narrow strait, and again crawl awkwardly with jerky movements, up the black rocks—quite a dozen of the huge fellows. We look in vain for mushrooms where they used to be, but as we are seeking for them we come upon the nests of the terns in multitudes, at the verge of the cliffs and along the ledges of the rocks. Just a little cup-shaped depression in the grass or moss, with the most remarkable variety in the colouring of the eggs, even in the same nest. This is quite a peculiarity of the tern, and sometimes there is far greater difference between the eggs of a single bird than between those of different species. Late as the tern is of nesting generally, it seems still later this season, very few of the young being more than a day old. "I found a nest with two eggs and a fluffy youngster," says a skirmisher, and his description is that of the bird we are seeking, so we set off in search. The eggs are there—lesser black-backed gull—but the youngster has taken warning and disappeared, only to be captured as it nestles into the corner of a rock some yards away, similarly coloured to its own grey fluff. Meantime the eye of a maiden, as quick as it is merry, has discovered the nest of some duck under a rock; and the eggs have been already abstracted and examined ere we reach the spot and endeavour to replace them in their den, far under the overhanging boulder, for the eggs are within a day of hatching, and they prove to be those of the sawbill (*Merganser*), whose young have never been successfully reared in this quarter. But oh! those ladies. Here was another nest of a gull with eggs near maturity, and they have disappeared in a most mysterious manner!

In a pool close to the beach we find quite a mass of tadpoles, late enough of appearing, and the excessive restlessness of the sandpipers, and the wild anxiety of an oyster-catcher, point to young ones skulking in the crevices of the rocks or under some sheltering tuft. Everything late this year, but as the whistle is sounding, and the smoke has long been encircling our potato pot in the cave, we must not be late for our welcome meal. We would willingly have lolled and joked longer around the snow-white cloth, and watched the peregrine soar away from the invaded premises, and arranged the blaeberries and the hill heather to the best advantage, but Lismore is near, and Tirifour "Castle," that ruined broch, is a novelty to some of the party.

The beach is rough, the tide low, and the cliffs ragged and steep under the ancient Pictish tower, but the ladies wander round the rough stones of the shore, and strike inland in search of a shop. Actually there is a shop; but we are obliged to waylay them further shoreward, and delude them back through the long clover of the limestone island to the boat. They will rather face the cliffs than the rude shore again, and we feel like driving a team of unbroken fillies over a mountain road as we gather them shorewards along the rude path. Carefully we hand them down the last rough stage, but a leap is inevitable, and recklessly faced by the merry hearted. What did you think, my friend, as your comfortable companion shrieked and fled from your waiting arms? We own to perturbation, in spite of the laughter mingled with the shrieks of horror. Some frightful calamity, surely! but it only turns out to be a somewhat rude treatment of the contents of the new patent incubator! The destruction has not been so complete or disastrous as was anticipated, and after consigning the broken egg and contained embryonic black-backed gull to the waves, the "patent incubators" seemed still well supplied, and the ladies more careful of any rude approaches. For not only the gull's but the duck's nest had been surreptitiously stolen from, in hopes of successful incubation. Once the ladies had reached home and "unbosomed" their cares, the eggs were placed under a clocking hen, and, no doubt to its astonishment, next morning three goosanders made their appearance. Beautiful little creatures, and wonderfully droll they were; but only one now remains alive, and that does not promise a lengthened sojourn among us. This is to be regretted, but the troubles that await pets are innumerable. One was drowned, another was abstracted by the paw of a cat through the wire netting; and our little black-backed gull, after being a source of pleasure and amusement for several days, as it toddled about the house and played with the children, at last wandered too far, and was found in a rat trap; from whence it was removed for the benefit of our tame kestrel, now in full beauty of plumage.

The children levy blackmail on Lismore, in the shape of a big bunch of its rich clover for their tame rabbits; and then we shake up our little sail and stand homewards. But first, ere we enter our own loch, we run our boat alongside Tern Island, just to see the multitude of nests, and ascertain the progress of the young. None are more than a day or two old, and it is wonderful to note the instinct of the little fluffy creatures, with the bright white spec at the point of their bills, as they cower quietly beside the unhatched eggs, or slip with scarce perceptible movements into the heath alongside, and crouch immoveably under some little tuft.

No bird is so easy to rear as a gull, but a sea-swallow requires fish, and is most difficult, if not impossible to keep alive, except in very favourable quarters. Gulls will eat anything, and we learn that the other day, as a farmer was ploughing near us, a large gull, presumably a black-backer, swept down before him and went off with a mole! Rather strange game for a sea-bird, but " all is fish that comes into the net " with that omniverous bird.

One of the peculiarities of the human mind is a love of dexterous imitation, and this takes various forms. Perhaps the most unpleasant is the imitation of natural objects in unnatural substances, and we acknowledge the same feeling towards an imitation sealskin that a bull is supposed to bear towards a red cloak. Yet the mind is pleased with a dexterous copy all the same, and perhaps the pleasing feeling that we have discovered the analogy, or at least that we fully appreciate it, adds to the agreeable sensation produced by a really beautiful form.

The Polypodies, known familiarly as the oak and beech ferns, are common enough all about us, and, from being thus common, attract no attention, although none the less beautiful on that account. But the parsley fern (*Allosorus crispus*), or rock brakes, is less familiar to the eye anywhere, and is seldom to be found in Scotland except in confined localities. We have often resolved to hunt up this fine plant in its "native wilds," and as our stout young friend is on the hunting path, we must make up our minds to give a day to the chase. The sun has been shy all the summer, so we cannot expect a dry walk, but will ignominiously keep to the road as long as possible ere starting off towards the rock haunts of the pretty plant that has stolen its graceful fronds from our kale yardie and keeps demurely among the hills, as if afraid to be found out. Away up in Glen Dubh, that black glen among the hills, on which an eternal gloom seems settled as we look up from below, and where a heavy mist seems ever hanging to damp the spirits of the unhappy visitant, we must seek it. We are traversing a rude road towards the glen, wondering what sort of vehicle can hold together over the rocks and through the bogs, and occasionally forced to consider which road to take when it divides. But we need not bother, as there is but one way after all, and the double road is occasionally caused by the cart being turned aside in wet weather by a bog, or in the other case in frost by the slippery rocks. Scarce a sound is heard, and the feathered inhabitants of the woodlands seem to have been thoroughly depressed and crushed by the damp sunless summer. A few chaffinches about the main road, a fugitive blackie slipping off through the brush, and at last the harsh squeaking of a pair of jays is all we meet in the still mist-clad wooding. We have been keeping to the neighbourhood of the small stream near which we left the main road, and now after a long scramble through wood and over boggy land we approach the river Teighl in its higher course, before it plunges along over the long range of falls and rapids on its way towards Barcaldine Gardens. Here we find a sudden outcrop of civilisation in the shape of two youngsters with a huge rod seeking to emulate Izaak Walton on the skirts of the clouds. Surely no fish can possibly pass these falls, and yet here are plenty of trout of good size playing in the shallows, and lying lazily working their gills in the deeper pools. How came they there? is more easily asked than answered; and unless we could positively assert they were never introduced, it is useless to look for other explanations. No doubt trout are capable of very wonderful gymnastic performances, and eggs, too, have been carried in strange ways, but the very extended course of the stream in the glen would naturally lead to its being stocked, if not otherwise supplied.

Now that we have arrived at the glen proper, we are surprised to find it a fine vale, with a broad, wooded bottom, and steep sides sprinkled with natural wooding, and seamed with wild watercourses. Here is the neat cottage of the shepherd whose children we met by the river; and the neat, well-kept place and little garden, with the patch of oats and potatoes, and good stretch of grazing for his cow, show how snug and comfortable thrift and energy can make a family even in a rarely-visited Highland glen. The bog myrtle scents the air as we trample through it, but the heath is everywhere dull, save where the bell heather shows in brilliant purple patches. This heather seems very frequently to spring up when the common heath has been burned down, as if it had been lying perdu, crushed by its more vigorous and prosperous connection, and ready to take immediate advantage of its misfortune. The sphagnum moss is deep and wet, and we have to pick our steps warily; but the whole glen is workable and drainable, and those who live in the moist West cannot look upon it as uninhabitable, in the face, too, of the particularly vigorous dwellers in the cottage by the river Teighl. Quite a fine domain it would make, with a glorious view towards Linnhe and Morven, and Ben Breac looking down with complacent self-satisfaction over the wooded snuggery beneath it. The river still flows free and strong, and we are approaching the very top of the glen, where it is met by the sloping guard of hills. What violent torrents all those streams are in the winter and the rain time, when the cloud king hurls them downward impetuously, with heaps upon heaps of fractured rock in their train.

At the very top of the glen, on the left hand, there enters one such wild torrent called the "torrent of the cleft" *Esnagara*, over quite a morain of small boulders; and up this narrow gulch we keep towards the summit of the hills. Ere we proceed far we have to cross again and again the stream that rushes downward, and so find that the rocks we have to traverse are of a character such as to try our feet severely. Only those in the very bed of the stream are water-worn, the remainder being sharp edged, as if fresh blasted from the steep cliffs on either hand. Was not this the cliff where Donald captured the eagle, and that where the raven loves to build its nest? Steep enough all the way, and yet all clothed in greenery of bracken and heath, and young of the birch and mountain ash, save where a new, fresh-cut face tells of a recent fall of rock. Huge boulders, water-worn, there are also here and there; splendid granite of many colours, from cream colour to red, from whence brought or how it would be difficult to say without a careful survey of the neighbourhood. This mass seems similar to the granite of Bunaw, on the other side of the hill; but that is like nothing we know in the district. What power short of a glacier or an iceberg could have thrown that monster boulder in the middle of the stream, large enough to build a church? Has it descended from the summit as the stream cut its path under it through the hill, or only been undermined as the gully widened?

"Here is one!" shouts our comrade, and sheltering under a large stone is a little group of the friends we are seeking, and have scrambled so far to obtain. We still clamber up, however, and conjure up the placid smile that would scramble up the cheek of our shoemaker did he but know we were in such quarters. Round a corner, and a wonderful grey mare's tail falls in a side basin, whence a scudding streamlet joins the one we are ascending. Quite a fairy corner, and we half expect an apparition of a fairy chieftian in kilt and claymore to demand our credentials and punish our audacity. We have left the stream, and are crawling up the loose and dangerous streams of broken rock that a careless step would set rolling indefinitely. Here is a bit on which the heath has got a partial foothold, and has tied the stones together, and from this vantage ground we can now reach the plants we are in search of, whose fronds in enticing bunches now peer from the loose stones alongside. Plenty of them and to spare, and, by carefully removing the stones around, the whole plant, and all the soil it has gathered about its roots, can be safely carried off. We are very busy, and the rolling stones tell of the whereabouts and the progress of the one to the other. Greedier, too, we grow as we proceed, for no sooner have we removed one plant than another far more beautiful is sure to appear. Oh! that bird in the bush with the brilliant plumage, while our poor little friend in the cage there is dull as peat water! As we crawl carefully downward, with our backs well laden, clutching anxiously at the rotten heather, and dragging with us the wild thyme, the blaeberry, and the wild strawberry, we have the consolation of knowing that according as our eyes have been greedy our backs will be bent. What a power is water, and what a water power is there; and what a force, too, is a simple idea, that has dragged us through the muir and over the mountain debris in search of the successful imitator of one of our commonest garden vegetables, known to the initiated as *Allosorus crispus*, and to lovers of a simply beautiful form by the much more euphonious title of the *parsley fern*.

AUGUST, 1881.

It is odd how one sometimes comes upon a "find" in one or other domain of nature, and blindly, almost with intentional perversity, neglects to take advantage of it. When scrambling over the Black island last month, we came upon quite a number of the brilliant tiger-moths, mostly in a lethargic condition, and apparently unwilling to be disturbed. The female of this species gets the character of being inactive, no doubt this meaning *during the day*, which might well be anticipated from a night wanderer. Two we placed in a little match box, and on opening the box after our arrival home, we found the metal lid carefully coated with a great array of small circular eggs evenly spread. Another that we pinned down for preservation committed the same indiscretion on the board to which it had been fixed. The brilliance of this moth is most striking, and the manner in which the individuals were openly laid on the hillocks or the out-cropping rocks, showed they trusted all the same to their safety being assured. How could such a number of brilliant creatures be unseen in such prominent positions, and amid quantities of birds; and what did they specially resemble that diverted the suspicions of its insectiverous enemies? The marked distinctness of the crimson and black body and wings, and the prominence of the cream-coloured spots on the rich forewings, could scarcely have permitted their escape except from some resemblance not apparent to our eye. Although a nocturnal insect, these specimens were all openly spread upon the turf or the rocks. The tiger moths (*Chelonia*) are by no means rare, but we understand they are local in the north. A friend made his appearance with a variety, in the shape of a ruby tiger (*Arctia fuliginosa*), whose more refined construction and smaller dimensions were amply compensated by the intensity of the pink and black hind wings, with the rich, rose-coloured border, half-concealed by the semi-transparent fore wings. What a field for the young naturalist is this of the moths and butterflies, and how gently it draws him into a proper appreciation of the beauty of structure through admiration of the more patent beauty of colouring. No one could long collect moths without wondering where their caterpillars fed, and how they arrived at their particular arrangement of hues, and whether the brilliance of the caterpillars was in accordance with the gorgeousness of the mature insect! This does not at all seem to be the case; and so young heavy-head, who has made no great appearance at the school or the academy, who has but managed to scrape through college, draws himself up and promises to do great things when the "ugly duckling" has developed into a swan. Not even botany will more insensibly draw the lover of beauty into love of science than the study of the fleeting flower-petals that dance in the sunlight, or deck with seldom-seen elegance the autumn twilight.

What a droll fellow! Quite in a state of excitement over our friendly visit, and determined to show it extravagantly about our legs. A little nondescript dog that has followed us among the gooseberry bushes, and there, sooth to say, follows our example, and freely partakes of the product of the over-burthened branches. We do not recollect seeing a dog make such liberal use of fruit before, but the little fellow actually demolishes the hanging berries, taking them off with a satisfied snap. A very interesting fact this, showing how sympathy and imitation will direct the original carnivorous instinct into more peaceful channels. No doubt it commenced with the gooseberry jocularly handed to it by kindly hands, just as some dogs will only eat the food from the table of their master, and will even eat obnoxious morsels if from his plate.

A curious development of an opposite character came under our notice a week ago. The ducklings of a neighbour disappeared mysteriously, until our little lady, in her peregrinations, observed a large bird appropriate and devour one of them as it was entering the stream. Watch was kept, and the result was that a large heron was caught red-handed, and gradually appropriated for the keep of our little kestrel, whose stomach requires considerable attention. No doubt a duckling is a mere trifle to such a powerful bird as a heron, but we were not before aware that they become so omniverous as to emulate the gulls in the vicinity of the farm-yard, and thus devour young birds. Indeed, we still believe this to be quite an exceptional and abnormal occurrence, and worthy of being chronicled.

Our little kestrel grows in interest and increases in beauty of plumage. It makes a very tame pet, and is greatly pleased to be taken notice of by any one passing the cage at the kitchen door. It flies upon the galvanised wire-netting, grasping it and spreading its wings, while crying in the plaintive tone that seems so poor an endowment for such a fine bird. Here comes some one with a carefully-plucked sparrow—the idea of plucking anything for such a dextrous stripper of a bird—and hands it through the wires. Its feet are occupied, so you see it is forced to take it from the hand with its beak; but no sooner can it regain its perch than it seizes the bird round the neck with its foot—we were almost going to write hand, so like to the action of a hand is the grip of the bird—and holding it up as it stands on one leg, tears it to pieces with its beak. Large soft eyes, and the curious restless movement of the head out and into the neck, gives the kestrel a strange mixture of gentleness and watchfulness difficult to describe.

What does it mean? To-day has been comparatively good, but the wind exceedingly changeable, and the sun is going down with a very stormy promise. As we strain at the oars against a strong head wind a voice exclaims "golden plovers," and, sure enough, there is a flock of half-a-dozen skimming down the wind. One of them leaves its companions, and sweeps around till it settles on the grassy slope by the sea, where it peeps at us from the grass while we pass. There is no doubt about it, we are too close to be mistaken, if we *could* mistake the flight and cry of this graceful bird. The tide is the highest for months, and it is down at the verge where the dark fringe of sea-weed skirts the green bank. What can it mean, this sudden early appearance of a group of winter visitors? are they driven from the north by promise of a severe winter, or only carried southward by the nor'-wester!

On Sunday last we were surprised at the movements of the collected swallows of the district. In place of sweeping gracefully around, they gathered on the beach at low water, flying to and fro like a flight of sparrows, and sitting on the tops of the stakes in the water in a most undignified and common-place way for swallows. The reason for this conduct on this day we scarcely appreciated, for it has not been repeated since. No doubt the weather was very heavy and depressing, and all insects would be in the lower stratum of the atmosphere; but why settle upon the foreshore and on the seaware, except to demolish marine insects? and if upon this day, why not upon any other day when the tide was low?

We have often seen stray swallows skimming over the seaware and nipping up an odd insect; but quite the swallow colony of the whole district to congregate on the beach, and behave with the reckless disregard of appearance of a "family at the coast," was an unusual occurrence.

Our loch has been very destitute of life for some time, and gulls more especially are not common with us. On our way in by boat to our little bay, in the dusk this evening, we started a very large flight of small gulls intermingled with vociferous curlews, all settling again on the little cairn-covered island near us. They must have been driven in by an approaching gale, and the curlews, too, seem to have already reached the coast for the winter, after incubating among the moors during the summer.

We so frequently hear of the remarkable force of instinct, and how it triumphs over habit and early training, that it is notable when we find a very marked instance to the contrary, and discover a case where early associations triumph completely over inherited peculiarities. The young ducks that take instinctively to the water, to the horror of their hen foster-mother, is within the experience of every keeper of fowls; but we have an amusing duck that formed part of such a hen-incubated brood, and, while its companions have all joined the other ducks, and daily frequent the sea and the stream, yet it has attached itself to our chickens, from whom it is inseparable. We have in vain sought to drive it into a sense of its wider field of labour, to show that it was born to "conquer the flood;" it remembers only the kin of the foster-mother!

There is a class of fishes not well known even to collectors, and seldom found in any quantity by those who are interested in noting them. We allude to those that are not deep-sea fish, and within the influence of the beam trawl; nor foreshore fish within the reach of the rambler; nor such as will take a hand-line bait. They dwell mostly near the coast, but perhaps in rocky ground, or where the seine net alone will reach them, and then only casually. We were assisting at the attempted capture of a shoal of "herring" apparently, whose movements rippled the water all about and around where we had carefully spread the seine. Slowly the net came in on the dark beach, with a bit of moonlight occasionally glinting through the clouds, while those around anxiously awaited the arrival of the expected haul. Again and again a hand is withdrawn as sharply as it is lowered, when it finds only the huge armed head of a bull-head (*Cottus*) in place of a more edible prey. They turn out only to be immature herrings of too small dimensions for the net, only one having been foolish enough to remain entangled in the meshes, accompanied with some small whiting and a few rock cod and flounders. "Only a small flounder," said a voice, as we lifted a little fellow; but the darkness did not prevent us distinguishing something about our little capture that was *not* floundery. In the first place, it was round and most remarkably plump; and next, as we peered at it in the dim light, we observed that its mouth was turned towards the left hand, a sure indication that it belonged to the turbot family, as all the flounders look to the right. Only a little fellow truly, but how plump and beautifully shaped when we come to have a good look at him! Among those flounders and dabs it looks like the aristocrat it is, the scion of a noble family, one of the genus *Rhombus !* Why should the fact of a fish looking to the left, like the turbot and the brill, make them superior in flesh, in appearance, and in flavour, to those that look the reverse way! One thing is notable; these left-looking members of the flat-fish community have much larger mouths than the flounders proper, and so in all probability have more ample opportunities for filling their stomachs, and this must tell in the struggle for existence. It is soon clear our capture is a top-knot, of which only two species are figured as having the dorsal and anal fins passing under the tail, and both are comparatively rare. Indeed, they have been constantly confused in the minds of naturalists; and we believe they have been still further rendered difficult to identify through the occasional outcrop of a third species or variety (of which our capture is a specimen). The fish is but a small fellow at the best, not at any time much over 6in.; consequently it is not a very important contribution to the national cuisine; but it is a very handsome species of flat-fish, and consequently an elegant addition to our fauna.

We have had the dredge plying very frequently of late, having the rare fortune of a companion equally enthusiastic and willing to join in the labour, which to those so interested is a pleasure and no toil. Many a boatload of rubbish have we lifted from depths where it might naturally have expected to sink into oblivion and clay, and much careful sifting have we gone through for very little. What a strange idea one gets of the isolated *locales* of certain species that do not seem to cross over into the ground wholly devoted to other varieties. One time the dredge comes to the surface full of moving life that makes our lady companion shudder with instinctive repugnance. Now, hand over that dish full of sea-water, and look at our captures more carefully. We pick out of the living mass of brittle stars that in thousands fill the dredge to the mouth, several specimens, and place them in the dish. See the beauty of the limbs, the marvellous variety and beauty of colouring, the numberless delicate ray spines and flexible cirri; just one of those creatures well depicted on a sheet of paper would be charming; but there is an *embarras des richesses*, and the multitude horrifies you. The dredge must have been passing over tangle, and gathering these wriggling creatures from the fronds. Now again the bag is full of the shells of the *Turritella*, those long pointed shells that must be extremely numerous in the loch, where we have more than once taken several thousand in a single draw of the dredge. When this is the case few other species are found among them, no doubt the carnivorous character of this shell fish sufficiently accounting for the absence of others.

The ladies are shrugging their shoulders; beauty, indeed, amid such rubbish, and joy over such a creature too! A miniature elephant's trunk to appearance, we thought, as it came out from the mass; an elephant's trunk about 7 inches long we think it now as it stands before us in spirits. A sea-leech, or skate-worm, covered over with tubercles and fine hairs, (*Pontobdella muricata*); it had settled itself by means of its sucker foot upon the back of an ascidian, and with its sucker mouth was wandering around, extending and retracting, seeking something to catch hold of. To the finger it attached itself with unpleasant sucking action, but showed no sign of teeth, as in the leech proper. What is this inside the ascidian? Several small shells deeply embedded in the body of the creature, and apparently quite at home in that position, (*Modiolaria*.) How they breathe is difficult to determine, as they are not at all necessarily in the life currents of the ascidian, but fixed in the stiff gelatinous coating. These shells are of the mussel species—a class that frequently seeks to hide or cover itself, and some by means of their byssis succeed in surrounding themselves with quite a little heap of miscellaneous articles. Those in the ascidians are beautifully delicate and daintily marked, and many have evidently taken up their abode in the body of the creature from their earliest infancy, all sizes being found in the same animal.

Here we are upon sandy bottom again, for the sandstars —those fragile-limbed starfish without ray-spines or cirri— are wriggling in numbers among the contents of the dredge. Then these little shells, so sober-toned on the outside, where a dull cuticle covers them, and so brilliant inside, where the mother-of-pearl gleams on them like silver, are quite numerous whenever we get into the deeper waters. We come to look upon these *nuculae* as quite elegant, so plump do they feel, and so careful of their internal charms. We have the "pelican's foot" in the loch, too, and in a living state; so you need not fear to get a specimen by and bye, my young friend. Thus we continue to prosecute our search, and at length among delicate *tellinae*, and quaint-looking *corbulae*, and silver bosomed *nuculae*, dull, hard working borers, like *saxicava*, that drill their way into odd corners, and blunt-nosed specimens of *mya truncata*, we find a solitary *pes pelecani*, or pelican's foot, with the very carnivorous possessor "at home." Of course, we occasionally obtain *Cypræa*, the beautiful little cowrie, and here is one with a dark cuticle all over it. Take care, now! look closer at the line gradually widening down the back, for the little animal is withdrawing the "mantle" that expands and covers it all over, and now it has once more the appearance of an ordinary, neat, ribbed cowrie. It has folded away its cloak inside the shell.

We have been promised a fine week among our home weather prophets, but the big prophet at the door asserted the contrary, for, with a northerly wind blowing for some days we have had no tide to speak of, a sure sign of unsettled weather. So last eve the little gulls, in a perfect cloud of white wings, made their appearance again before the door, swirling past on their way to the cairn in front; and these were soon followed by a steadily rising wind, which blew a hard gale all night, and is still blustering savagely, with all the proverbial severity of the "black nor'easter."

Yet last Sunday we had a pet summer day, such as we have seen few of this year, and we walked down by the sea shore to enjoy the pleasure of looking into the placid waters. There was an especial abundance of the purple laver seaweed, looking more like a delicate film of oily matter than a vegetable growth; and despite the extreme placidity there was a general feeling of life and motion that we could not account for at first. Gradually the eyes, as they scanned the depths, discovered the million cirrhi of the barnacles in ceaseless motion, and working with seemingly exceptional energy, for the long waving fans were protruded to a great length, no doubt the calmness and clearness of the water giving the creatures the confidence to work thus, knowing they could more readily catch sight of an enemy in such weather. The effect altogether was very remarkable, and although we have many a time watched the interesting creatures as they swept their delicate branchlets from between their door-plates, they never before appeared as they did that day—the prevailing life of the rocky shore.

In front of us, on the long muddy foreshore at low tide, the traversing stream is at present literally black with minute crustaceans, and all the "dubs" left by the tide are in a similar condition. These belong to the *Mysidæ*, and afford just now a most interesting subject for close examination. They are stalk-eyed crustaceans, and the great eyes—for such a small creature—are the most prominent features they have. We sweep the hand net along, and gather a number, but they are very small, so the net is laid flat in the advancing stream of sea water, and soon the larger ones are hurried inward in multitudes, for all life washes shorewards with the entering tide, and they bring activity along with them, too, for it requires a smart movement of the net to gather those that cross over it. A certain number thus collected of those that looked bulkiest in the water we remove to a tumbler, and endeavour to examine them. They are mostly too gelatinous for us to see them properly, but we pick out two with darker markings, and bring a lens to bear upon them. The great eyes are very remarkable, while the long probosci are equally so, and beyond these the delicate antennæ stretch so fine as to be scarcely visible under the strong lens. Quite miniature lobsters they are, only the tail flap does not fold under them, but they are doubled-up at the middle like an old man. This gives them the shape ordinarily of a boomerang. Their ciliated legs in front inclosed in many instances a large semi-transparent sac of very tough membrane, and this, when opened, showed a series of strangely shaped objects, not unlike Prince Rupert's drops, or better, as a friend suggested, "like a lot of commas." These proved to be eggs of the little crustacean, and in one or two instances they were distinctly eyed. Does this little fellow really carry them about until hatched, and are these minute creatures even more highly organised and better provided than the large crabs and lobsters, obliged to carry their ova in multitudes open under their tail flap; while the mysis has a select few only, in a secure sac. One peculiarity about this huge appendage is, that it is attached to the chest under the front legs, which close around it, in place of being under the abdomen, as in the larger crustacea!

We were recently carrying out a slaughter of the by no means innocent crabs, whose love for oysters clashed with our idea of the fitness of things. We were on the point of crushing an ordinary-sized common looking fellow (*C. moenas*) along with his companions, when a peculiar condition of the abdomen attracted attention. The crab could not have been more than a year old at the outside, and yet it had quite a number of very large barnacles securely seated on its carapace, and several smaller ones on the joints of the legs, on which there were also prominent the small green fronds of an ulva. But the poor fellow's troubles did not end here; under the abdomen, as already suggested, there was a peculiar protuberance forcing it open as if it were heavy with spawn; and this turned out to be two mussels, one of several months' growth, the other smaller, well secured by their byssi, and so placed as to force the false legs apart and askew! Yet the crab looked healthy and active, while all its sedentary parasites seemed equally so.

What do we know of the motives of the lower animals after all, and is not the life of some of the commoner creatures around us much more complicated and difficult for man to unravel than he is always willing to admit? Here we have been rowing up and down the loch at all hours, and yet even at an hour when we were hurrying homeward to bed, and the sun had crept downward in beauty behind the Kingairloch hills, throwing the black firs of the wooded Appin knolls into beautiful relief on a field of silver, the rooks were still sitting silent, and almost motionless, on the same bit of foreshore and gravel beach. Day after day this has been the case, with a regardlessness of strangers, and apparent quiet self-absorption, that is remarkable. Not a dozen or a score of rooks! but when they rise the air is black with a cloud of wings, and one would say that all the rooks of Benderloch were thus assembled on the Appin beach. So far as we could observe, and they permitted the closest scrutiny, they were not feeding at all, scarcely moving at all, and most notably silent, for their vociferous race. If a rook Parliament, there was no Coercion Bill before them; and if religious, thay must belong to the Society of Friends; but really what brings them together daily to the same spot is beyond our ken.

A very large proportion of jackdaws accompany the rooks whenever they are seen flying overhead; and, however silent the rooks may be, their smaller friends are sufficiently loud-voiced. But in these silent assemblies we did not see or hear any of the jackdaw race.

The Lapwings are already banded together, and back from the moors like the golden plover, and no doubt they will soon be on the move to the south. The oyster catchers are also back in a great, bright, band, with their black and white plumage flashing in the sunlight last eve ere the sun went down. The shores have been dull enough since the departure of these birds.

One of the most shy and careful birds that enters Loch Creran is the Saw-bill (*Merganser*), and yet a mother and four youngsters had entered the stream in front, and passed up nearly to the road yesterday. The young birds were full fledged, but small and backward, having evidently been very late in making their appearance. Indeed we never found the eggs of sea-fowl so late in any season as this.

Around the farm house the fields of grain are steadily advancing towards maturity, and some days ago, ere the colouring had become so marked as it now is, we noticed near the dykes and close along the hedgerows stretches of oats, whose heads were as white as their neighbour's were green. That birds could cause such an extensive devastation at first seemed impossible, but as these white, grainless heads only bordered the haunts of the sparrows and other smaller fry, we were gradually forced to accept this conclusion. On pursuing the subject, we found a shrewd neighbour cutting his hedges close, in order to drive the birds away, which was successful so far, as they became alarmed at the open unsheltering condition of their haunts, and "went over to a neighbour's!" It was curious to note how the birds kept mostly to the fringes of the fields, whence they could give a short skip on to the swaying ears, have a good feed, and then skip back again. The ears thus cropped withered in the heat, hence the different shade on the edges of the fields compared with the natural green of the ears.

Where have you got all those night-moths, and have you been treacling the trees? we ask a young friend and entomologist. We learn, in reply, that he has not been nearly so successful with treacle as with a natural trap ready to his hand in multitudes in every field about. He had only to go out in the gloaming to the flowers of the ragwort, and upon these he found the moths in multitudes in a sort of stupified condition, as if the powerful smell of this "stinking-william" was too much for them, and attracted them all the same like so many gin shops. There they were to be found, at anyrate, quite unable to escape, and waiting with stolid indifference to be boxed.

SEPTEMBER, 1881.

They have got to the end of their tether, that is certain, we exclaim, as we observe the stately flowers of the foxglove nodding their gay heads from the top of the stem, with row after row of withered or empty calices below them. "What a pity the noble plant does not flower all at once," remarks an observer; while the rest of us think it very advantageous to have it remaining with us so long in flower, and very sensible of it to dole out its treasures in moderation, in place of making a great show and away. Anyway, we are all sorry to see the flowers at last at the very tip-top, and to know that the end is near for it. Interesting it is to note the wide difference between the earliest flowers, with the tapering series of bells above them, each taking up the fallen mantle of those below, and advancing steadily to the summit, compared with the rows of departed glories that the topmost bells have to look dolefully down upon.

But we have been little on the land and much at sea these latter days, wooing what has behaved very cruelly to us, as to many others, that last bitter Thursday night. If ever anyone wants to appreciate properly the derivation of Loch Creran as the loch of "miry clay," according to an accomplished neighbour, he has only to attempt to draw up a dredge made of fine cheese cloth from 20 fathoms deep. Up it comes, and the eager hands that bring it on board are pretty tired of its thoroughly receptive character ere it comes in over the gunwale. But what cannot enthusiasm endure, and how can you reconcile the fact that those hands sunk well over the wrists in the slime of the bottom belong to very sensitive minds, and are fed by decidedly squeamish stomachs! With what delight does the investigator draw out from amid the mass some stray specimen of a *velutina*, and how keenly does he glean the sediment for some hoped-for rarity. The minutest sea-slug is handled with regard and affection, and a shout of joy heralds the appearance of a small webbed star fish. A star fish webbed between the rays, whose presence is, indeed, such a rarity with us that we have never before met with it in Loch Creran. We must draw a veil over its latter end, so far as we are concerned, nor say how it managed to be again committed to the briny. I'm afraid, my friend, you thought more of those delicious pectens than of their companions in misfortune.

That last draw was in the dusk, and the contents had to be removed and examined by daylight next morning; and well that it was so, for how could one be expected to see in a rough examination in a rough boat the two delicate organisms we drag from a branching *Sertularia*. Minute crustacea they are, about half an inch long, and not unlike a *mantis* in their movements and appearance, being extremely fragile and threadlike, (*Caprella*.) Yet their eyes are comparatively large, their antennæ marked, their legs numerous, and they are altogether, from their tenuity and the great hooks at the end of every limb, admirably adapted for clinging on to the deep sea algae or zoophytes, and declining to be washed ashore. Indeed, they become naturally entangled by their hooked limbs in the small glass in which they were deposited, and could with difficulty be disengaged. But what is this! we caught a gleam of irridescence from the midst of the mud, and we soon drag from its enveloping dull coating a little sea mouse, with its fringe of brilliantly irridescent hairs, that make this one of the most remarkable creatures to the collector.

How impossible it is to appreciate all the beauties of these annelides with their varied characters, and how strangely they turn up sometimes! What is that gelatinous creature at the bottom of the empty pecten, we mutter next day, as we bring the lens to bear upon upon what appears to be a gelatinous yet fibrous mass. But the more we examine it the more it sinks from view, until nothing but a little jelly shows on the shell. We return it to the water, and once more the jelly expands into tentacles of most remarkable dimensions, and only the closest investigation shows that there is a minute hole in the shell, behind which an annelid is occupying a serpula tube, from which it thrusts its tentacles through the minute puncture in the shell! The various serpulae themselves are sufficiently deserving of attention, and not only the houses they build for themselves, but the animals that build them are notable. Why should some of them twist their tubes into endless entanglements, while others simply give one curl and curve upwards like a snake standing on a single coil?

In vain we attempt to evade the ascidians of all sizes, they come up in multitudes in spite of us; and full of riches they are too. Delicate sertularia all over them, dainty little sea weeds clambering over their rough hides, their bowels invaded with positive multitudes of these delicately-striped and finely-formed mussels, harbouring amid their gelatinous bodies.

It is getting quite rough as we throw the dredge once more to the bottom, and it has just found ground when Philip shouts out, "What is that white thing in the water?" We can only discern something unusually white a yard or two under the surface of the waves, and half anchored by the dredge, we row round towards it. Overboard goes our anchor, as the only mode of sounding the object, and we then perceive it is a magnificent specimen of a medusa, *Rhizostoma*, with a glorious purple circlet around the edge. It is too wary, however, to be caught with such a clumsy weapon, so, although we bring it to the surface more than once, it soon discovers our intention, and rapidly descends into the depths.

Meantime our dredge has got disorganised in the course of our movements, and before we get it into proper position, and once more start on our way, we have thrown ourselves so late that this haul must be our last. Hermit crabs of several kinds; and why are you fellows without your trousers? We chuck the largest into a dish, and note that his undefended extremity is tougher than if it had just emerged from a shell, while the claws that enable it to hold on to its habitation are quite in working condition; so we conclude that it is merely on the look out for a new house, having lately left one on account of being too straitened for room. Bump! why we have been so intent over the tub that the wind has driven us ashore, so we may as well hurry home to dinner.

We take care that the heads are left upon them this

time at any rate, so that we can better judge of the exact character of our captures ; for we have again obtained some dozens of the beautiful little fish that we procured last June, and that appeared to us on a rude examination to be smelts.

We had exactly the same experience with these as with our former capture, and this is of importance in our estimation of their species ; for although that these are Atherines is unquestionable, are they really *Atherina presbyter?* They are not at all different in size from what they were last June, and it is quite clear that they are mature fish, although only four to five inches in length to the end of the forked tail. It was again on occasion of a very low tide that we observed them passing inwards towards the stream in front of us, and rippling the whole surface of the water. Not in a mass, but in active, constantly shifting, playing multitudes in broken detachments, breaking the surface of the water from no ostensible cause, as they were not leaping, but only splashing. Their extreme activity, and the peculiar colour of the back of the creature in the water, prevented them being readily observed, even when you were within a few yards of the ripples, so when pressed on shore it took one all the more by surprise to find them to be living strips of silver. The large scales give to the back the appearance of being checkered, the prevailing hue being dark green ; while from the tail to the pectoral fin a band of pure silver, in which all indication of scale is lost, is the most marked characteristic of the fish. The portion between this band and the belly is only less silvery, while the blue-black eye and iridescent cheeks make this little fish a thing of beauty.

The Atherines are said not to be found on the East

Coast of England, and they are not common in Scotland while they have been captured in the Firth of Forth. Does this not mean that with us our nets are too large to capture such a small fish, and our fishing population too careless of what is set down roughly as "fry" to pay any attention to them? Again, Couch describes the habits of *A. Boieri* as being very different from *A. Presbyter*, *which always swims deep in the water;* and yet the captures we made, except in being smaller, closely resemble what is falsely termed the smelt in some districts, *A. Presbyter;* the proper smelt being a large fish of a different class. Although we only managed with a small hand net to secure a few dozen specimens, we saw them in multitudes at the mouth of the stream ; and others, who were further out in a boat, spoke in exaggerated terms of the number of barrels playing around a half dry rock. It is quite clear that these fishes are now of their full natural size, and they were in really beautiful condition, so that, despite the sharp bones with which they are provided, they proved a most tasty dish when fried and eaten with oat cake. That there are different opinions as to their gastronomic value may be due to the attempt made to include the back-bone in the mouthful; but if this is withdrawn these little Atherines are as delicate as any fish we have ever tasted, fat as herring, without being oily. They were sufficiently plentiful, too, to make their capture worth attempting, but how can one take such small fish in quantity without a net whose meshes would be indefinitely small? We fear they will be permitted to afford food to the seals and the sea-birds, and by wandering about the loch delude the dwellers thereby into trying for herring or mackerel. Our attention was first attracted to the fish by the extraordinary splashing and antics of a large diver, whose energies were evidently devoted to reducing the number of the large shoal that was approaching.

The specimens captured were in milt and roe, and we found that the females were far more numerous than the males, as has been observed in those in the south of England. It is also noteworthy that, when cooked, the silver stripe dividing the fish lengthways was even more distinctly marked than when in the water. It seemed to be more than superficial, and that the flesh underneath was darker along this clearly defined band.

Meantime, there are two natural questions to ask respecting them. If the same as the common atherine, why are they so small : for even if limited in their range to our own loch, there is a plentiful supply of food in it for any fish? And, again, why have they departed from the accustomed ways of *A. Presbyter*, and adopted the peculiarly specific habits of the still smaller and somewhat dissimilar *A. Boieri* as described by Couch.

This last tide has been the lowest we have ever known in our loch, and at Connel Falls the force of the current was exceptionally severe, owing to the depth of the tide below the usual level of the water. This gave great facilities for any one desirous of examining the beach at a depth rarely reached, and as the cause of the great ebb was partly the severe north-east wind that blew with severity for some days down Loch Linnhe, it at the same time threw much that was of interest on the shore. Delighted at an easy opportunity of watching the products of the deep, we marched, basket in hand, along the water's edge, and thereby found many objects we do not commonly meet even in our deeper water wanderings and investigations. We were satisfied, from the numerous large shells of the great pecten, that it must be an inhabitant of the loch; but notwithstanding our long examination of the neighbouring waters, we never succeeded in discovering a living specimen until during the ebb, when our companion discovered one stranded at low water, with its rows of brilliant eyes seeming to seek for a way to escape, and its many feelers grasping around helplessly. These active fish keep to the deeper waters. Thrown up by the same breeze, no doubt right across the loch, were many fine samples of *Solen-ensis*, or the razor-fish with the curved shell. These shell-fish are not common in Loch Creran. They are somewhat small compared with those on Loch Linnhe, as is the case with most of our sea productions. Why, we cannot say, as our salt water is little less salt than the Atlantic itself; and we should think there was not less food in the more inland waters. A kind friend has just remembered that there are lovers of razor-fish under our roof, and a dozen beautiful shell-fish have made their appearance from Ardmucknish Bay. These prove to be noble examples of the straight-shelled razor-fish *Solen siliqua*, and, for beauty of marking, elegance of proportions, clearness of mother-of-pearl, and generally fine growth, we have never seen them surpassed. The quantity of food in one shell is by no means contemptible, and a dozen such shell-fish would represent to most people who could enjoy them, the nourishment contained in a pair of spring chickens. We do not recollect finding *S. siliqua* in Loch Creran, nor receiving *S. ensis* from Lochnellside, so that each species appears to retain control of its own locality.

The disturbance to the equanimity of the foreshore

caused by such a sharp breeze at lowest ebb, is further evident from the many shells of *myae* and *astarte*, and *venus*, all dwellers in the mud and sand, that have been uncovered and thrown shoreward by the wash of the sea. Here, too, is a fine specimen of rose star, and overgorged five-fingers are plentiful enough. We wish we could destroy them without so much trouble, as the only security is to toss them high and dry; but the foreshore is too far off for a starfish to be thrown beyond it, and as for lopping off the limbs of a heartless creature, with sufficient life to exist in a fragment, it is only duplicating the foe.

In the quieter hollows the *mysis* is now to be found, with its abdomen enlarged still further, and some of them are quite dark, almost black, in colour. Great blotches of striped red and white gelatine are sea anemones left in the lurch, mostly huge specimens of *crassicornis*; and close beside them are limpets, so rarely away from a meal that they are of exceptional size and very fat, much superior to those near the summit of tide mark.

Why! One is continually obliged to ask, why, even concerning the commonest events that are daily occurring around us, and that still remain to our minds unanswered. "Why are those rooks on the road at present?" asks our friend as the second rook we have passed rises slowly and heavily, and flies unwillingly for a short distance. "For some time back I have observed them singly on the road, and they don't seem to be there for food, and yet when they fly off they return at once to the same spot in an uncomfortable, sickly sort of way. What can be wrong with them?" We ourselves have observed this peculiar conduct on the part of individual rooks of late, and attributed it to their desire to dust themselves, or need for sand and similar matter to counteract their ordinary fushionless diet. Our friend suggests that the birds as a community are just now flying to such great distances; to Lismore, the tops of the hills, and the further shores of Linnhe, for crowberries, that they are tired out, and are glad of days of occasional quiet, when they haunt one particular spot, apparently doing nothing, and not even saying much. We have seen them on occasions when we could not thus explain their lethargy or indolence, and no doubt a rook's mind is more complicated than we are generally willing to allow.

The horse chestnut trees are now well laden with fruit, and we are a little careful when passing under them, as the nuts dropping from a high tree top give no trifling knock to any civilised head. The crop is exceptionally good, and we lazily pick up some of the large thorny articles, and cut through the thick rind to the inner kernels, still white and bean-like amid their matrix. Why is the nut of this tree covered with prickles, we ask ourselves, as we thrust the jaggy little ball into the hand of the astonished youngster who demanded it? That there is some good practical reason for them we do not doubt, but what is it? If the tough, thick rind were to remain closed until it was decayed, and thus throw free the inner kernels, we could understand the prickles were to prevent it rolling away, and so obliging it to lie and rot amid the decaying herbage. But when ripe the stout husk opens and permits the escape of the kernels, so we must suppose some other reason. Perhaps they saved the nuts from persecution by some horse-chestnut eating animal until the escape of the kernels to the ground gave some of them a chance of taking root. Indeed the chances are that *Nemo me impune lacessit*, thus strongly adopted as a motto, meant some foe of a most distinct and persecuting character at no distant date; if not in some other habitat even at the present day itself.

This has been the week of the Oban Games, in which the athletes of the district turn out in force. We cannot help being astonished at the marked deficiency of the neighbourhood in men of physical mark. This is the more to be noted as there are certain local families who would be remarkable anywhere in the world for the magnificence of their physique, more especially among the well-to-do class. But the great proportion of the original inhabitants, although hardy and sturdy, are of the small, dark, so-called Iberian race, incapable of comparing favourably with the men of the East Coast or many parts of the Hebrides. Athletics are also of quite recent introduction, and have not taken firm root or grown kindly as yet among a population who are too hard pressed to acquire mere subsistence to have much energy left for special culture.

We stop the children and empty their pockets of the pods of the laburnum, which are always understood to be most injurious. Yet the friend at our elbow asserts he has eaten at least a whole pod with impunity, while his school fellow ate still more. Are they really as dangerous as they are supposed to be, or will some youthful stomachs defy the most outrageous treatment?

Curving high over the road is a fine tree, graceful and uncommon, and, looking upwards, we discover it to be laden with russet-cheeked fruit of a very tempting appearance. We will tempt the children with the gay apples of the wild apple tree, or crab, we say; and a stick tossed upwards brings down quite a shower of little beauties.

Sharp teeth are driven into them as we reach home, but the task is too severe even for the youngsters, and our native apple is voted a delusion and a snare. But what a crop the tree bore; while another tree in the garden we have just left, is equally weighted for the first time. In more than one garden about, there are trees this year yielding abundantly that never before showed more than a handful of pears or a pocketful of apples. This is, no doubt, our legacy from last year's fine summer; but what can we expect from next season after this heatless year? The water in the sea was cold enough yesterday for the month of January.

This morning the loch is as calm as crystal, and the mist is lifting from the water and the fields, and creeping along the face of the hills with weird-like stateliness that contrasts strangely with the previous day; for our stooks, that were in capital condition for leading, were suddenly scattered by the severe southerly gale, and then deluged by the succeeding torrents that continued throughout the day. A day of such a character accounts for a vast deal of the difference between the actual returns to the farmer and the natural expectation from the seed sown. A careful husbandman, and skilled observer informs us that he has frequently counted the grains on a single stalk of oats here, and found that the average was not under twenty-five, while we are content in this part of the world with about four returns. Where is this vast difference between four and twenty-five to be looked for? No doubt a large number of seeds are unfertile, many more have the vital part of the seed destroyed by insects before it can sprout, and birds must be credited with another proportion; while grain that is thoroughly ripe and has got thoroughly wet, when it dries again shakes out of the ears in quantity at every movement. Were it not that the straw is of more consequence to us here in a way—as farmers—than the grain, we would look to much more careful cultivation doing for oats what has been done in special instances for wheat, namely, create a class of large-grained, strong stemmed grass more readily controlled, that would be planted like potatoes in place of sown broadcast. This is a result not at all difficult to obtain, as has been shown in the case of wheat thus treated; but the single stems are so thick and glazed with silica, that it would not suit the primary object of our straw, as wintering for our stock. To those who look to a peasant proprietory living upon their agricultural produce, however, this is a direction in which important results may be looked for, as enabling the husbandman to obtain a more reasonable proportion of the possible and natural return.

Young frogs of the size of small beetles continue to make their appearance after every fresh outbreak of wet weather here, and yet they cannot have been produced from fresh thrown spawn, we fancy, for we have seen none since the spring, and are consequently led to suppose the tadpoles have, through untoward circumstances and surroundings been prevented completing their transformation until later, and remained longer in the tadpole state. We saw one year a quantity of tadpoles in a dark, dull pool in the wood near this in the month of November, and supposed their change had been arrested through want of sunlight.

We saw fresh dog-roses in flower at Barcaldine two days ago, along with the hips of the former crop, and very much out of place they looked in a landscape whose brightest colouring is now obtained from the fast fading berries of the rowan and its still more brilliantly and variously coloured leaves. Indeed, as we passed up towards the falls on the little river that sweeps so gracefully by Barcaldine garden, we feasted our eyes on the rowan trees, gleaming in shades from the palest yellow to the richest carmine, in which the moisture still glistened; while through between the branches the eye still rested on the cool green fronds of luxuriant ferns in the sheltered nooks on the banks. Where a few weeks ago we could stand on the little wooden bridge, with greenery all about us, and peep through varied summer tints at the cups and the curves, the poised boulders and the trembling undermined rocks of the bed of the wild mountain torrent that dashes beneath our feet, to-day it only impresses our friend with sadness, as the water sings a doleful dirge over the waning year, and a brilliant leaf of carmine from the rowan slips from its hold and circles downward into the waters like a sympathetic tear. *We* have no such feelings, but think only of the bold embryo that has pushed its predecessor off, telling it jocularly that it has had its swing, and has departed gracefully from the scene! What more can any of us do? We look in upon our friend at the garden, who surprises our companion by showing him all the latest novelties and improvements in agriculture, at which he is an adept. Any one who is only acquainted with old fashioned times and old world ways, must be surprised at the progress made of late, and no improvement effected is more ingenious or effective than the supply of artificial combs for the bees to work upon, and save their time and energies gathering wax; for one pound of wax is said to cost more labour than 20lb. of honey. A number of dead bees lie outside one of the hives, where they have been killed when seeking to make their way in, for they were aliens and belonged to a neighbouring community! The bees look large, for they are crossed with the Ligurian, but they have not managed to do any good this year, when few indeed are the days on which they could have worked outside; and flowers, even when somewhat plentiful, were deficient in honey from the lack of sunshine. It is very interesting to find the latest beehives, supplied with artificial combs and a queen-bee screen, in our somewhat isolated locality, and we should much like to see this industry developed more extensively among us.

Two wounded stags, after a somewhat severe chase, took to the water; but one was sorely stricken, and the pursuing dog, on reaching it, with surprising courage and intelligence, got upon its head and sat there, despite its struggles, until the animal was drowned. Its purpose was quite clear, and carried out with resolution and success, and seems worthy of note as an instance in an animal of shrewdly considering how best and most easily to attain a definite object.

We were sitting in a beautifully-situated farm-house, with the wild and graceful bay curving before us, and, nearer still than the splendid beach and the bathing-tent on the green, a well-filled and well-ordered garden. With patriotic devotion to the national emblem, a nobly-grown thistle thrusts its sturdy head before the window, and we listen with amusement to the discussion that proceeds as to whether this is *really* a Scotch thistle or not. We never before had the question suggested, nor, indeed, ever doubted that a "Scotch" thistle was a specific variety of the most readily recognised character. No one could suppose that a sow thistle or a ground thistle was our national emblem, except in so far as the prickles went; but that there should be a possibility of such great divergence of opinion as to the particular species of carduus that properly represented "Caledonia stern and wild," we never imagined. We find, however, that these great thistles in cultivated gardens are not, properly speaking, the true Scotch thistle, which is a *Cnicus*, or *plume thistle*, and not a carduus at all; so that in future we shall remember that we are only properly represented by *Cnicus lanceolatus*, the true Scotch thistle, as it is also one of our most common species. We yet believe all the same, that such a cosmopolitan race may be sufficiently represented by any thistle, so long as it is hard enough in the prickles and sturdy enough.

OCTOBER, 1881.

We are informed of a remarkable instance of the mirage in Glen Creran on Sunday last about sun-down. Our informant and his family all witnessed the various displays of castellated towns and towers, while it was accompanied by a still more unusual phenomenon in the infinite multiplication of the sun to the eyes of the whole party, various coloured "suns" being visible on the rocks, the herbage, and the persons of the party. We were along with a friend on the shore of Loch Creran, about the same hour, and saw nothing unusual in the sunset, so that the atmospheric condition must have been peculiar to the glen itself. The sun went down in a red glare, and the contracted, mountain-embosomed glen may have been better supplied with moisture than our wider landscape. From the description the vivid appearance of the various-coloured multiplied suns seemed to be more external optical phenomena than simply in the eyes of the observers from the glare of the sun itself.

Instances of affection in animals during captivity are sufficiently numerous, but it is not so often that we find them rendering themselves mateless through unbridled passion. The pair of young peregrines that were removed from the Black Island in the summer grew apace, and became very handsome birds; but some time since, either from quarrelling over their food, or from their naturally pugilistic tempers being aggravated through continual confinement, they had a domestic jar, which ended in the female depriving herself thenceforward of the company, as well as the rivalry, of her male companion. The hawk tribe are rare examples of female superiority in size and strength, so that Mrs. Peregrine was merely asserting her natural prerogative when she put a tragic end to the weaker vessel. The crime does not seem to rankle in the mind of the survivor.

We found ourselves the other day introduced to a novel mode of exterminating small birds. In a friend's garden the sparrows have become a nuisance, as they are so frequently found to be whereever they can get a footing; and as shooting them is a costly and troublesome operation, the members of the household resorted to a very simple and effective mode of thinning the ranks of what had become a common enemy in the fruit season. On the gable of the house the ivy was thickly growing, and in this, every evening at dusk, the gathering sparrows sought shelter, keeping up a continuous chatter for some time, ere all had found their allotted corners in which to spend the night. Ivy is always a great haunt of small birds, and, more especially after the nesting season is over, young broods and old birds cuddle together under the thick evergreen leaves, particularly if the gable covered thereby is warmed from a good snug room inside. Knowing all this, no sooner had the birds thoroughly settled down for the night, and got well into their first sleep, than one or other member of the household, armed with a long stick or hoe, slipped outside and commenced to beat the ivy from top to bottom. The birds are too startled all to rush out on such an occasion, but so many always seek to hide, and remain to die. The havoc made on some occasions is considerable, and only the stretches of grainless oats and the devastated garden can still the conscience when the morning light reveals the dire result.

Yesterday morning was bitterly cold and frosty, and all are crying that winter is upon us. The day before had been warm in the sun, and many butterflies were abroad, and so next day they also started for a ramble and endeavoured to shake their frosted wings. Those we met in the shelter of the trees, where the atmosphere was milder and where they had protection from the wind, were sufficiently lively—notably quite a number of Northern browns, but one of the same species we met in the open was so benumbed that it could only stagger insanely about the side of the road. Butterflies have all been very scarce this summer, owing to the low temperature and exceptional moisture, so that with the advent of dry weather, albeit somewhat severe, they are making a last effort to flutter among the leaves, now equally brilliant with themselves.

A huge box it is—heavily laden with bivalves and gravel, and outwardly stayed with heavy weights—so we endeavour at low water to lift it from the ground and fix it to the stout boat, meaning to float it into shallow water as the tide rises. But the rope declined to stand the strain of the waterlogged and water-filled box, and it returned with a tilt to the bottom. So a fresh day saw us with a new manila rope, a very low tide, a peaceful sea, and fresh sinews, with the needful appliances for reaching the breeding apparatus that had for months been lying fathoms deep. The boat is anchored, the ropes, after long manipulation, affixed to the mass, and we are on the point of bearing on the anchor when we observe a slow ungainly motion, a dark, stealthy figure among the sea-ware, and then a show of white as it turns up its wing. A skate, close at hand too. This was too much to let pass; so the boat is slewed round as far as the ropes will permit, the split handle of the iron graip brought to bear, and a bold thrust and a dexterous toss sends a delicate thornback into the boat.

Once more we tackle our object, and with toil and labour draw it shoreward. What will have settled upon it during these months we seek eagerly to know, that some idea of the seasons in which the young of marine creatures are thrown may be obtained; for no subject is more difficult, or absurd to dogmatise upon, seeing the seasons may be more than one, and are frequently very extended, while the variation of temperature doubtless affects marine creatures to as important an extent as those on shore. Here, at any rate, are a vast number of ascidians of various species, many of them very well grown indeed; several pectens of larger growth than we should have anticipated in the few months the box has been in the water, several purple seaweeds in many individual bunches, and a patch of serpulæ of quite recent attachment, showing they are late of spatting this year, as last. We are glancing hurriedly over the many ascidians, and detach one beautiful transparent specimen, and admire the perfect purity of the gelatinous body; some delicate foreign matter apparently moves inside, or is it merely the natural flow of liquid from the entrance to the exit moving some portion of the organism? A more careful inspection discovers a most interesting fact, that inside this simple organism, by some means or other, a fragile specimen of the mantis-like crustacean we have formerly described (*Leptomera*) was circulating. The ascidian itself had grown to its present dimensions in a few months at most, even if deposited so soon as the box was sunk; so if the crustacean was drawn into the orifice as spawn, it must have matured rapidly; while if it entered accidentally there was nothing to prevent its exit when it pleased. On the whole we are inclined to suppose that this extremely fragile and delicate creature sought shelter within the secure and tender body of the lower organism, whose constantly circulating water supply brought to the parasite the necessary nourishment; as the larger and coarser ascidians shelter, and apparently provide for, the embedded mussels so frequently found in them. Is it not possible that these ascidians may yet prove admirable hunting grounds for various classes of sheltering creatures, as an entomologist exults over a toad that has made a heavy meal upon rare nocturnal insects?

Like those suddenly stricken with fear or sorrow, our mountains have turned grey in a night, and this morning the snow is creeping down the heights, and peeping into the gullies all around us. To-day, although Loch Creran is "folding her arms across her breast" and composing herself, she showed another sight yesterday, with the whole waters curled into foam, and the bursts of sleet and hail scudding over it in mad revelry. The hail was such as we rarely see in this country, the average being of the size of large peas, and so hard frozen that they came dancing down our chimney, over a good fire, into the middle of the room, and even after some time could be picked up and found as hard as chips of ice. The effects of such a gale as we have had, when it strikes upon shallow water, is scarcely conceivable in the rapidity with which it raises heavy waves. We were watching a series of concrete ponds of only a foot or two in depth and twelve yards long, on the foreshore in front of our dwelling. Over this short range the wind tore in fitful gusts, sending the accumulated wavelets dashing over the further wall in a constant heavy wash. To appearance it seemed as if they would have been emptied entirely in a very short time; and in reality they were very rapidly reduced in depth of water, although the wind veered continually, blowing from the south to north-west and back again, throughout the three nights and two days' gale. The very short duration of the gusts that characterised this storm gave but little time for the growth of heavy waves, but they seemed to make up in virulence for the short time each lasted. One could better appreciate the fact that a shallow sea like the German Ocean gives especial facilities for the growth of a rough sea in a short spell, after glancing at these vicious white fringes to ponds but thirty-six feet long. No wonder that a shallow sea is a dangerous one, and our Eastern coasts so frequently and sorely tried.

During the gale, which was especially bitter and keen when from the north-west, various birds entered our loch, and displayed unwonted familiarity. A large cormorant was actually disporting at the mouth of the burn about eighty yards from our door, although one can rarely get within shot of them on Loch Creran at any time, they are so wary; but the unexpected severity of the weather so early in the year appealed to the feelings even of this hardy bird. This was followed by several sawbills, neither so rare nor so shy, but yet careful enough; and yesterday, about mid-day, half a dozen wary youngsters skipped and played in the most contemptuous manner, still nearer to us. "They are quite close, you must go and shoot them," were the orders given, as the ladies hankered after the breasts of the little beauties; for are they not all grebes, with delightful delicate plumage, and have they not thrust themselves providentially into the hands of the fowler? We smile sarcastically as we fill a tube with No. 6, and with the utmost dexterity reach a point of vantage. All down! that is strange, for whoever saw every one of a band of a half a dozen grebes by any chance dip together when in proximity to danger? The fact is suspicious, and we are still more careful in our movements, but soon a little head bobs up well out in the middle of the bay, followed by another and another, until all the little creatures are skipping and diving together in a compact band well out of harm's way. They are so uncommonly sharp, and so readily catch the smallest movement, that the chances of coming upon them thus is very small.

Why do bees desert their homes occasionally without notice given, not only when they may have nothing wherewith to pay their rent, but even when they are well supplied with the needful to meet the stern tax-gatherer and rent-collector who fails not to call upon them? A friend has more than once suffered from such a "midnight flitting;" on one occasion the hive was between others, and when it was examined it proved to have about nineteen pounds of honey in it, while, except a few plunderers from other hives who had discovered the store, not a bee remained therein. Why did not the other hives quit, if the complaint was one of situation; it could not have been of starvation, or a bad year, and a special objection should surely have been discovered earlier? A mouse or a toad would have annoyed all as well as one. We suppose bees are as much troubled with "fancies" as other living creatures, and such a dense community will no doubt act as hurriedly under the influence of unreasoning panic, or equally unaccountable fancies, as the occupants of human hives; indeed probably more so, from the still closer communion, and greater likelihood of "mesmeric" infection.

What is it? We look at one another as the ghostly figure looms above the bank in the dark night, and then simultaneously we recognise a portion of an old white horse, where no white horse should be. This portion soon resolves itself into the whole animal, that had dragged out its tethering pin, and wandered off into better pasturage. We possess ourselves of the tether, and lead it through the darkness to a stookless portion of stubble, and on the way our friend informs us of a horse that could roll itself up to the peg in the ground to which the tether was attached, and then easily hoist it straight out of the ground, a most intelligent performance; while we are equally interested to learn from our experienced companion, that many horses can free themselves by steadily bringing a strain to bear at the full stretch of the rope on the one side, and then by a sudden rush to the opposite extremity, sending the pin flying out with the recoil. And yet we are told this is only "instinct," and that a horse cannot reason!

At low tide this week we ransacked a pool in the rock to see if any small fishes had taken refuge therein. A pure white doris, or nudibranch mollusc, was sheltering under the seaware, and as we proceeded in our search we brought to light five different species of fishes in that one small rocky pool. Several beautiful gobies—two-spotted —bore the palm for beauty and interest, while a young pipe-fish (*syngnathus*), several butter-fish (*Gunnellus*), a fifteen-spined stickleback (*Gasterosteus*), and a small freshwater eel, kept up the interest of the natural aquarium. On our way home we could have added a good sized sea eel, several flat fish, another species of goby, and a shoal of two-spined sticklebacks to the collection of the morning, over a stretch of a few hundred yards.

During the day the wind gradually recommenced from the south, wore round to the north-west by the evening, and blew a vicious gale from the north-east all night, so that this morning (Friday) there is plenty of jetsom on the shore, as what rational marine construction could stand such a long strain hammering at them from all sides of the compass. Our sailing boat has "gone into winter quarters" early, and against our will, while the gale still continues without any sign of weakness or hesitation. A "depression" has crossed not only the Atlantic, but the minds of those who "do business on the great waters."

It is now nearly a fortnight since the stormy weather commenced, and we have only had one day's calm since. Wednesday was as severe with us as almost any day since the commencement, and last night was quite on a par with the disastrous night of Thursday last week.

The peculiarity of this series of gales is that they have steadily progressed round the compass. They commenced with south and south-west, and after days devoted to the different "airts" of north-west, north, north-east, and easterly, finished with the bitter south-east gale of last night. As we write the howling of the blast has ceased for a time, but we don't feel at all secure, although, after such a complete occupation of "a' the airts the wind can blaw," we are hoping the week may finish more peacefully.

The succession of gales have ended, so far, as they began, with an exceptionally intermittent display of energy; the squalls being constant throughout, and whether from south-west, north, or south-east, equally bitter and disastrous. While driving along by the shores of Ardmucknish Bay yesterday morning, we were surprised to see the Oban fishing boats skimming along in the then increasing gale, and settling down to the whiting fishing, well out in the exposed bay. The rising gusts, after a time, drove them off one by one, until about the middle of the day the last boat bundled and went, having delayed until it had the utmost difficulty in escaping from the white squalls then beginning to churn Loch Linnhe into spindrift. Shortly after mid-day no sail could with any rational hope be hoisted in our surrounding waters. We sat wondering what was to be the end of such a long-continued spell of rough treatment, and watching the black and white squalls succeeding each other, and racing madly seaward from the beautifully-situated loch with a southern aspect—on whose beach one sailing boat lay bottom up, with the scantiest likelihood of ever again dipping her bow in the briny sea after Thursday night's treatment,—when a crash outside announced a further catastrophy. A heavy wooden roof, with plenty of exit for the entering wind, and no rational excuse on account of extreme youth for indulging in such vagaries, took a flight heavenward and fell with a crash on the lawn near by. It was not in a corner, it was heavily timbered, and was simply a wanton piece of recklessness on the part of the squalls, and proof of their sheer strength. The stones along the sands on which sea-weed was hanging were rolled about by the wind with the greatest ease, even up to very heavy weights; and we are not so much surprised at our disasters as amazed that the list is so small.

Yesterday morning, before the gale came on in its severity, the rooks were circling about in great multitudes overhead at an exceptional height, corroborating the popular faith; while to-day, now that the gale is upon us, they are skimming hurriedly and anxiously close to the waves. Before the evening closed in a great flight of sea-gulls made their appearance in front, to their favourite haven in a gale, so that we were justified in concluding that the storm was not yet over. After an hour's lull it once more howls around us, and throws the loch into breakers against our shores.

While traversing the beautifully-wooded vicinity of Lochnell's ruined mansion it relieved the eyes to turn them from the sea, in mad revelry, to the wondrous beauty of the foliage and the exceptional display of berries. The great thorn hedges were in rich crimson garb from the masses of haws, while the rowans were here still in perfection, although about Barcaldine shores they have long been withered, and valueless for purposes of display or preservation. One tree greatly attracted our attention. The leaves had entirely fled, and the berries hung still in rich masses, fresh and unwrinkled, while every branch was coated with a luxuriant growth of grey moss, against and amongst which the gay berries hung strangely, like the bright cheeks of wholesome age when their owner's locks are like the snow. We continue peering into the foliage, when we come suddenly upon what to our eyes is a novelty. We rarely, indeed, recollect finding berries growing freely on the yew tree, but here on some magnificent old yews of Lochnell we find the dark green foliage all dotted over with the beautiful, quaint red berries. These are certainly somewhat "fushionless," but we believe quite innocuous, and many eat them with impunity, while a preserve is made from them by others. Seldom, however, are they procurable in such multitudes as on these noble trees this season, and we are quite charmed with the elegance of the dark branches, with their finely-coloured drops of luscious-looking jelly hanging underneath the foliage. Here and there a number of small "acorns" hung alongside the gayest berries, caused by the undeveloped disc of the female flower having taken the appearance of the cup of an acorn, in place of completing its growth into the surrounding jelly. We were forcibly reminded of the interesting transformation witnessed by Gill in the mountains of Thibet and Northern China, where the holly ran into the oak and the oak into the chesnut, for here was the yew with imitation oak berries alongside its more perfect fruits, showing how slight is the difference in development between them.

Can a rational pig swim, or an ordinary pig swim rationally? That is the question! We are crossing the ferry in the aristrocatic company of four good pigs, and as we approach the landing-place the growing excitement of the porcine mind culminates when we are still within a few yards; so, despite its tethered limb, one plunges overboard. With the customary contrariety of the clan, it goes right under the boat, and starts for the centre of the current, just then racing for the entrance of Loch Etive with great speed. Of course there was an excess of excitement, and great waste of eloquence, while there was rowing in hot haste after the half-mad animal, now rapidly commiting suicide in the midst of the current. For it never managed to lift its nose above the water, but continued to propel itself with considerable speed just on a level with the surface of the water. Had it simply tilted up its nose one inch or two it could have gone on merrily; but, as it was, before the stern chasers had reached it and slipped a rope over it so as to keep its head above the water, the current had swept them well nigh through the Falls of Connel, and they could only land it exhausted on the shore it had left. The pig was fat, and the ordinary belief that a fat pig cuts its throat in swimming would perhaps have sooner or later been realised; but does a pig in its senses, and without an undue excess of flesh, really drown itself through stupidity? We cannot suppose so, and must put down this fellow's action to the debasing influence of civilisation and an over-paternal government!

We are all in the position of the Welsh electoral district, when their member promised the electors whatever weather they all agreed upon as suitable! The ferrymen and seafarers were in sullen despair up till Monday afternoon, while the groups hurrying on their potato digging were chuckling over the gales, even when these were stripping their roofs; for so long as the high winds continued the dreaded frosts that were threatening would be kept off, and the rains that might equally suspend operations would only be sampled in showers. Cart after cart, heavily laden with rushes, and strongly-growing marsh grass, have been passing from Barcaldine to thatch the now completed stacks, and repair the old-fashioned roofs of the cottages and byres, for our population is gradually awakening to the value of their straw to an extent never before displayed; and so far as this wild product of the Barcaldine woods can be procured and utilised, to that extent is the artificially grown product saved as winter fodder and bedding for their stock. This woodland and upland growth, however, can only be obtained through the courtesy of the shooting tenant, and at such times as the game will be least disturbed; and considering this, and the ordinary lethargy of the neighbourhood over small savings, it was quite remarkable the promptitude and wide spread energy displayed by those who could make use of the thatching. The shores of our seas have been so severely handled all the season that little was thrown up during these gales, partly, no doubt, because the tides were varying so little at neap. All along the shores of Loch Creran the "waning of the year" was of the most marked description, and the line of seaweed that marked high water during the gales was rolled into a huge rope, with a line of parti-coloured leaves just beyond, succeeded again by a band of yellow needles from the fir trees, and yet again by an infinitely finely-ground "olla podrida" from the particles of crushed leaves broken up in the war of elements. Along the stretch of beach we traversed, the whole was swept as with a mighty besom; and a series of mussel beds, lying with the peculiar vicious propensity of this shellfish on the outlook for naked feet, and with their sharpest points uppermost, were severely handled for their perverse peculiarity.

For the gale, probably driving before it a stretch of gravel when the water was shallow over the beds, had nipped the points of whole stretches of these mussels, of course destroying them utterly, as they not only lay exposed to the driving sand and small gravel that soon silted in and choked the already sadly bruised mollusc, but they were thrown open to the restless oyster catcher, now delighted to have an open feast without wearing down still further their hard bills.

The rapidity with which the cold weather has painted the landscape is more like a transformation scene in a pantomine. Our walk through the thinning woods last Sunday was almost overpowering in the lavish wealth of colouring. The rich blue of the hills, with the sunlight gleaming over them, and hiding in the richer light the scattered patches of snow; the dark waves, as the terrific squalls swept down the glens and whipped the dark sea into white waters, swirling the gay leaves in myriads before them as they crossed the charming "water-colour exhibition" between the hill-side and the shore; the dark, stern silver firs, erect yet swaying amid the nodding and crouching foliage of the birch and other deciduous trees, presented a succession of scenes as exquisitely beautiful as the mind could conceive. How often do we say still, as we have already said, you who come to the "somber north" cannot have the wildest conception of the lavish beauty of Bonnie Scotland, until you see her in the Queen of Months, when she holds her drawing-room on the mountain side, or in the woodland glade, and gathers the beauty and fashion of her gay world "for a few days only," to dazzle the beholder with the splendour of her court.

That hillside has been a source of delight to many a

jaded Southerner, and must have thrust itself with persistent determination among visions of gay dresses in many a brilliant ball-room, when the tired eyelids fell upon tired eyes, and wholesome thoughts thrust themselves—thrust themselves—that bunch in the hedge is never natural! It has thrust itself so persistently upon our mind, that we are forced to withdraw our eyes even from the heaven-tending hills, and examine it more minutely. The hedge has been getting bare these latter days, and so has rendered this knot somewhat more apparent, otherwise it would not have been noted even by our practised eyes; for it belongs to a little builder that is as dexterous in its choice of a locality as it is skilful in the use it makes of it. Here is this low hedge, not three feet high at the most, crushing into the road, for there is no footpath, and threadbare at the best, even when in its fresh toggery. Yet where our coat must have brushed against its encircling twigs, and the stamp of our passing foot have shaken the youngsters in their snug retreat, a common wren had built its nest, with the moss thoroughly interwoven amid encircling twigs of thorn. Even a finger can scarcely be inserted, but the little troglodytes had been gliding in and out amid the thorns, and yet evading the eyes of the schoolboys and the passing wayfarers until its snuggery was completed in a most workmanlike fashion. There is no doubt that a wren can secure a dwelling-place from ordinary human observation in a manner such as no other bird can pretend to, and we have found half-a-dozen of their nests in the thinned hedge, 50 yards long, in which our most careful and by no means unskilful scrutiny could not make sure of one, when the mother's heart was panting and "summer was green."

NOVEMBER, 1881.

"Ichabod! Ichabod! the glory is departed," we exclaim, while traversing the woods, now nearly cleared of their brilliant apparel. But there are lovely peeps to be had still, although the wind, with the bitterness of jealousy, is swirling even the tenacious leaves of the oak tree after those of the plane tree, the horse-chestnut, the lime, and the birch. The beeches still hang on to their bunting in the sheltered nooks, but the larches have almost been stripped, except where their delicately-pale yellow needles have been well protected. In such cases, the effect of a cluster of young larches around the rich uninjured green of the graceful Douglas pine is most charming; for this pine, like the spruce, defies alike the teeth of the frost and the sharpened scissors of the east wind.

Our winter prospects are rather cheerless, for already the snow has crept down to near the foot of Ben Breac —not with the surreptitious movement of a visitor, but with the quiet, self-satisfied confidence of a boarder that meant to make itself comfortable; so no wonder the brackens have completely struck their colours, and are retreating into the heath, while the varied ferns are pale with dread, and hang, cold, bleached, and shivering, awaiting the end. How beautiful is death, as it creeps upon them stealthily, and spreads its delicately-graduated tints from drooping frond to frond!

"What is it they are talking about?" asks a friend, as unwonted animation and earnestness pervades the faces of the natives. What indeed, but about the most serious question of the hour. How are your potatoes? Did the June frost hurt them much? Has the muggy weather of August and September done still greater damage by fostering the fungus that produces disease? Many are the possibilities of injury to potatoes between the first planting and the placing in pits, and even thereafter, ere they are converted into food or cash for the cultivator. Fortunately we are far better off than those in happier districts (for ordinary cultivation) are to-day, for most of the potato crop of Benderloch is secured. But disease has not wholly avoided them, and those few muggy days of early autumn have secured their prey; while the few days' frost in June have simply left certain sheltered portions of ground entirely clear of shaws or tubers, so far as edible quality or size goes. One peculiarity of our hardy blue potato is that it can be pitted during wet weather with impunity, a valuable quality in our moist climate.

Alongside a fair potato harvest for the majority of our cultivators, we have a most unusually successful supply of the second great constituent of a true Highland breakfast —viz., herring. Fish trains have been regularly dispatched from Oban for the South, freighted from the immediate vicinity with large fine herring; and Benderloch was not without a proportion of the harvest of the sea. But it was not so well prepared to take advantage of this uncertain produce as it ought to be, and, while we understand from a reliable observer, that Loch Linnhe was alive with a great herring "school," such as our venerable informant had never seen before, no boats from our quarter were able to participate in the fishery. A detachment, however, found their way into Ardmucknish Bay, and provided amply for those in the vicinity, as the poor fish were actually pressing on to the rocks of the shore, and were readily captured with the seine net. No sooner was this generally known than a rush of boats took place to the limited bay from all quarters, where they ranged themselves during *daylight*, thus effectually scaring the fish from the confined quarters, where judicious management might have kept them until the bulk were secured. The want of public spirit and co-operation of classes is ever a serious detriment to success in the Highlands, where, in the fisheries especially, there is utter want of foresight or regard for to-morrow. This is to be found even in long-established stations, and is not confined to the comparatively unskilled and ignorant landsmen, who alone prosecute our shore fisheries in the West. Still our people have participated somewhat in the good gift of the sea, and the few days the herring were hurrying shoreward will have helped to enrich a good many breakfasts among us : we should like to know that many more had been prepared to profit by such a rare opportunity. One night's fishing repaid the whole cost of a new net and left something over, and this ought to stimulate others to invest in a like venture. We are perhaps indebted to the severe gales, still howling around our neighbourhood, for these herring shoals, driven inward from their usual haunts around the shores of Mull.

The rooks have a busy time of it just now, as they make use of their nests throughout the year, and these have been so severely handled in the already severe "winter" that the poor birds were actively engaged repairing, these latter days, whenever the gales allowed them to carry their burdens. This has not been often, however, and some pairs we observed very disconsolate over their nests, whose fragments were being swirled over the sward below the trees. The poor birds will no doubt have to roost in the open until gentler breezes blow.

They were digging potatoes near Achnacloich, close to

the Oban line, on the southern shore of Loch Etive, when an unusually stately figure stepped out into the open, and slowly sauntered up towards the copsewood near the house. A potato digger lifted his eyes in amazement at the sight. No haunt of the red deer within ten miles, with the populous district of Bonaw between, and yet here was a stately stag in splendid condition. There was racing and chasing on the shore of Etive, for the sportsmen did not fail to hurry forth on such a rare occasion, and the wounded animal took to the loch, and started for the opposite shore near Achnaba, in one of the roughest days of the October gale. A small boat was launched and followed, landing as soon as possible, for the loch was excessively rough, and the crossing more dangerous than amusing. The stag yet managed to swim the distance, nearly two and a half miles, but was so exhausted that it was forced to land in the teeth of its pursuers. It proved to be a fine animal, that had apparently summered among the plantations of the district without being observed. Whether it had crossed through the populous district in the dark, or had swam Loch Etive before on its way to Lochnell district, would be difficult to say; but a stag of the same character was observed about our own hills a year ago, and may have crossed over from the same quarter that it sought when wounded. Its horns were hard, black, and peculiar, and its venison more like good *ox beef.* In all likelihood it had been driven forth from some herd in the Black Forest, or near the head of Loch Etive.

A good observer comes to trust to his eyes, and grows dubious about those of other people. No doubt this accounts for the onslaught of a keen-eyed correspondent on our "wonder of the world," Connel Falls. He must not expect it to get up an exhibition of its powers at all times or any time, and if one passes the ferry at slack water or neap tides, there is nothing particular to tell of the wild torrent that empties itself seaward in a big spring-tide at low-water. Add to this a heavy gale *with* the tide, and the ferry is then impassable; while a heavy gale *against* the tide is even worse to go through. "Circumstances alter cases," as the school line says. We recollect looking at a coal miner stripped to the waist, picking coal as he lay on his side in a narrow aperture, and being surprised at our guide asserting he "was six feet high and had bones like a horse." Connel can show well when its mane is up and the tide is low.

On Monday evening (7th) about half-past six we saw the finest meteor it has ever been our fortune to note. We had just stepped outside, when it swept down the heavens in a slight curve from the west, like a great "drop" of fire; and went out when due north from our position, in a brilliant violet flame. This occurred just as it had apparently entered the margin of a fleecy cloud, in which it appeared as if extinguished, as a flambeau would when thrust into vapour.

With a beautiful evening and a rising glass, the prospects of a good morrow were fair, but on our return homeward a little after ten, a splendid circle surrounded the moon and blasted our hopes. It was a more sensitive glass than the mercury, and a thoroughly wet day followed. The whole week, indeed, has been mild, but even before the more genial weather set in we were led forth in the evening, armed with a box of matches to supplement the moon, and employed in eagerly hunting the gooseberry bushes that the owner had discovered to be in blossom. They were not the outcome of the sudden mild weather, any more than the row of primroses along our hedge with a northern and western exposure, the daisies blooming as in early summer, the brilliant blue flowers of the periwinkle as vigorous as in spring, the auriculas, hepaticas, and candy tufts forgetful of the months, and the Christmas roses with a mass of fresh buds hurrying forth to join the gay and untimeous assembly. Here comes a fresh growth of bean stem hanging with blossom, but not with the vigorous scent of the summer, any more than the freshly-plucked head of the mignonette we have just had held beneath our nostrils. Roses, red and hardy or pale and delicate, are all around us, and we are wondering, like all the rest of "the world," what has driven them all forth at this time of the year, as if scoffing at the prophets who are predicting a severe winter.

When wading in the sea a few days ago we were satisfied the water was no milder than usual, yet our ponds were newly coated with a luxuriant growth of seaweed, both *ulva* and *ectocarpus*, the latter an annual that has disappeared some time since from its usual habit, and been thrown ashore in decaying heaps. So this is quite a fresh and unanticipated crop to defile the smooth sides of the concrete ponds, and the sea is quite as determined to be bizarre and singular as any bit of land about. Here, too, as we row along, is a bit of floating wood to mark and buoy a submarine structure we lowered to its place just a month ago. It looks dirty as we approach, and proves to be covered with a floating beard of seaweed already several inches in length! This, although at least three weeks of the month it has been there have been occupied by a succession of almost unprecedented gales, for the most part accompanied by very cold weather. So that we cannot look to the shelter and security of the ponds as the cause of the growth upon them, seeing this piece of doubly-exposed wood, thrashed, and tossed, and washed by every breeze, is at least as well occupied as the concrete.

The water is somewhat warmer as it deepens, so coming shorewards our feet are doubly chilled in the shallows, as we skirt the water's edge. There are some odd white blotches on that stone, a few inches deep in the coldest water. What are they? We approach carelessly, expecting to find a lump of quartz or some other simple white object, when we meet three dog whelks busily employed depositing their spawn in this same month of November. We have noted this in former years, and supposed it abnormal, but must come to the conclusion that the spawn of these and other marine creatures are thrown more or less throughout the year. The great ocean progeny could scarcely be else supplied with food, unless some one or other class of creatures were to throw the needful embryo throughout the various seasons. The young of the little *Mysis* have been only lately expelled, and now throng the seaweed and the shallows in countless multitudes, a store, no doubt, for the winter subsistence of higher and more vigorous organisms. Young gobies, also, now shelter amid the seaweed-edged rocks and boulders in active little colonies, hanging continually about the same limited area.

The cry of "herring in the loch" has been so frequently repeated, that the sight of a flight of gulls actively engaged near the supposed frequented area, sent us over to watch their operations. We were soon satisfied that they were occupied with very much smaller fry, but not having taken our weapons with us could not certify the exact character of the prey over which they made such a very great fuss. Three large herring boats returned empty from our waters this week, so we need not have cast aspersions on the character of the seals and the dookers for not having given us notice of an arrival that was wholly imaginary. There are herring in our loch, but these are probably few in number and *local*, remaining with us all the year; as they do to a small extent in most of our western lochs. We have seen few seals lately, but one was art and part in the onslaught made by the gulls, whatever may have been their prey. He was so intent upon his meal that he allowed us to approach very close, and watch him plunging not 20 yards from shore. But as one swallow will not make a summer, one seal and a pair of guillemots will not make a shoal of fish.

We had just donned our waterproofs in the afternoon, and started for Ledaig to see how a south wind treated the long sweep of bay, when the weather put on an extra spurt, and we had not gone half a mile ere every weak point had been discovered and made the most of by the rain, driven along as it was with the utmost fury. We had heard a distant grumble some time before, but, dissatisfied with the result of soaking our extremities, the "Clerk" began striking matches broadly across the landscape to see if he could peer more successfully down the chinks of our muffled neck. The flashes of lightning for a time were very fine, and would have been magnificent but for a stretch of sky towards the north-west that remained comparatively clear, and so prevented the gloom that would otherwise have prevailed. This led us to predict a change of wind in that direction, which followed next day, along with a marked change of temperature now that the stars are out.

The thunderstorm was overhead for a time, but kept to the hills, and passed on between us and Cruachan towards Glencoe. Despite the assault we still stumbled along towards the Ledaig beach, but before we reached it the gloom of the weather was creeping into the gloaming of these short days, and we could only spend a few minutes on the strand, listening to the rolling and the rattling of the small boulders, as they were tossed about in the mighty swing of the breakers. How they played with the beach, and swirled the boulders into cairns, while the restless sea made its bed for the winter, and threw ashore in heaps knee-deep the rich masses of discarded bedding.

Looking out on the masses of furious living waters, we decided that now was an opportunity for obtaining a supply of large specimens of *Helcion pellucida*, the beautiful streaked limpet-like shell fish that haunts and subsists upon the tangle (*palmatus*), so to-morrow we determined to pay a morning visit, and meantime, in the waning light, drew out two large tangle stems from the mass of seaware, and made homeward. After a rough transit, on examination one of them proved to have a specimen of the desired little mollusc well buried, shell and all, in the stem—while it is something remarkable that next morning, after two hours' careful examination of hundreds of stems, we did not find another specimen! So that our shot at a venture in the dark might have fairly and reasonably misled us into supposing we had merely to go and pick up a stem to find the mollusc in question.

Now, we had a definite and distinct object besides the mere gathering of specimens of what, although pretty enough, is by no means a rare shell, and that was the careful examination of the stems of those tangles thrown ashore, to see if they were generally much weakened by the *pellucida*, or sufficiently so to account in most cases for their having yielded to old Ocean's notice of ejectment. There were a goodly number of cases in which the stout, tough stems were wholly uninjured by mollusc or any other foe, except the error of its youth in laying hold of a foundation incapable of supporting its manhood. In these cases, the whole attachments had come away, bringing with them the masses of barnacles (*balani*) to which they had originally clung, and which had now failed them in their hour of need, and left the stones clear alike of barnacles and tangle. But by far the greater number of stems were eaten into a narrow point at the base of the portion thrown ashore, and this was often apparently well up the stem—eaten into great ruts, or eaten into the distinct hole that showed the dimensions of the limpet above alluded to. Many of these assaults were of a character that scarcely admitted of the explanation that they had been perpetrated by any shell-bearing mollusc, more especially a circular excavation in the very centre of the stem, and several inches deep, where the depredators had completely destroyed the power of the stem by eating away the central base. The molluscs, for the most part, where their assaults were distinctly traceable, had confined themselves to the former portion just inside the "bark;" but these others ate the soft tender parts in the interior. For long we failed to catch any individual that could give a clue to the ravager until we came upon a group of whitish grubs among the attachments of a stem that was thrown well up the beach. Having finished our examination we came upon another individual with two curious dark eyes lying in the trench he had excavated.

Cutting off a good piece of the stem with the grub attached, we placed it in sea water, in which it has been so busy that we cannot now bring our lens to bear upon it, as it has disappeared in the new "cutting" it has eaten its way into.

We found we were rather late on the ground this morning, as it was already occupied by a large flight of gulls, equally aware of the fact that a turbulent ocean-mother cast its children ashore. These masses of tangle and other roots are admirable hunting-grounds on ordinary occasions, so we went over a great number to see if we could obtain an insight into the dredging-ground outside. In almost every instance a goodly-sized mussel (*modiolus*) formed the nucleus, and these the gulls had invariably broken up, devouring the animal. The tide was coming in, so they had a long spell, and had gone over the length of the beach religiously.

The storm having come at neap tide had not swept the proper laminarian zone, but merely thrown ashore what could be readily reached in a good spring tide. So, little had reached us from deep water; nor did we see a single fish thrown ashore or stranded in the multitudinous rock pools where Dun Mac Uisneachan divides the rolling beach with its rugged sea-fretted base.

A capture was a specimen of a common barnacle, from a tangle stem, to which a serpula tube was attached; and thinking the occupants dead we removed them as specimens, in the dearth of something more remarkable. As we sat at our paper a short time after, we were disturbed by a sound of such a marked and distinctive character that we were forced to endeavour to trace it. A drop of water falling sharply from a height, or the sudden withdrawal of the tongue from between the teeth, was the likeliest sound we could think of, and it took us a minute or two to trace it across the room to an *omnium gatherum* of our specimens, and thereafter to the individual members of them. Judge of our surprise to find the sound proceeded from the barnacle, whose ciliæ were being extruded and withdrawn sharply as in its ocean home, but with a result that could scarcely accompany the movement in its natural element! Prompt transfer to sea water was an immediate cure.

"Disaster
Followed fast, and followed faster, till his songs one burden bore.'

We have hitherto calculated from the Tay Bridge gale, on which occasion the tide in Loch Linnhe was said to have risen higher than at any time since 1799, and consequently we have considered ourselves absolutely secure if our belongings were beyond the mark of this gale. But Monday night (the 21st) has changed all that. "The Tay Bridge gale destroyed my boats this time," exclaimed our stalwart friend amid the ruins of his many craft. For he had foreseen a storm, and drawn all beyond the furthest mark of that gale, and yet—— The fact is that the now celebrated gale that made such havoc with us in December, 1879, only lasted a few hours, however severe; while that of Monday night lasted until Tuesday evening with steady fury, varied with intermittent blasts of greater ferocity, when the breaking of the thunder clouds deluged us with rain and hail. Blowing thus so long from the southerly quarter, the water was driven up our western coast lochs to an unprecedented extent—rising *five feet* higher perpendicularly in Loch Creran than on the previous occasion, and carrying devastation into all buildings near the sea. The result of such a rise, in the darkness, accompanied with all the fury of a thunderstorm, is scarcely to be conceived; and as we looked at the complete wreck of the dwellings across our little sheltered bay, from which the inmates had escaped in time through the howling of their dog, the mind was enabled to attain some dim conception of what the sea was doing in Ardmuchnish Bay. Our friend's dog has a horror and great physical dread of lightning; and the vivid flashes had alarmed him so that he wakened his master in time; for the highest of the tide was not due until six, while the water was inside his house by four! At daybreak our first sight was a little grebe diving in the sea on the grass a few yards from our gate; while the boats, securely moored close by, had disappeared about the same time. The darkness, and the fury of the hurricane rendered all efforts vain, and the wreckage that now strews the beaches around Benderloch, tells many a tale of sorrow. "You can gather potatoes by the cart-load in Ardmuchnish Bay," says one; and a neighbouring farmer has had 200 barrels of them carried off from his pits, although an observer would have accounted these absolutely safe from the sea.

The gale still blows fiercely as we proceed up Loch Creran, and seek the vestiges of departed boats and the belongings of ourselves and friends, which the now receding tide has left; for if the gale had continued an hour or two longer the tide of Tuesday evening would have been again as high, and it was necessary to save at once what was possible. A timber vessel loading logs had added to the destruction, as these had been carried all over the loch, and employed dexterously as battering rams by the infuriated waves. We stoop and pick up an oyster from a heap of leaves under the trees, whither it had been carried by the sea, and alongside and now hopelessly stranded are multitudes of annelids borne off from their deep water beds by the scour of the water.

"Wurms for bait, indeed," we exclaim, as these appear in great coils along the path. For the sea water has been as impartial in its dealings towards the land annelids as towards its own children; and while it flings its own ashore, it has drowned the others out to keep them company. What a chance for Darwin to count the product per square yard!—for wherever the sea has reached the worms lie in dead coils. Where are all the ducks and sea fowl? ask those further up the loch, for is this not an unusually rich feast for them! We left all the gulls in our little bay, but have seen no ducks whatever, these having no doubt sought the inland waters.

We pass the newly-erected concrete breastworks, torn into fragments and strewed along the beach, and havoc, in deadly earnest, skirting every little bay. Here, trees are rocking in the wind, with their roots in the air for the most part, for the earth and rock they cling to have been swept away—others have their trunks all scored, for the stones and boulders of the beach have been washing about their stems by the hour; and others, again, have a good supply of seaweed hung among their boughs to replace the vanished leaves. This is the manner in which the wire-fencing has been swept away, when one would have supposed it could not possibly have presented sufficient obstruction to the rush of the waves. These first festooned it with seaware until it became so heavy as to weigh down the wires, and strain the posts, and then the obstruction was sufficient to enable the next rush to carry all away.

Those in front are excited and interested, as they stand

shivering in the storm of hail at Cregan Ferry, where the evidences of desolation are sufficiently distinct. Ere we reach the ground one of the interesting strangers they have been attracted by has disappeared towards the head of the loch, but the other is still to be seen battling with the waves in the teeth of the storm. Actually a little stormy petrel at Cregan! With what pluck the little fellow fights his way down in the face of the gale, dodging behind the waves, and taking advantage of every possible shelter they could afford. He actually makes progress, too, despite the fury of the blast that forces us all to leave the unsheltered promontory, and turn homeward.

Only once before has the old keeper seen this bird in Loch Creran, even in a time of gales. We had a porpoise in the loch on Saturday—a rare visitor in our so concealed loch. We were watching a little smack coming down the loch in the gale of Saturday flying like a racer, with mainsail and two jibs up, and every wave washing her from stem to stern. Rather anxiously we noted her lower her jib and reef her mainsail while she still staggered on, half the time under water, when the "pellock," coming down in the same course, but nearer us, met some of our marine constructions, and went skipping over them in two great leaps. It did not again show itself until it passed our point of sight.

We have crossed to the Ledaig shore. Carefully now! the breast wall opposite the smith's forge is away, and the stiffest neck in Benderloch could not stand a drop there. There is the famous rock of Ledaig still standing at any rate, although seldom in its "career" could it have looked out upon a wilder scene; and here is the poet's garden—well! at least half of it! The hedge and the other half—20 years of toil and care and affectionate tendance—*Ay de mi!* what good can they do to men or gods at the bottom of Ardmucknish Bay?

My good friend, I'm afraid our foresight in laying in such a stock of sparrow-hail for eventual rare feathered visitors will not avail us if this weather continues. Here has the glass gone down on Sunday morning as low as ever we have seen it, and now all day the wind and the rain are merrily sweeping over our devoted heads, lashing the water into fury, and rendering our ferries impassable once again. So we are pleased to think we have stolen yesterday from amidst the waste of desert days, with its wedge of frost driven in between the wet and storm, and its moonlight blink through the dreary branches of the desolate woods. How busy the squirrels were amid the tree tops, and how well they showed among the bare branches, with here a grey tail curled over a brown back, and there a dark tail over a grey back, as they sit on the stripped larches. For it is upon the larches they are mostly to be found at present, and we could not think what they could be doing upon them, until lately, when we took shelter one rough day last week under the still covered head of a neighbouring Scotch fir. From the mosses under our feet, at present so rich and green, our eyes wandered to the high over-arching trees, and there at the end of a branch appeared a nest of a contour that set our wits to work to decipher the builders. We watched it long without success, when suddenly the "nest" tilted over and dropped head first to the next branch, there to continue in motion ere again assuming the stationary position. The squirrel, for such it was, had been intent upon its labours in the midst of the severe rain, with its umbrella tail yielding such protection as it might; and our further observation proved that it was really busy among the many small cones, now conspicuous on the larches through the absence of the leaves. We scarcely expected them to be at this work so early in the year, and are the more surprised seeing that friends who partook of a squirrel pie lately described them as not at all turpentine tasted. No doubt the aroma of beech-nuts and acorns was not yet eradicated. Of these last the supply here is not very important; as although the climate and soil is well suited to the oak, and these trees prove most valuable timber in Barcaldine, yet the fruit is very small and badly grown compared with that of more favoured districts. The finest acorns we have lifted in this region would not approach in size or flavour those of eastern Perthshire, let alone more southern counties.

We stroll along noting the abnormal growths among the trees, and particularly interested in that graceful vegetable product that occasionally plays such ungraceful antics—the birch. No one who has peeped much amid our forest foliage but must have noted and wondered at the bunches, like nests, that appear on the birch, to which we have formerly alluded, and which are formed of multitudes of twigs intertwined. Here is a small specimen, with a small-sized enormity, and we examine it closely, if perchance some younger and less complex production will furnish us with a clue to its origin. We find a less and a lesser, until we come to a very young bunch indeed, being merely the growth of a season. The branchlet has forked, as 'tis its nature to, and one end bud has seemingly been broken off. This has caused additional energy and flow of sap to the wound, and been followed by a *number* of buds, that have succeeded in growing twigs some inches long. The branch has not been strong enough to support more than one or two there, and the others have died down; the wood consequently thickens with the increasing power of the branch, and a fresh lot of buds crop out over it and grow to a certain length of twig, a proportion again dying down, and aggravating the original habit of expanding the knot by multiplication of twigs. The result is a congeries of twigs *dead and alive*, interminably interlaced around a thickening stem, and a bundle of exaggerated bud-bearers. Here are two conterminous birches, veterans of their race, the one graceful and delicately drooping as a birch should be, the other stiff and knuckly all over its branches, even to the furthest rigid, ungraceful twig. There is not a single " bunch " of twigs upon it. Yet its stem and its branches have surrounded themselves with a continually increasing aggregation of excrescences, in the shape of knots, that become hard and finely grained, and, when "skinned" and polished, make beautiful ornaments. This peculiarity of the woody fibre seems quite to have absorbed the extra vitality of the tree, and, while the twigs and branches are alike foreshortened, it is free from the other deformity. The appearance of the two against the sky is so dissimilar that they could scarcely be recognised as the same species.

We come upon a magnificent silver that has fallen to Tuesday's gale (the 22nd), falling with its forked stem on either side of a large beech, and stripping it of branches until brought up tightly wedged. It is impossible to separate them, and they must go together. The enormous roots of the silver have stretched far, but they have been completely undermined by the rabbits, and these have unquestionably weakened the hold of the giant

G

upon the river bank, and helped to complete the destruction of an enormous mass of vegetable matter.

The tide of Monday the 28th, although a neap, was as high, but not so rough, as that of the Tay Bridge night, so that we could well understand our venerable friend suggesting that the land may be really sinking to meet the waters. After the subsidence, two oyster catchers, with unexampled daring, sported but a few yards in front of our door, as they anxiously and hurriedly devoured the sickening earth-worms that had escaped the former inundation, only to succumb before this fresh and uncalled-for assault. Yesterday the little coletits in numbers were busy in terrible earnest, and regardless of our presence in the woods, probably anticipating last night's storm.

The most interesting and important stranger that has lately fallen to the gun in our district is a phalarope shot at Barcaldine. This proved to be a red-necked phalarope *(Phalaropus hyperboreus)*. These rare lobe-footed swimmers are of a remarkably tame and confiding character, apparently little used to human neighbourhood. We have only observed one before in this district, when it flew about our boat in such a confiding manner that we did not shoot it, although pressed to do so.

We observed on this occasion, as after the former severe storms, that the pheasants were afraid to trust themselves off their legs, having become thoroughly demoralised after the tempest.

DECEMBER, 1881.

"Not bad weather for the country," says one, with emphasis; "very good weather indeed," says another, sententiously, as we pass along in the pitiless rainfall, in a blink between the hurricanes. For old-fashioned gales have departed with old-fashioned tides, and it is hard to judge now whether the wind or the tide is to further transcend its ordinary movements. This week the tide was again as high as that of December, 1879, although nothing approaching that of the 22d November, which has burthened the Lorne Roads with £1800 of damages! When we consider that the wholesale destruction of boats will necessarily throw more work upon the roads, the ordinary wear and tear will in all probability be above the average for a considerable time. But the weather is good for "the country!" What is the country? Are those portions of our palmated coast subjected to those watery influences not part of the said country, and are those who go down to the sea in small boats, and reap their harvest, in part or in whole, from the waters, not part and parcel of the country? It seems a paradox to say that what is bad for us is good for "the country;" yet there is still a picking for stock on the half-green hills, and the labours of the husbandmen may be conducted with ease where last winter all labour was frozen. Certain it is that rain and mild weather have combined to make the mosses of all kind simply perfect. The brown leaves have been swept off the sward under the trees by the savage gales, and the undergrowth of moss and fern is so rich and green that one almost fancies the green leaves have simply dropped *en masse* from the boughs for a pic-nic under. Here is the fine bole of an old oak, with widespreading branches, that is in itself a field for the mycologist, with its bark completely hidden under lichen, moss, and fungus, and grey fronds of *polypodium* here and there, where they have obtained a precarious foothold. We are "wreckers" among the mass of sea-driven spoil far over ordinary highwater mark, and yet the mosses are gay and exquisitely constructed far below the banded seaware. There is a beautiful grey lichen creeping over the rocks, upon which a little red fungus has settled, sprinkling it all over with vermillion spots of various sizes; and, indeed, scarce a spot they can get a hold upon but is covered with some cryptogamic plant of beauty that will well repay gathering for closer inspection. See those green puckered d'oyleys, with grey beads, hung all over that other tree stem! Some young ladies' boarding school in the vicinity has been holding an exhibition apparently—but no, they are only the leathery lichens, growing in a circular form all over the bank. Green, and slate, and purple, to rich black, they are festooning or adorning the trees around. Now, why is it that the fir tribe are mostly in happy ignorance of this rich adornment? for, except a sapless grey lichen on the branches of the larch, all are upon the deciduous trees. The oak is perhaps richest in specimens if not in species, while the beech has some especial beauties upon its dead logs, and no small display upon its living stem. The birch, too, is in no want of extraneous clothing, and yet the beech and birch more especially are smooth-stemmed trees, and give no more foothold to the spores of these plants than the various pines, nor anything like the facilities of the wrinkled hides of well-grown larches. We want "more light" on this subject ere risking a theory of any sort. It may be that these "foreigners" are too recent interlopers to have created or adopted a set of hangers-on of their own, while trees like the British oak have been so long acclimatised that a numerous family of dependants, have been created to flourish around them, and add grandeur and richness to their "giant boles." Can the presence of turpentine be an objection to these growths, and protect the pines from their hampering clasp? Yet in the *Mycologia Scotica* there is no lack of fungi growing upon pines, and we are forced to seek elsewhere for a reason. These woods, in all likelihood, were originally composed of our native deciduous trees; and the cryptogamic flora flourishing upon them must have consequently been of the class more particularly belonging to these various trees. When the larch, silver, and other pines were introduced some century and a half ago, in a very young condition, the seeds of the fungi belonging to them would not have been present; or could not exist under the changed conditions, until the growth of the trees prepared a matrix for them. It would be interesting to know whether the rule held good, that deciduous trees scattered in a pine forest were comparatively free from cryptogamic plants, and pines of species scattered in a deciduous forest equally free on their part?

Well! now, look here, Donald. How did these come here? A good number of limpet shells among the moss well up the rocky bank, and not showing any sign of having been brought there by birds. The oyster-catcher would have devoured them on the rocky shelf from whence they were taken, and never sought to fetch them here. No boy has been at these, so far as our judgment goes, and we do not think the crow would tackle a limpit; although it is very hard to say what a cunning grey crow, that so often frequents the beach at this season, would *not* do for a meal. Yet we are not satisfied that these look like the work of crows. What do you suppose they are, or it is, that has brought these shells from the beach? "If not birds they must be rats," is the reply. Rats! Did you ever hear of rats eating limpets, now? "Yes, I have often heard of them eating limpets." This leads to close questioning of our careful and shrewd friend, and we find that a friend of his found a rat on one occasion with its lip caught by a limpet shell, under which it had slipped when pushing it off its hold. It seems absurd to fancy such a strong animal as a rat could be held by a small shell-fish, but the strength of hold of those molluscs is so great that 30lb. to 40lb. can be held hanging on to the shells without dragging it off; and once the shellfish gets notice of your attack, you may kick the toes off your boots or the shell to pieces before it will give way. So, little chance would a rat have with its lip in the grip of the creature. "I once landed on the Island of Dunstaffnage to cut grass, and it was so full of rats that I was afraid to go on; and the grass was so full of limpet shells that I could scarcely use the scythe, and had to keep sharpening it all the time," adds our informant. This was the place where the limpet had played at "pull baker, pull devil," with the rat, and had the best of it; so no doubt the rats had been driven by stern necessity to capture the only food available. It is very questionable, however, if ordinary rats have sufficiently studied the habits of the mollusca to be able to obtain a meal in this way!

With all the wind we have had of late—sufficient, if stored in an accumulator, to keep us in power for years—the country is a huge sponge, and the rain still falling in "buckets." This evening, however, it came as sleet, and the hills around are white—we hope a harbinger of frost and quiet.

A long-delayed excursion to the head of the loch was

entered upon on Monday without the smallest misgiving, but about two miles up we came upon a belt of ice that stretched across the very broadest part of the loch, and impeded further progress without an amount of damage to boat and oars that was not to be thought of. Here we saw quite a number of heads of seals in the loch, along the verge of the ice bank, giving a most Arctic character to the wintry scene. Why they should have deserted the loch lower down to congregate here we do not understand, unless we are to conclude these were properly the ordinary occupants of the portion of water covered by the ice—about $1\frac{1}{2}$ miles wide by 1 mile deep; for once we had landed and journeyed by the Appin shore to Cregan Ferry, we found the water there quite clear of ice, and the dwellers on shore unaware of its vicinity, until the crashing of a steam yacht on its way through drew their attention thereto. We attributed this ice phenomenon to the enormous rainfall of the period preceding the frost, which had found its way with a rush into the loch, there to float and freeze upon the surface. This had already helped to clear the water, by removing the fresh water from the depths—for we have rarely seen the loch so clear after so great a rainfall. But the weather was evidently still unsettled, as the seafowl and migratory ducks were excessively wild; and we peeped down at the sea bottom with the wistful gaze of one who had been long a stranger, and feared to be soon estranged again. Our time was short, and all we did was to bring to the surface a strange crab from a fathom or two that had especially attracted our attention. It proved to be only a hermit, apparently the common *Bernhardus*, under peculiarly unhappy circumstances; for he had outgrown his dwelling, the dog-whelk shell which now only covered his tail, and into which he could not withdraw his shell-clad body. He knew well his awkward position, for no sooner did we bring him aboard than he bolted out of his stolen abode, and tried the "injured innocence" trick. But his appearance was decidedly against him, like the battered nose of a prize-fighter, as he had lost pieces—not joints—off two of his legs, while one of his big claws had also been torn off. This last had just commenced to grow again, about three-sixteenths of an inch long, while the other nipper was two inches long. We picked up a bundle of barnacles on Saturday last that proved to be on an old whelk shell, while well inside the aperture a serpula tube was growing with the live annelid in it. On our return home we found the further presence of a hermit crab that had seemingly left the worm in possession as a "blind" to hermit hunters.

Last week we noted a crab with a plentiful supply of roe, another instance, if more were required, of the almost continuous "seedtime" of some marine creatures.

The herring have once more paid a visit to our southern shores, and yielded a second harvest to the more enterprising residents on Ardmucknish Bay; but coming in the midst of severe weather, the success of the fishermen was not so pronounced as it might have been. Many of these herring were in roe in *various stages* of progress—some almost ready to be thrown, and some not in a state to be deposited for a month or two. The herring were also of all sizes, one that we assisted in finding safe quarters for, measuring 13in. long and 3in. deep. We were lately discussing the "great herring question" with a venerable and experienced fisherman, more especially with reference to the name of *garvies*. He described the herring sile as being occasionally driven ashore on Loch Linnhe side, and on one occasion he witnessed them thus thrown on the rocks by the assault of a great shoal of saithe. The fish not only forced them out of the water but actually risked being stranded themselves, so far inwards did they pick the herring off the rocks. Among these small fry were a good many of a larger size—the size of garvies—that went by the name of *Garavack* or Garvock, or " or big little ones " as our informer sought to explain. What more particularly interested us was his account of the grey crows hastening to the prey, and hurrying off to the hills with several of the larger ones in their beaks, not to devour but to *hide*, returning to supply their immediate wants. So that if this keenest of crows has not yet arrived at salting herring, they have, at least, got the length of storing *garvies*.

These saithe, that prey upon the herring in their hobledehoyhood, equally stick by them in their maturity, as the multitude of coal-fish or steinlock—the full grown saithe—that follow herring shoals and devour the herring in myriads, is almost incredible. We have heard of one man in Barra who declared he could catch a ton weight of them at a spell, if his hands could stand the strain of the line; and we have seen 15 full-grown herring taken out of one of them! Yet with all their delicate feeding, —and what more delicate feeding than herring for all classes of fish?—the coal fish is one of the coarsest and least oily that comes out of the water. Black, as its name implies, large flaked, and fibrous, it is a standing protest against the theory that you can possibly feed a coarse nature into a fine one.

Talk of desolate homes! Just fancy the poor sand martins returning to their cliffs at Shian, once more to occupy the nests in their sandy faces. All gone at a sweep, and only the very back ends of one or two left to show where they once had been, for the sea has cut the bank away for several feet back. The boat circles round the stony point into the still more exposed bay of Ardtinny, and our attention is too much occupied with the force and direction of the wind, and whether we shall risk a more extended journey with that threatened storm held over us, to see all that has taken place of late. What of those sand cliffs riddled with rabbit warrens, and that other great bank, that was little but a cliff, turned into a thicket with bushes and brambles? All completely cut away; and if poor, little fudfud were at home, the whole colony must be buried under the tons of sand, and gravel, and the bushes that have fallen *en masse* into the sea, when the foundation was undermined by the lash of the waves. What consolation could it be to the most philosophical rabbit to think that he is to be *unrocked* by some very post-diluvian geologist beside himself with joy at discovering such a rich find of skeletons in the *Old Red Sandstone* of the period? Meantime, if the rabbits have really perished as completely as their warren, it will be a lucky wind for the neighbouring farmers.

"The world belongs to him that can wait," but when you have to wait three months for a calm day at low tide, a few years more or less must appear of little consequence when attending mightier eventualities. It has come at length this morning, with a light frost and no breeze, and we quite hopefully watched the darkening shore creep seaward, and the active figures of the oyster catchers follow the water-line, while the voices of curlews receded further and further from the door. Quite an unaccustomed appearance has the loch in front to-day, for the eye has become so used to the rush of the waves, and the howl of the wind has been so familiar that, like the historical miller when his water-wheel stops creaking, the stillness of a normal day comes like the stoppage of a great pulse. There is a sudden break in the smooth surface of the sea, a white streak gleams along the water, and a huge figure appears defiantly conspicuous several hundred yards off. The atmosphere gives it an unduly prominent appearance, and as the Northern Diver—for such it is—rises and flaps its wings, it appears far more important than it usually does in its "native element." Only on Sunday last, before service, when the sea outside was sadly ruffled in temper, and bipeds ashore were in an equally unbecoming state of mind, a large specimen of the Great Northern Diver was disporting itself at a few yards' distance from the shore in front of our dwelling. But this is a week day, and the weather is fine, so we need not expect such a display, and therefore content ourselves with seeking the edge of the water like the seafowl, and looking like them for unconsidered trifles cast up by the late boisterous days and nights of bluster.

We have not far to go until we meet an ungainly but interesting figure in a very forlorn plight; for once again a huge-headed, gaping object, with its formidable array of teeth prominently displayed, and its fishing apparatus much out of repair, has been left hapless by the inconsiderate force of the waves and thoughtless hurry of the receding tide! A fishing-frog *(Lophius)*, with the "bait" torn off its angle, and a series of holes driven into its soft but tough skin by crabs and buckies, is now before us, and we proceed to draw it shoreward with our boat-hook, that we may examine it at leisure. We have never before met such a large, fine liver in any of the specimens we have examined, and it bore every evidence of being in a capital condition—the liver weighing not less than 1½lb. Why are you thus, my friend, and wherefore were you left lamenting, as so many of your species so often are? Not a ventriloquist, it yet must speak from its stomach, so we cut out this organ in quest of the answer to our question. As in almost every case that has come under our inspection, when thus stranded it had come into shallow water in pursuit of skates, and in this creature, 3ft. 3in. long, we found a skate-fish 2ft. long and 16in. across the wings. The skate was uninjured by the formidable teeth of the creature, and yet it was curled up in the huge sack of a stomach, with its tail turned back and its wings folded over its back, just as if the angler had carefully packed it for immediate despatch. That the devourer had not been injured by the nature of its prey was clear from the fact that the remains of a second skate, consisting of the teeth and jaw-bones, with a few of the vertebræ, lay alongside the other; so its career of usefulness had been cut short apparently simply through being stranded. The only other contents of the stomach were of a character to demand consideration in any less gluttonous fish, but in such a gormandiser the presence of a handful of withered *Zostera marina* and a large blade of *sacharina* seaweed might mean nothing but that they had been swallowed by the omnivorous creature, along with its more legitimate prey, blindly and without intent.

It so happened that the skate in question was not the only one that came into our hands to-day, one of more notable dimensions having fallen to the skilled hands of Donald; and as we are at the "table of contents," we may note the result of a *post-mortem* just concluded.

Big crab, little crab, crab of a middle size, seven of them all in a row, one nip and a gobble, and there was an end of it. What is this now? Coming in among the crabs it is conspicuous, and very soon proves to be a *Mya Arenaria*, the large bivalve shellfish that burrows in the clay and mud at low water. You have been more successful than we were to-day, old fellow, for have we not been wandering, three-pronged graip in hand, seeking to dig up a nice set of *Mya* valves, mostly without success! We were at a loss to understand how a skate fish could capture a *Mya*, but on carefully examining the object, we came to the conclusion that it had caught hold of the end of the long siphon tube, and torn only so much of the creature out of its shell.

Now, skate fish abound in our loch, and we have examined many of them, yet what is it that makes this one so very interesting to-day? The fact is that it contains multitudes of eggs in various stages of progress, and quite overturns any theory of breeding months we might be tempted to entertain. In fact, we scarcely ever capture a female skate fish in the loch that is not well supplied with embryo eggs. In this instance none were ready for emission; nor, indeed, were any provided with the horny gelatinous shell; but there was really no difference between the condition of this fish and one captured in the summer. The eggs so closely resembled those of hens in embryo that we determined to try whether they were edible, they looked so tempting on the plate. So, half-a-dozen or more were boiled in milk, with butter, flour, and condiments in addition, but although the result was quite palatable, and without the strong taste we anticipated, yet the eggs were so doughy that our experiment merely proved that skate eggs may be eaten with satisfaction when you are hungry, and nothing more delicate is at hand. Even this is something, and may be considered sufficient result to justify the by no means disagreeable experiment on our vile body. We present the information to those whom it may concern.

It is curious how certain scientific ideas or observations become public property, and the rough general conception comes to be accepted without question by the multitude, while others rap in vain for admittance into the category of their faiths. The population have come to talk as glibly about the Gulf Stream as if they had been occupied with the thermometric readings along its lengthened course. Must we really look to some marked alteration of its course for the comparatively high temperature of our western sea this winter, and the consequent increase of activity in the reproductive organs of marine creatures? It would not be unreasonable to suppose that, apart from the cosmical influences whose action directs the prevailing currents of the ocean, the local result of an exceptionally severe winter in certain Arctic regions might partially divert the warm stream from the Gulf, through earlier contact with the cold Arctic current. The importance of this stream to Arctic explorers north of Europe has been repeatedly acknowledged, and the wide difference in its effects from year to year upon the ice of the Arctic seas is probably due both to changes in its movements and its temperature. For no doubt if the prevailing winds, when it is traversing the temperate seas, are from the northwest, it will arrive upon our coasts not only somewhat farther south, but vastly colder than if it had been subjected throughout its course to the warm hurricanes from their cradle in the Gulf of Mexico. We should thus anticipate that when, as last winter, we had a prevalence of northerly gales, the influence of the Gulf Stream would be reduced to a minimum; while this season, with our succession of south-westerly hurricanes, its influence upon our waters should be increased to a maximum. Certain it is that our short notes of surprise at the spawn of various marine creatures must be accentuated since we have had at length an opportunity of traversing the littoral during a really low tide. Never in our experience of the sea shore have we witnessed, winter or summer, such a display of spawn, more especially of whelks, as we did during last week, when over a great stretch of shore dotted with stones at verge of low tide these were literally white with whelk spawn mostly newly deposited. We could have collected bushels of it from a very limited area, so that the excessively wet season we owe to these same south-westerly winds might be naturally looked upon as the cause of the unexpected whelk harvest to follow.

Although the local temperature of the air can have little influence upon our seas, yet the same prime cause —the prevailing mild southerly gales—has influenced our gardens and woodlands, probably to their early sorrow. For not only have the leaves pushed themselves well forward on the sanguine woodbines, but the rose bushes have themselves been deceived into showing strong buds. Still more unusual and much less acceptable, if persisted in, was the lively assemblage our friend met on the highway this week. For the sun was playing mildly on a bosky corner, and had enticed thence quite a lively band of gnats, ignorant of the unkind trick the great luminary had stopped to indulge in. The Great Shadow would not be long of overtaking them, however; and no doubt they would all soon be ready for the simple and natural little epitaph, "Since I am so early done for, I wonder what I was begun for?" and not a single swallow in Benderloch to answer the pertinent question!

With what charming readiness mankind throws names, and sticks to them persistently! One class of mind is foolish because it differs from ours, and all manifestations of intellect out of the accepted groove are ignored, when they are not stigmatised as mechanical. Thus we have come to talk without further consideration of the mental action of animals as instinct, although we might probably with equal reason treat the ordinary intellectual displays of average humanity as similarly mechanical. Yet seldom can one pass a day without noting little deviations from the ordinary course of life among birds and beasts, that can only be accounted for by intelligent adaptation. A little dog that plays presistently and harmoniously with a half-grown kitten, worrying and teasing it to an amusing extent in a neighbour's parlour, shows how surroundings and upbringing eradicate a supposed instinct on the part of the dog; while the fact that the cat will hunt the doggie all about in order to have a romp with it, speaks to equal alteration of mechanical aversion into sensible regard. In similar lines ran our thoughts as we tramped along the road in the rain, and scarcely glanced at the dreary moorland alongside. As we came down upon the loch the dull hue of the ploughed land was here and there marked with the darker specks where the rooks were busy; but what was our surprise to note, a hundred yards from the water, carefully hunting the same ploughed land, a large flight of a bird livelier alike in colour and in action! A flock of oyster-catchers were busy, along with the rooks, well away from the water side. We had thought, after the great storm of November, that an oyster-catcher eating the drowned-out worms was a novelty even a few yards from the water, but here was a great band quite in their element. We have never taken anything but shell-fish from their stomachs, and have certainly never before seen a similar determination to have a share of what was forthcoming further inland. Have the birds been driven by failing supplies, now the tides are getting small; or have they reasoned that, if the rooks persistently find nourishment along the foreshores, they may in return invade with satisfaction the hunting grounds of the rooks? Limpets are, no doubt, the ordinary diet of oyster-catchers with us; but if they find a soft diet of worms is easier for even their strong bills, they may in time somewhat alter their characteristics. We suspect the younger members even now fight shy of the more difficult and vigorous species of limpets, for last Friday (23rd) during the best of the tide, we observed a flock of these birds busily engaged among the stones on a gravel spit that runs well out into the loch. Although much frequented by them, we did not believe they were feeding much, and so carefully examined one that fell to the gun on this same ground. Its stomach was certainly full of limpets, but they were so small that the bird had eaten shell and fish together in every case, while in the larger specimens they, of course, only eat the fish. The beak of this bird was not worn down, so we concluded it was this year's growth, and had not yet reached the necessary skill to succeed with the colossi of the limpet tribe, for the meat contained in one good limpet would have far surpassed the contents of all the shells in the stomach of our specimen, and would have attracted its attention at low water had it been capable of detaching one such.

JANUARY, 1882.

What a pretty picture they made, to be sure, in the comfortable room with the cheerful surroundings and every evidence of affectionate interest in the animal creation around them. Cats you call them? you say, as soon as you have recovered from the natural start as one huge barred animal leaps upon the table and another awaits with impatience, but with dignity, the proffered morsel. Cats, indeed!—tigers that have become domesticated, so far as size and appearance goes. Just look at their large soft eyes, however, and the extremely gentle ways of the beautiful creatures, and you will be better able to appreciate the fact that they have descended in the same family for generations, and both by inheritance and culture are thoroughly civilised and cultivated. Perhaps you are inclined to doubt the statement until one impatiently notifies its desire for a share of the meal, and with well-bred grace removes the Brussels sprout from the lady's fork, and continnes to "look for more" until the whole are consumed. We have all seen a cat eat grass, but one with a passionate love for such vegetable delicacies as Brussels sprouts is surely a rare creature to meet. Yet both these large, gentle carnivora showed a marked partiality for this vegetable, even from the midst of the plate full of well-fattened turkey. We are all wonderfully accommodating when food that more especially suits us is scarce; but it by no means follows that we should become more especially enamoured of a food not naturally suited to our ordinary physiological condition. But these cats had become almost vegetarians in their preference for a delicate sprout to a piece of turkey.

"I don't like the way the rooks are flying," says our

driver, while the white-tipped waves are hurrying shoreward opposite the Poet's Nook. Terribly restless are rooks and sea-birds, but we blame the actual more than the prospective weather for their conduct, and pass onwards to our destination.

We skirt the edge of a young plantation of evergreen pines, in which scores of the trees have been "browned" by the wind, almost as if burnt—the continuous severity even of the comparatively mild south-west gales having at length affected their vitality, perhaps by shaking loose their foothold in the peat. The snow is only in isolated patches on Cruachan, as we skirt the Etive shore, and the ever-increasing violence of the gale shows that the rooks had good reason to be restless and anxious. We are keeping a sharp look out for that finely-growing specimen of *Pinus nobilis*, to learn if it has stood the continuously severe weather, and happily the straight, graceful, trim figure comes in sight by the old church, as distinctive as a redcoat in a crowd. We should like much if this beautiful pine were to thrive generally in this country, as it would add a most remarkable figure to the landscape, and give a style to ordinary plantations that many seem to lack. Here is the palace. We descend to shake hands with "The Queen," the most noted figure, as it is also the best known and most buxom presence, in Benderloch. She details with quiet good-humour how her hens were carried off by the terrible gale, and shows the corner whence she escaped from her garden, while we look with interest on the specimens of fowls with reversed feathers, so rare now-a-days in Scotland. They all look as if they had got such a blast in November that their feathers had never recovered their normal position. Yet they really belong to a curious and interesting variety of the ordinary fowl. As we pluck from the stakes alongside her palace garden a few beautiful fungi, nicely scolloped and elegantly coloured, we find the dye come off at once upon our fingers, and wonder more is not done with these various cryptogamic plants in the way of extracting their often brilliant hues. Even the most sober-hued were largely used in former times as sources from which to extract most useful and durable colours, far surpassing the more fugitive or native dyes that have nearly driven them alike from our knowledge and our memory. On this southern side of the hills the fungi are more abundant still than with us, as the clouds first strike this face and pour their contents down the cheeks. Even the broom and the gorse, dry as are their stems, and hard in the grain as is their wood, are hanging with pink and yellow clusters of brilliant-hued fungi. This side of the hills is also the one to which the hares, and game generally, more especially resort in the winter, as they are perfectly aware that the mild winds, rain-laden though they be, keep it clear of snow and frost, if at all possible. But our eyes have been twice on the loch for once they have been on the paper this last hour, watching with anxiety the progress of the four-oared boat in the teeth of the gale, and as it has borne its burden shorewards at last in safety, we breathe more freely and lay down our pen.

It has long ceased to be a question of how many years have passed since we have had such and such a storm. Now it is, whether to-day's storm or yesterday's was the most violent. So far as our own feelings went (and we passed during Friday over the greater part of the region specially exposed to its visitation), we should have said the gale of 22d November was the more severe. But the consensus of opinion is everywhere against us, and the injury done to vegetation is in favour of the superior virulence of Friday's tempest. Unfortunately, it seems difficult to obtain reliable scientific data, and the widely differing figures, from places close together, lead us to acknowledge the very variable and local character of the more specially bitter squalls. Crossing by rail from West to East during the height of the storm—from 11 to 12—the clouds seemed to be travelling at the rate of the train, say 40 miles an hour—no doubt an estimate far under the speed of the exceptionally energetic bursts. We sought in vain to arrive at some conclusion respecting the direction of these more severe assaults, but the trees had been snapped in twain and overthrown in equal progression from the south round to the west, and the fact that they fell apparently as readily when under the northern shelter of a hill-side as when they faced the south-western gale on a brae face, showed the uncertainty of any ordinary calculation. It cannot for a moment be maintained that the weakest have fallen before an exceptional strain, for we have just returned from an examination in which we found many of the best rooted and best protected from position among the slain, while others, without the same advantages, and close alongside, were quite uninjured. These pointed to sharply-defined narrow bands of concentrated fury, and these lines were occasionally clearly indicated by a row of trees, not brought down the one by the other, but lying quite clear, the top of the one as it lay being some yards from the upturned roots of its fellow in misfortune. Weaker trees on either side in many such cases had escaped unhurt. Again the storm seemed to swirl over the hill top and pounce down upon some particular tree in the centre of a group, either cutting its head sharply off or levelling the whole. Here, for instance, is a well-rooted birch-tree surrounded by occasional exposed evergreens. Yet the latter have been spared, while the leafless, widely rooted, small branched birch has lifted its enormous foot almost as high as its late summit. Individual opinions under such circumstances can be of little value, and observations over a wide area are necessary to arrive at any conclusions. Fortunately for the West Highlands, the tide was ebbing ere the storm reached its height, or the record of disaster would have far exceeded anything previously recorded. As we are apparently threatened with other severe gales at high spring tides, it behoves us all to be prepared for them, and avoid as much as possible leaving removeable property within their influence. In Loch Creran no one living ever saw such a sea, the loch being one sheet of spindrift, through which the squalls cut lanes in the excess of their fury. But we are not, and have not been, cold. No sooner does the traveller cross the snowy ridge about Killin than he begins to enter a black land, sharply defined from the white region he is leaving. The south-west winds have warmed and blackened all the land up to the hill-tops, save where this wet, warm season has greened all the slopes with grass and sphagnum. As we left the road this evening, and wandered off under the lonely trees and around their fallen fellows, we could scarcely credit our eyesight at the presence of multitudes of delicate green trefoil leaves, strewn all among the dingier but still cheerfully coloured mosses. Even in our northern exposure, too, our friends hand us a beautiful opening flower of rhododendron, and we naturally expect animal life to be as plentiful with us as the vegetable. In place of this, there never was such a scarcity of life at this period of the year; and except the multitudes of gulls keeping shoreward from the constant succession of storms, there is no novel bird-life about. No doubt they are keeping to their summer haunts in the North, as we learn that even the redwing—a constant winter visitor to Ledaig —has this year refrained from taking winter lodgings beneath the kindly shadow of the famous rock.

"A mouse or a rat?" said he—just at our feet, the impudent, fearless creature! It has run under that stone on the pier-edge, so we step over to examine it carefully, when—pop! out goes the creature, and slips under another, within a foot or two of where we are. There is no fear, no haste, no undue excitement, and yet the sober-hued animal that suggests a mouse or a rat is simply a bird, and no other than our constant attendant —the quietest, most reliable, "common object of the seashore." A mudlark you call it in the South, because it always frequents sandy, muddy shores to prey upon the minute insects. A rock-pipit it is properly called, as it not only constantly hops about the rocky seaboard, but it is really difficult to imagine a portion of our rough coast without this active little bird, scarcely observable, it is so like in colour to the ground it affects. In Scotland it is often misnamed the "shore lark," of brilliant plumage, not uncommon on some parts of the East Coast of England, but extremely rare as a rule in this country. The rock pipit (*Anthus Aquaticus*) is both very common and very familiar, and its gentle little chirp, as it suddenly alights in your immediate neighbourhood, is frequently the only cause of your discovering its proximity.

An observant correspondent asks us what is the so-called "cheepuc" that occasionally startles the quiet fisherman, as he sits in his boat on the bay, or off the silent shore in the dusk? Can any one suggest any other creature, marine or terrestrial, that is likely to make night alarming or interesting, and would answer to the peculiar name of "cheepuc." It is unnecessary to name snipes, beetles, or any of the fish called gurnets, that are well known as being musically inclined.

We are quite "at sea" this week, revelling in the unexpectedly fine weather, and unable fully to comprehend the extent of our beatitude. We had come naturally to hum the verse—

> "The weather is not as it used to wis,
> The nights are terribly damp,
> And I always his the rheumatiz-
> Except when I have the cramp."

But we are still in the middle of the winter in moist Benderloch, although it is almost impossible fully to credit the fact. Now that the weather is calm and dry, the extreme mildness tells more forcibly. It is not enough that primroses are full blown all around our dwelling, that the birds in the stricken woods are singing as merrily as in the opening spring time, but all nature is out of joint and staggering about, like a schoolboy awakened during a moonlight night and told that it is morning. About a month ago we saw what we fancied a bird issue from a shed and skirt the edge of a house, but our companion declared it to be a bat. We had discredited his sight, and forgotten the incident, when two days ago in early dusk we found ourselves the centre for the gyrations of an unmistakable bat, that continued to hunt as steadily as in the summer time. It had evidently been awakened by the mild temperature from an attempt at hybernation, and finding its stomach awakening at the same time, had gone forth to seek its prey. It is now some time since we mentioned a flight of gnats, and small flies are not uncommon, so perhaps Mr. Leather Wings, as the children call him, may actually find its customary food. Indeed, a friend just informs me he saw another bat "on another shore" in the gloaming, and, what is more to the purpose, saw actually a trout leaping in Loch Nell mill-dam yesterday! What would a trout leap at except at a fly, and if there are flies for trout why not for our friend the bat? At any rate, the fact that a trout has been leaping at a fly; and a bat on the hunt for gnats in the gloaming, and duckweed in green splatches all over the ditches, points to a most extraordinary condition of nature in January. Notwithstanding the gloomy damp weather at the end of last week, the clouds seemed to have broken at one point over "The Craig," and upon this hill, so beautiful in sunshine, the sun poured down a subdued wealth of light, that showed it up with all the hues of early summer; for it is even now well clothed with grass and mosses, and stealthily disports itself in all the borrowed livery of May. On Monday the wind was still blowing smoothly, and a cormorant perches on an uncovered rock in the water, extending its wings as to make a cross, and allowing the wind to blow steadily under its plumage. "It is facing more east, and the wind will go round in that direction, says a voice at our elbow," "for we say that the cormorant will always face the way the wind is going to blow." Very rarely do we note a cormorant in such close proximity, and we half expected the promised gale in consequence; but next day there was the same bird again, in the same position, and facing still more east. Still another day found the bird imitating the orthodox scarecrow figure, and yet more to the east did it face; and certainly the wind has not been less easterly than before this stray meteorologist made its appearance, no doubt having been sitting at the feet of Mr. Wragge and Ben Nevis during the summer.

Most sportsmen know how a non-aquatic bird behaves when it is either suddenly forced to take to the water or falls there to the gun. Not only does it make a terrible splashing and sputtering, but appears really alarmed for its safety in this unknown and dreaded element. No class of birds is less aquatic than the gallinaceous—birds of the wood and the heath, the rock and the mountain. Yet even these birds seem to accommodate themselves to circumstances in a remarkable way, as the following occurrence will testify :—The plantations have not been shot over for black cock for some weeks; but the other day a wounded bird was encountered that had evidently been subsisting during the intervening period without being able to take flight. When pursued it eventually took to the stream at a deep portion, and not only swam steadily and freely, with its wings close to its side, but actually went under the bank and took refuge in a hole, as a wild duck would do. As the bird was captured in this position there is no doubt about the species, and a very fine specimen of a black cock it was, in beautiful plumage. Unable to escape from ordinary danger by flight, it had acquired the art of swimming, and took naturally to the very arts that specially appertain to water hens or coots. That birds of this class are particularly helpless on the water is abundantly evident from the dislike of our domestic fowls to entering or encountering water; and the case of a hen with ducklings is often referred to as an instance thereof, not even its affection for its apparent offspring inducing it to leave the shore. A still more definite measure of incapacity was met with last autumn, by a shooting party on Loch Creran. They could not imagine what strange objects they were approaching near the middle of the loch, and were more than surprised to find a brace of hen pheasants with their heads down and feet in the air; exactly in the same condition as the poor little page, who got no quarter, but who was found "with his heels in the air and his head in a water butt." Not a sign of shot or other violence was to be found upon them, and as they were quite warm, it was supposed they had just attempted to fly across the loch, and, having over-estimated their powers, fallen into the water to perish helplessly. For the pheasant is an unwieldy bird, and of no great power of flight. Yet it is scarcely credible that any bird in its ordinary state should be unable to keep itself afloat for a reasonable time, and the seemingly sudden surrender together of two hen pheasants is as remarkable in its way as the intelligent adaptation of the black cock to its altered circumstances.

A very simple and natural explanation, surely! The oyster-catchers have continuously been frequenting ploughed land, and we received the very sensible reply to our query, "Why are these birds forsaking the shores and taking to wandering with the rooks and seagulls?" that the shore had really been so cleared of food by the long-continued and severe gales that no shore bird could readily obtain its usual prey. There must be something in this, and the numbers of limpet-shells we noted on the foreshore to-day seemed to tell of greater loss than the usual wear-and-tear of a shore existence.

Our boat has been skulking in a corner all these weeks, fearing to follow the fate of its many fellows; but the tide had been told it would be a big one, and evidently thought so to, and took a good race down for the upward leap. Such a display of seabottom had not been vouchsafed us for long, so we were not slow in mustering for a scamper on the loch. The sail has said goodbye to the yard in the gale, and the mast is looking for wreckage since November, so we must fain trust to our oars for a run down to Aird's Point. Unaccustomed hands settle down to oars with satisfaction, and after a preliminary canter, to see if a small flock of widgeon would await closer inspection, we turn seawards. The morning is beautiful, but just as we get well clear of the point and out into the open water, a sharp sniff comes from the south-west, and we look at one another questioningly. The American gale predicted to-day, and the "chart" threatening all sorts of evil, are we wise to proceed? Trusting in the fine tide as a sure indication of good weather outside in the Atlantic, despite the white horses now rapidly rising, we venture on. The loch is found to be full of widgeon all as wild as possible, and even mallards are not scarce, although they frequent more the head of the loch. Down we go easily, for we are following the tide, and soon arrive among the struggling waters, and turn to cross towards the islets in the midst of the turmoil of the current. The tide turns sooner here, and we suppose it is near slack tide, but are soon undeceived, and have a desperate struggle ere we slip behind the banks of half-submerged tangle and reach a rocky haven. It is months since we *could* have landed here, and long since we have done so, and we can scarcely credit our eyes at the lavish prodigality of growth everywhere manifest. Our lady comrade is wild with delight at the brilliant-hued multitudes of *Trochus Zizyphinus*—that crimson-tinted spiral shell so finely shaped—crawling everywhere upon the rocks. The tangle seems never to have ceased growing, and is a perfect forest of great stems and magnificent fronds, and were it not that we are seeking other treasures we could well spend the few half-hours that the ocean can afford us on this rock in studying the various capers of this vegetable growth. Here is one fine stem that has actually coiled round upon itself, and formed a granny knot, afterwards spiralling off towards the frond in a remarkable manner, considering the usually straightforward growth of this great seaweed *Fucus palmatus*. Again, as we proceed, remarking upon the quite exceptional character of such conduct the like of which we have never before met, we come upon a beautifully spiralled stem of *Saccharinus*, like a great corkscrew. Only in such an ocean corner could similar growths be found, for here the currents meet and fight, and whirlpools swirl perpetually, and no doubt these stems have received their youthful bias in some such turmoil. We scramble over the rocks, and hunt the pools deep with sand from broken shells, with quite childish delight, so long have we been cornered and cabined by the gales, but nothing except the hardiest growths reward our exertions. Here and there a brilliant sun-star is found by the edge of the water, strangely beautiful, and with none of the repugnant appearance of the equally interesting and wonderful five fingers. Little five fingers are all about, and as they appear curled up on some object, the gazer cannot fail to corroborate the naturalist who finds the sea-urchin is but a star-fish with its toes together. The common doris is as numerous here as are the big buckies, and both are spawning as vigorously as in the heat of summer. The strangely and beautifully spiralled spawn of the nudibranchs is, indeed, in masses all about the shore, and all had an inkling of the destination of a large proportion of it in an individual of the dog-whelk tribe, that in one case had set itself calmly down to devour the freshly-deposited offspring of the higher class mollusc.

One unmistakable result of the mild season was the fact that the hermit crabs, whether in barnacle-covered houses of the whelks, or brilliant-zoned *Zizyphinus*, or rough old dwellings of the buckies, were always in pairs! Fancy two hermit crabs making love to one another! They put one more in mind of Diogenes in his tub, or two scolds abusing one another from contiguous cottage doors. We are carefully picking the animals from the interior of some specimen of *Zizyphinus*, when a poor boiled hermit crab answers the summons of an inserted pin. Ay! and here is the result of the Gulf stream bringing tropical manners into the sedate winter seas of the North, for you are as well supplied with roe comparatively as the finest berry lobsters! Sticking here and there about the rocks on the very verge of the lowest tide, are a lot of fine rock oysters, not too close to interfere with one another's dinners, and so all fat, and fresh, and flourishing. The late Frank Buckland started the question as to what side it was natural for the oyster to lie upon—whether the concave or flat side should be downmost. No doubt these oysters you find lying free in mud or sand are usually with the flat side downmost, because that is the natural side on to which they would be rolled. But those oysters found sticking to rocks on to which they have attached themselves in their transition state, have invariably the concave side downmost. This is only as one would predicate, because the oyster of our shores, being an inhabitant of the foreshore, and, consequently, obliged to be occasionally out of water at spring tides, can keep a supply of water in the concave shell, but with the flat side downward scarcely any moisture can be retained. We do not recollect ever having seen an oyster attached to a stone or rock by the flat side.

No sooner do we get clear of Eriska Sound with the entering tide than the cry of "the Yankees are upon us" rises to every lip, but after a desperate pull to the shelter of the "old wife's rock," the fitful blast has shifted and permits us to dodge home, with a prospect of dreaming of endless tangle stems, and tangle fronds covered with *pellucidæ*, and surrounded by crimson barred *trochi;* while dog-whelks and great sea anemones and multiform and many coloured zoophytes, gleam through the waters around.

FEBRUARY, 1882.

We have had a charming day ending in a beautiful moonlight night, and the whole of Benderloch has looked its best under the double smile of sun and moon. To-morrow is full moon, and we are hopefully looking forward to decent weather, although a most unwelcome radiance surrounds the moon to-night, as if it had the will but not the way to form a warning halo; and the peculiar snakes in the sky as the sun went to its rest seemed also to presage wind. In the meantime we have enjoyed a thorough summer day, as we wandered through the low-lying land "between the lochs;" and not only were the gnats busy at mid-day about the roadsides, but the bees themselves were afoot, and there was no reason whatever to prevent them finding some little honey in the unseasonable flowers. Everything seemed out of place and time, so we stopped in our path across the still growing sward, and watched the movements of a young horse, half-hoping half-fearing to see it strangle itself on the wire of the fence. Will it put its foot through the lower wires and complete its entanglement, will a stray dog scare it and disorganise its movements, or does it at all appreciate its danger? With its head between the highest and second wire it cooly scratches itself, first on the one wire, then on the other, regardless of our presence, and with unhurried assurance. When satisfied, the head is straightened and withdrawn with ease and celerity, when he at once turns and proceeds to the application of an *a posteriori* argument against the utility of wooden stobs and ordinary iron wire! If a young horse had a very little more intelligence it would never become an old drudge; and the result of severe labour on horse as upon man is to divert power from the brain into the muscles, and stimulate the little intellect that is left more to avoid imposed labour than to perform it skilfully.

"I'm so glad you left the stone circles," said the enthusiastic archæologist, to the improving farmer on whose land we are now, regardless of the fact that the trouble of removing so many great stones was the only safeguard they possessed. We pass close by them, now little raised above the moss, and seek the summit of the serpentine mound near at hand, from whence we look towards Loch Creran on the one hand and Ardmucknish Bay on the other. A serpent mound, most unmistakably some would say, for it winds along from the moss near the foot of the hills, and with a few simple gaps continues along under our feet, and around behind the old castle, until its diminishing and still more twisted tail ends in the moss towards the shores of Loch Linnhe. But one portion of the mound is solid rock, and a great portion water-worn gravel, and another portion of still larger water-worn stones; and to suppose the moveable portion, however symmetrical, to be artificial, is to imagine our ancestors to be more numerous than the ignorance and folly required to erect such a supposed artificial mound could have possibly enabled them to be. No one can stand where we now do, and look from sea loch to sea shore, without concluding that the great moss between did not always interrupt the waves of the one from washing into the other, the level even now being but little above the sea. Between us and Ledaig two clear beaches cross the country, that evidently mark the retrogression of the waters through the elevation of the land; and the broken snake on which we now stand is most likely a still prior beach, on which the billows tossed pebbles of all sizes, here and there breaking through the softer portions, and rolling through that dip into Loch Creran. For our friend has pushed a fishing rod 18 feet down through the peat moss of that narrow depression between firmer ground, by which the waters no doubt rolled into Creran through the break alongside, ere they retired to form the next beach about a mile distant, leaving an uncommonly good snake to crawl across several miles of Benderloch. There is almost sufficient evidence of design and workmanship in its regularity to bolster up a theory of a Roman fortification, if such were not absurd.

As we approach the stream, swollen by last night's rain, we find the stepping-stones unapproachable, and yet an hour's labour with a spade would divert it into its old course, at present silted up with sand from landward and seaward. This is to be done "to-morrow;" and tomorrow, if it comes seldom in the Lowlands, never arrives in the Highlands. Cockles were lying all about, for the disturbed sea has dislodged them from the sand, and they too, will be preparing for maternal arrangements at unseasonable and unreasonable times, no doubt deluded by this troublesome weather. For we cannot suppose that it is really normal to find even mollusca spawning at all seasons of the year; but we must place them on the same footing as unusual flowers. A huge horse mussel (*Modiola*) that we brought from Loch Linnhe last week proved to have 1¾ oz. of meat in it, and of this weight about half was spawn in a condition almost ready for throwing; while oysters are already as forward as they should be in May. We are proud of our potatoes in Benderloch, and usually they do well for us, but this year no smacks seek our coast with open holds, and the mild weather is sending the pitted roots into a dangerous state of restless activity, that will force our farmers to sell them in the shape of beef and dairy produce. "It never rains but it pours," and what with acres of our finest seaward land covered with gravel by the storm, and heaped with sand still further inland, even the farmers as they progress with their spring work, and look with satisfaction at the picking even now on the hills, consider we have no more reason to murmur on sea than they have on shore. How can a wind damage a stretch of agricultural land? we asked ourselves, and here is the answer in covered acres; while our friend tells us dolefully of a year in which the wind blew seaward with such fury that, on the light sandy soil of Ledaig, all the *seed* was blown from the fields into the sea, and might be seen floating for days on the top of the water. The sea water is no doubt injurious to agricultural land, but, on the other hand, the evidence is in favour of its action on pasture. On lands close to the sea that are covered every spring tide, the produce of butter is improved, and we learn of a dairy-woman who always noticed a marked improvement in the first churning after every spring tide! This could not arise from its action on the grass, so much as upon the cattle themselves, the salt no doubt acting as a stimulant to their secretions, as cows are always fond of, and advantaged by, a proportion of salt.

We were wandering yesterday along the edge of the stream where it cuts its path through the blue clay, and where the sea was soon to rise several feet deep. Here and there the shells of *Myarenaria* were sticking tenantless out of the clay that had been cut away from about them, and the smaller but still large *Mya truncata*, that other siphon shell fish, were scattered all about, either emptied by the long bills of the curlews, or the owners having given up the struggle in disgust. Suddenly the bed of the stream was obscured for many yards by a moving curtain of a hazy character, and we stopped to examine the phenomenon more closely. Why, the *Mysis* were casting their young in August and September, and yet here are absolute myriads of them about a quarter of an inch in length, thronging every corner of the stream, and filling all the pools in the clay foreshore. What is the meaning of this; and is it a quite exceptional infliction upon our waters? We know that this small class of crustacean forms a most important portion of the diet of the very largest marine animals, and it is more than presumed that the herring also obtains a large proportion of its food from among the same class: is there any connection between the two? There are two herring invasions into our western lochs, one in the autumn and another in the spring, and on both occasions they come prepared to breed; but also many come with no such parental object in view. Do they time their visits to suit the spawning periods of these small crustacea and other such? At the same time it must be noted that we never observed such a quantity of young of this creature at this season of the year on any former occasion, and it may be quite exceptional. For we have observed many classes of crustacea spawning this winter; not only the ordinary green crabs, *C. mænas*, but among the hermits scarcely a Bernhardus turns up without a plentiful crop of "berries."

A fresh bag on the dredge, we push out into the loch and try for scallops on the best scallop ground we know of. For have we not a lady on board who has the sense to appreciate these delicate bivalves, and who looks to be rewarded for wet feet and a seat in the cold wind by a delicious repast! The wind blows us sharply off the shore and across the swiftly running currents, so the dredge is hard to keep in proper trim, and do we not wickedly take advantage of the said wind to allow our boat to drift into deeper water than that in which the *Pecten opercularis* is mostly found! The tow-rope is out to the last inch, and we are punished by vainly dragging the dredge through soft mud and bringing it aboard through all the extra fathoms without the smallest result. But the wind again favours the naturalist more than the "gourmet" or the pot-hunter, and we once and again drag up evidences that the iron has been deeper than the primary object of the expedition warranted.

At last the dredge comes up heavily weighted, and

evidently straining the linen bag to the utmost, so we confidently anticipate we have gone deep among the blue clay, and expect to see a bucket of this very aggravating material—that escapes but slowly through the close bag—come up to demand careful manipulation in the sieve. But, no! We have actually reached the ladies' treasure-house, and a good supply of *Pecten opercularis*, as beautiful as they are delightful, have arrived on board. Now that we have struck the ground, we cannot possibly escape our responsibilities, and soon the bucket is well supplied with the chattering, restless beauties, and the mass of life is too great for us to examine between times. But one thing is apparent to the meanest observer, and that is the gregarious character of many of the creatures brought on board. The *P. opercularis* came up in a body when we hit the proper ground, and the *turritella* shells in many hundreds when we hit their proper muddy habitat, while scarcely a single ascidian is met on their ground. We move a little further out of the course of the current, and lo! the social tunicates appear in great bunches, not one being obtainable from the ground in the vicinity. Each class seems to monopolise to a great extent the ground it affects. We have clearly not been much among the tangle, for only one specimen of *P. varius* shows itself, and this partially prickly and more elongated species sticks mostly to the rich fronds of the larger seaware by means of a byssus like a mussel, and thence spreads its delicate double fringe of ciliæ into the surrounding water. Whew! as we dive into the last bagful, is there not a fine specimen of *P. maximus*, all alive O; the second only we have rescued from oblivion in the mud, although the empty shells in numbers are found on shore. Deeply cupped on one side and flat on the upper, this large species is clearly accustomed travelling —for they are very active—on the convex side, for the flat side in this instance is heavily freighted with the domiciles of serpulæ and barnacles while the other is rubbed clean. Another proof of the steady use of the lower shell for standing the brunt of locomotion is its superior strength, not only of form but of construction, while the flat shell is almost invariably of more or less bright colouring, the other being dull and colourless. This would naturally be the result of continuously facing the light in the one case, and being debarred from it in the other, as we see in the back and belly of a flat fish. Plenty of growing *Opercularis*, from half an inch to an inch and a-half, are there, and the shrewd provider, with much foresight, is tossing them into the briny sea for future attentions. We are just in the nick of time—for not all *small* pectens are necessarily young ones—and we rescue two fine specimens of a small species(*P. tigrinus*), beautifully marked, and one of them quite an inch in length and the same in breadth—a large specimen of this gracefully-shaped pecten or scallop. These, too, are darker and more richly coloured on the one side, and a few delicate and minute whirls of serpulæ (*Spirorbis*) are attached to the side least subjected to friction.

The lamp is lit and the tub lifted on to the table while we examine carefully the various heaps of trash, lest something of interest may have been omitted in our rude prior examination. Only a little fellow, but a welcome one, for you are the second we have met in Loch Creran of the "web footed" starfishes (*Palmipes*); so you are carefully transferred to a roomy aquarium. Again the search is rewarded by the discovery of a sea-mouse of moderate dimensions, and with its irridescent "hairs" very dull indeed. It must have got sadly squashed in the passage of the heavy bag through the water, with its load of pectens on the top of it. This is a visitor from the mud; and so is the next on the list, a live specimen of *pes-pelicani* or pelican's foot shell, and it is also transferred to the receptacle for the temporary wanderings of creatures whose future lot has been undecided. Alas! for the careless act. When we went to seek our small *palmipes* it had disappeared, and not a single possible adversary, but the pelican's foot was within the bounds of habitation. The myriads of turritelli and other uninteresting specimens have been run over, and we have lifted the last handful of muddy sediment to run it through the finer seive, when in doing so we find a lump that has somehow escaped us, amid the mud in our hand. A novel species of sea-anemone most certainly, we exclaim, and once it is washed clean and transferred to a transparent glass our surmise is to us a surety. This also is the first specimen of the interesting *Adamsia* that we have met with here, and we watch its reawakening life with much satisfaction. "Send for me when it has shown its character," says our friend; and seeing we have been so long over this bucketful, we will set it aside, and indulge in a supper of *P. opercularis*, which we are thankful you are not here to rob us of, as the smell would overcome your severest prejudices, and the beauty of the dishful undermine your most unselfish instincts.

Stories of nests coming from all sides, we were wondering whether those birds that nest earliest in ordinary seasons would also be deluded into starting operations, like the redbreast and the sparrows. So, finding ourselves in the vicinity of the heronry we wandered through the sphagnum, that is gradually reasserting its sway over the fields these moist years, until we arrived under the fir trees, where the long-limbed birds do annually congregate for nesting purposes. The heron is one of the first birds to commence building, but not a sign of herons or nests was to be seen, and even those of last year had, without exception, been blown to the last twig out of the trees. It was quite clear they had no intention as yet of setting to work; and the gales that have once more returned, to whistle all the day and shriek all night through the woods, are not such as to induce these unwieldy birds to fly about with over-balancing sticks among the tree tops. At anyrate, both herons and rooks, regardless of blooming primroses and wonderfully green hillsides and fields, await with dignified patience the proper time, so that they must have an almanac to go by, of which we poor mortals have not been able to discover the secret.

The huge tree is leaning across the road, and its roots will carry a stretch of paling along with them should they turn up to the heavy gale, so the saw is hard at work through the tough roots of the beech where they have buttressed up the stem. Ominous cracks come suddenly: and as the blast strikes with a warning howl and a 'sough,' the mass is toppled over, and falls with a crash that gives a schoolboy-surge of delight to the most callous onlooker. Enormous branches, like young monarchs themselves, stretch onward in a circle eight or ten feet from the ground, and two of them are bound indissolubly together. A good foot through is the joining, and it is hard as heart of oak; for the beech is a hard tree of itself, and this portion is particularly so. We stand and watch the axe playing upon the joining, curious to observe how the junction is effected, for it is a type of many similar vagaries in the forest. Well! the smaller branch, some four to six inches in diameter, has simply grown straight through the larger one, *and still retains its bark*, although deeply embedded in the hard wood. Yet, outside, the barks overlap, and there it was really impossible to say exactly how the junction had come about. On this great tree there is scarcely a straight stick, although it may represent twenty carts of wood, for every few inches along the branches there are knots like the fist, apparently caused by insects distorting the growth. These microscopic mites exercise a great influence upon forest trees.

We lay down our axe and step under the shelter, for the blast is bitter and hail-laden. A group of Highland cattle are standing in the field, where the storm lately cast some great branches from that stately oak tree. They have not left a single twig of it, and are now busily engaged chewing the branches assiduously. We should have supposed that oak bark thus partaken of would have had a very injurious effect on the interior arrangements of the cows; but perhaps they feel the lack of fodder at this season of the year, and find a dose of astringent bark act successfully in reducing the undue summer capacity of their stomachs!

Just like children! we mutter, as, looking out of our little window, we note the sheep on the foreshore. The tide is coming in, and the stream, so lately a comparative driblet, is now several feet deep with the brackish water. Sheep, "of course," don't think, and only act from instinct and "follow my leader." Down the gravel bank comes the foremost sheep, walks steadily into the water, and swims across to the grass on the other side, followed by all the rest, except one! This fellow comes quietly down the bank, walks just over its feet in the water, looks at the grass at the other side, peeps through the water before it, casts a half glance backwards at the grassless gravel as if ashamed of itself, takes another step forward, and tries to look as if it merely went in to cool itself. "I'm not the least afraid, and I can swim as well as you," it says to those already over; then quietly turns and walks sedately ashore! Now, why did it not follow its neighbours? It evidently decided that "the game was not worth the candle," and said, "I'm not such a sheep as I look," as plainly as possible. We have been lately amused with the habits of our ducks compared with the fowls. It is the custom with us to give them a feed in the morning ere they start on their peregrinations, but the ducks will rather want their matutinal meal than take it before they have a swim, while the hens will rush at it with energy. No matter although the food is at their feet the ducks have a plunge in the sea and a good swim, and return "hot foot" to what may be left.

Yes! the disappearance of our webbed starfish was a mystery; and next morning the soap would not lather, and we thought our hands must be salt from dabbling in the salt water. But neither glycerine nor brown Windsor would do, and the more we rubbed the less chance there seemed of ultimate success. So we hurriedly tried the soap direct upon our persons, but the water would not take it off, and it gradually dawned upon our awakening senses that there was a reason more potent than badly made soap. Our damsel had transferred a ewer of sea-water from our stock aquarium to our bed-room; and although she looked as innocent as a sucking dove, we have a strong suspicion that the enemy that so struck at our domestic arrangements had no especial affection for starfish, webbed or otherwise.

We had a share of the gale of Saturday last, and by Sunday it had gone round to the N.W., with the result that unexpectedly the lowest spring tide we have known for years was experienced. Stretches of sea-bottom were exposed to the vulgar gaze that had not seen the sky, except through water, for an indefinite period. The consequence of such a low tide, along with the severe gale, was soon to be seen in masses of seaware along the beaches, and among some of it we were surprised to note quite heaps of skate eggs, looking so fresh that we supposed them newly thrown on the neighbouring cairn. On investigation, however, they were all empty, either through the exit of the mature fish, or, as in some instances, through having been devoured by some small borer. As we strolled along it was remarkable to observe how clean the beach was, the gale having thrown loose all freely-growing seaware; and we could well appreciate the joke of our shrewd friend, who insisted that his companion was so lazy he had not cut the seaware on the foreshore allotted to him for so long, that when he went to it, hook in hand, there was none to cut, the gales having swept it all off and thrown it up on his neighbour's beach. Suddenly, we came upon a long-necked shell-fish, with its protruding black siphon tube, and immediately thereafter we found these in heaps that would have made barrow loads. Now this is an admirable shell-fish to eat *(Mya truncata)*, and vast quantities of delicious food was here being lost, but no one could help it. They must have become so numerous on the sand that this lost its coherence, and the dash of the waves at the lowest of ebb had flung them all in helpless masses out of their holes. A similar result has followed the great increase of the razor fish (*Solen*), which were thrown ashore one year in Ardmucknish Bay in great quantities. So that in the case both of the seaweed and the shellfish the onslaught of humanity, when not excessive, is a protection to the species.

Ha! you rascal! That is the way you manage is it. Here is a large star-fish with its arms around a shell-fish (*tapes*), or rather the shell-fish fixed at the angle of two of its rays, and despite the dash of the waves it is busily occupied, having already *sucked* a great part of the fish out of the shell.

If it *is* Sunday, said everybody, what does it matter? to-morrow is the second day after the moon, and the tide ought to be better still. But Monday came, and the wind was again stiff from the south-west, and the waters elected not to face it, but to remain quietly in the loch! The tide is passed, and we have missed it, now said our little world, dolorously; but we will make the most of what little there is, and enjoy a day at the "shore" on Loch Linnhe. The boat is supplied, and we turn seawards, while all the morning anxious eyes have watched "the carry," if perchance there might come north in the wind. North it is distinctly, and when we reach the islets off Aird's Bay it is clear that the waters have made a bolt of it out to the Atlantic, for such a tide we have rarely seen. All the littoral ocean world is caught napping, as foot after foot is exposed, and we revel in the wonderful profusion of life displayed amid these current-haunted rocks. Life creates life; evidently here it is a "London town" with the higher life grazing on the lower, and a score of currents bringing nourishment from many a varied foreshore and sea-bottom. The great horse mussels are as thick as they can lie in the shade of the great tangle fronds. These are 6ft. long in the great stem, with an equal length of frond, and this does not at all represent their absolute stretch, for other tangles grip with their roots the upper portion of the stem, and add greatly to the length, this occurring in some instances several times, so that the end of the last frond must have been quite 20ft. from the original attachment. This original stem had correspondingly strengthened to hold it, and was sometimes quite 3in. in diameter. Our hands are scored among the barnacles, and we can scarce keep our feet among the slippery tangles; but down, down goes the tide, and the islet we have lately landed on by boat is now to be reached from its larger neighbour. With some care though, and as we cross and recross with our feminine burden, just to let her eyes behold the wonders under "that rock," we stagger like a giant in drink. But what a sight! The wonderful colonies, rich in orange or yellow, or delicately white, known as dead men's fingers, are no longer fingers, but are hanging from the roof of the little ocean cave in masses like the closed hand and wrist. Yellow, and purple, and orange, and violet, sponges almost cover the rock—of the most varied texture are they too, and all exceedingly beautiful; starfish, from the huge bloated fellows 13 inches and upwards in diameter, to the delicate, fragile, brittle stars, are crushing themselves into the crevices; while the suns, in many-hued beauty, are lying at the bottom of the pools scoffing at the great original that threatens so soon to burn us up. But what are those moving their beautiful limbs; all about are little creatures, rosy tinted, gripping on to the rock above them with their tentacled centres, and awaiting the return of the water that never before so left them in the lurch? "Encrinites," we exclaim, as for the first time in our experience we come upon quite a haunt of the beautiful Comatula rosacea, the only British species of crinoid. How beautiful they look thus at home, although restless under their waterless condition; quite a score of them among the rock oysters, the lovely-tinted Zisyphinus shells, and the other wonders that embellished the little cave; while close alongside, attached to the tangle stems, grew masses of purple dulce, richly toned and glancing in the light.

We suddenly make a plunge at an object that especially interests us, wedged in at the bottom of a pool. This is a scallop or pecten of a particular species. Should we meet with certain species we know, the chances are they are from a considerable depth, while another is generally attached by its mussel-like byssus to the tangle fronds at low water of springs; and another small species is a free swimmer from whatever depth our dredge can reach. But we did not know exactly whence to say Pecten pusio came. Unlike all the other pectens, it attaches itself like an oyster to the rock or some other hard attachment, and grows its commonly rough, twisted, and contorted shell, while remaining firmly fixed in some secure corner where it is not easily got at. We no sooner find one than others are forthcoming, and we discover that it is not uncommon even so far up towards the foreshore as is reachable this day. The wide range of action of the Pecten family is thus remarkable, from the active, beautifully-shaped deep-water *P. Maximus* and *opercularis* to the lightly attached *P. Varius* and the securely anchored *P. Pusio*—the most degenerate in appearance and character of all the tribe.

The rush of a wave startles us in the midst of our cogitations, and it is clear we must leave the haunts of the sea nymphs for an indefinite period. "Stop the boat a moment." Our boat hook is swept out, and in comes a sun indeed—quite $6\frac{1}{2}$ inches in diameter, as large as a dinner plate, and tinted with all the glories of the sunset. Murmurs of admiration break from all. "Back the boat," we call, as we seek to stay it in the current, "and examine the fragments of the feast Mr. Sun was engaged upon." "Flowers of the sea, or delicate sea-weeds!" you exclaim. Well, the cannibal was actually devouring its own kind. No wonder it was a sun, for it was building itself up on the rays of a star-fish, large as our finger each of them!

MARCH, 1882.

We were coming up the Sound of Eriska, and were then a good mile from the Appin shore, when one of our crew observed that there was a weasel on the shore. We smiled at the idea, for to see a brown weasel on a dusky foreshore at a mile distant was a feat we believed no eyes in the boat could accomplish, and even our own are fairly telescopic. However, there was really no mystery whatever, and the most ordinary vision could discern the Stoat in its winter robe of white, in a state of intense activity among the seaweed at low water. What it was about remained unknown, but it continued for a length of time to chase something all about the seaware, and may have been hunting some of the smaller fry, such as mice. We do not suppose the tribe eat crabs, at least we never heard of it, and the greater probability is that the exceptional tide may have induced the smaller mammalia to emulate the larger, and have a constitutional feed among the marine herbage. How conspicuous the creature was even at that great distance, and how its natural protection in an ordinary winter betrayed it when thus exposed to our mild season.

The rooks, it seems, have really been betrayed into commencing operations a fortnight ago in our neighbourhood, and quite little heaps of sticks are growing on the trees. The last three days' gale stopped their labours, but this morning they are again busy; so the great bunches of primroses, the yellow daffodils, the bushes of flowering currants gay with strong-scented flowers, with the apple-blossom showing in some corners, and all the gooseberry bushes getting green, have started these wise birds, despite their ordinary almanac. We wonder if that sparrow's nest on the side of the public road, evidently already filling, had anything to do with it? The rooks are so much earlier than all small birds that they must first have grown bewildered, then ashamed of their delay, and finally aggravated at the impertinent sparrow's progress, and rushed, regardless of consequences, into the matrimonial market and the building trade.

Well! a tortoise is nothing to you. We have had you for a week at least, and you have not succeeded in walking round the tumbler. *Pycnogonum littorale* they call you, too, and of all living creatures with which the ordinary world is best acquainted you resemble the active, industrious, self-reliant, and determined spider. It is, however, only in a very superficial way that you bear any likeness to an insect, for you are really a crustacean of sedentary habit—parasitic upon cetacea, say the best authorities. Now, where the cetacean came from or went to, that you were originally, or intended to be ultimately, attached to, it would be difficult to say, although it is certain you are intended by Nature, and your parents, to obtain your living without too great an effort. The little pig-like snout and the half-dozen limbs will scarcely take the trouble to turn or move, and if you draw all the limbs out one by one you can finish the operation before the one with which you commenced has drawn itself half-way back again. And yet most ordinary crustacea are especially active in your condition, for you have a great deal to look after, a little bag with many hundred eggs covering the whole under surface of your body. At the end of every limb is a long sharp claw, and the main purpose of its existence is clearly to get a hold of a fat sinecure and hold on to it tenaciously. We should suppose that seals are the most likely bodies in which these parasites exist, and the only two we have seen here seem to have been brought on oyster shells from Linnhe Loch. But what chances and possibilities of existence must surround such a creature? By what likelihood is it ever to meet a seal, seeing it is incapable of hunting for them; and the seal met, and found desirable, how about the likelihood of getting a hold of a quiet, retired croft at the junction of some of the flippers with the body, where it would do as little as it could except at meal-times, and be quite safe from the evicting habits of the Laird? Then such snug corners must be scarce even on the larger cetacea; and what would become of them if all these eggs of this little crustacean were to mature would be a serious question. Indeed, the question between the parasite and the animal it seats itself upon is altogether a most interesting one, and no doubt the lethargic habit of the body of most parasites enables them to do a great deal in the way of patient waiting for "something to turn up," seeing they are unable to do much in the more natural way of hunting suitable pastures. We have been told of the amazing quantities of fleas that suddenly appear in desert places on the advent of humanity or any warm-blooded animals; and, therefore, these more active parasites must have a similar power of waiting for a godsend.

There have frequently appeared accounts of the dexterity of observing travellers, in determining the points of the compass from the growth of mosses and lichens on the stems of trees. The principal involved in their calculation is a sufficiently simple one, and appeals at once to the reason as a most natural reading of a very likely fact. The prevailing wind of a cold country is, say, from the north, and in consequence the side exposed to such severe blasts must be quite denuded of the surplus coating that so freely gathers on the bark of trees in sheltered nooks and crannies. On the other hand, one would naturally suppose that in a district where the prevalent wind is from the south-west, the side exposed to these genial moisture-bearing winds would be certainly well supplied with the damper mosses, fostered by the warmth and the moisture. Keeping these views before us, we have been examining for some time back the woods here, deep and sheltered, and the copse there, narrow and exposed, the rough-barked trees with plenty of hold and freedom of lodgment for the spores, and the smooth-barked with hardened surface, and facing without protection the fiercest winds that blow; but not a single fraction of difference can we perceive in any one of them in any direction, north, south, east, or west, except for some merely individual reason, to be quite ignored by the one close alongside. We were somewhat surprised at this result of our observations, as we fancied the long continued gales from the south-west would have had a distinct effect in this locality, both in the bent of the trees themselves and in their coatings. It seems not.

As our loch had turned its back on the heavy gale, and was racing for Appin at a mad gallop, while the outlook was dour and drumly, we resolved to turn our back on the loch and seek the racing streams. For these, too, had given over dancing and frolicking, and were heedlessly hurrying to the sea. On the road itself we felt sufficiently disturbed in our ideas of seasons, for here was a redbreast sitting on a bough and piping manfully—its breast, in all the glow of its spring uniform, rising and falling with the swelling notes. There, close alongside, at the end of the winter, with the buds breaking forth all about, is a holly tree well supplied with brilliant red berries still. Surely no hungry-bellied songsters have been in your neighbourhood, most seductive-looking repository for seed-eating birds! We turn aside from the highway, and there are the well-grown plants of the foxglove, green and vigorous, as if they would soon be entering the field as the observed of all observers. The roe-deer are all about us, and very regardless of our presence; and, even to the sharp whistle we give to startle the graceful creatures into activity, they only take a few elegant leaps and turn round inquiringly. Such a mild-eyed, staff-encumbered wayfarer will not disturb their equanimity, so they recommence grazing with delightful nonchalance.

Here is another dweller in the woods! He lives amid the silvers and labours among the flowers, and we know by his face he has something to tell us. Of course he has; is there not a fine owl in the house that he captured last evening before it got dark! The poor bird only flew a short way when he secured it, and although it refused nourishment, and finally died before morning, still it is "a beautiful corpse," and he is sure would interest us.

We have not seen any but the white barn owl in the neighbourhood, so follow our leader to his home under the beautiful many-armed silver fir, that proves a sort of sword of Damocles to the household during these constantly recurring and terrible gales. For all around them have fallen silver and beach of loftiest and most luxuriant growth; and why should not this vegetable giant some of these nights, when the furies are afoot, also bow to circumstances and persistent onslaughts, or even throw off a mighty limb to the destruction of a household? To us there is an air of solidity about him, and we enter the doorway without forboding. Not so fast! You imp of Satan! Are you the mute at the funeral, or can you be vociferous as well as mute? "Not a moment stopped or stayed he," but toddled back and forward with one eye turned upwards at the intruder, and looking what he most certainly was, an impudent, tag-rag specimen of the most impudent and interesting of pets—a tame jackdaw. You are living enough, at any rate, despite your ragged appearance; but where is the poor owl. "Forth they bring our warrior dead," whether from the result of violence at capture, or from some complaint, is not quite apparent; but when it is lifted up it is so very light that inability to obtain food or make use of it is the most natural explanation. Beautiful indeed is a white barn owl, *Strix flammea*, yellow owl, as it is termed; with its snowy breast, exquisitely-tinted back, and wings of a prevailing yellow ochrish tinge, finely marked with darker shades and deeper colours. Only a barn owl, we say, just as we'd remark as we lift some odd volume, *only* Burns, while perhaps we expect some of our latest novels. Only, indeed! and where can you find such another bird for delicate downy beauty? What novelty and curiosity-hunters we all are, to be sure. The last time we handled one of the species alive was on the occasion of finding it dying in a hedge in the evening, into which it had seemingly thrust itself to escape persecution from small birds, and out of which it could not extricate itself.

As we tramp up the hill, we find the rivulets running full, and all about the mosses are of exceptional growth. Into the luxurious beds we sink up to the knees, many of them at present with dainty seed vessels ripe and full. At this time last year the same mosses were all richly dyed with varying shades up to the deepest red, this season they are still as green as the meadows in May. Here and there, if we look carefully, we may catch a peep of yellow, or a suspicion of cinnamon, but the eye as it rests on the cool soft patches finds nothing but what is fresh and invigorating. We have been tramping downwards, still kneedeep, when we come in view of the rushing green waters of our *river*, green that is to the eye, for the prevailing colour of the bottom so reflects the light to-day—a very delicate slate-coloured green, with sparkles through it where the ripples leap and go. Ho! Miss Woodbine. So we have caught you at your toilet on the quiet, before you come forth to delight the beholder with your full adornment. What a knowing trick to play, and what a quiet spot to come to. There she had climbed up the leafless limbs of that blackthorn over the river, and from her point of vantage can arrange her tresses, and titivate herself in the mirror of the water.

Your raiment is still a little scanty, but you do look charming in that delicate green—Hem! Nobody heard us, my dear, and we would'nt for the world let out the secret of your toilet. We cover our eyes with our hand, and peer through our fingers, as we turn down the stream.

Winding round picturesque rotten old stumps, crowned with ferns and mosses, we are scrambling along under the budding trees when we are arrested by the plaintive cry of " whitow, wheetow," constantly repeated. At last it irritates us somewhat from its persistent melancholy, and we mutter, little widow, little widow, supposing you *are* a little widow, why make such a row about it. Could you not for any sake borrow a leaf from the Japanese, and tie up your feathers to show your widowhood, and whether it is an absolutely inconsolable widowhood, or one open to conviction ! We follow the sound up the hill, and come upon a colony of titmice of various species, all actively engaged among the twigs of a group of alders. These stand out bare and hard against the skyline, with their living fruit hanging all ends up from the various branchlets. For a few minutes we stand under a neighbouring oak, on which a pair of brown creepers are desperately busy, and then quietly but openly walk over to the alders and stand underneath. Our intention was to examine the condition of the trees, never anticipating the usually-vigilant coletits would remain, but most of them went on with their labours, which consisted, as we expected, in examining the various buds—now thrusting forth their purple tops—in search of insects. Nearer and nearer they came to us, branch after branch was denuded of buds, until at length several. were hard at work a few feet from us. What a charming sight it was to see the little creatures, their feathers tossed to and fro in the hard breeze, as they poised themselves on a branch end, and with a dexterity and rapidity that was almost incredible, stripped every bud on almost every twig. How the little sharp bill went, now a lightning dab, now a strip of the mandibles, and the branch had been examined by the sharpest little eyes, and the sharpest little beak imaginable.

Did we not catch sight of a bullfinch as we came up the wood, in splendid spring livery too; and if he makes as thorough an investigation of every bud as the tits did, the statement that these being insect feeders are only supposed to attack those buds in which insects are secreted is, we fear, an unreliable one. They are much too busy to bother over minute examination, and don't trouble their little heads about a handful of buds more or less.

"I love the merry, merry spring time, and here it is," sang Cock Robin, as we stepped out at the door. There he was in his rosy waistcoat, piping his bravest on the tuft of an Austrian, while his sober little sweetheart was hopping about on the sward near by. "I'm not so sure of that," said she, pushing her gentle head through the hedge, and smelling a "bite" in the air that made her shiver—"it was pretty sharp frost this morning." He paid no attention to the statement, but proceeded to sing something like "Come under my plaidie, my ain bonnie lady," to his own great satisfaction. She was not to be cajoled, however, and insisted that no one else was preparing, and Mrs Grundy Redbreast would vote them a pair of fools to think of beginning housekeeping so early. "Why, the first frost all the grubs and worms will be deep in the earth, and wherever will we get what will keep us going, much less what will be sure to come, you know," and her face almost emulated his waistcoat for a moment. "Pooh! nonsense! Why, the sparrows have their nests finished already, and the rooks are long done building, and just look how the bushes are pushing on, they'll be covered with caterpillars before—before— I mean by the time they're wanted, said he. Sparrows, indeed! nice birds to imitate! and I'm not a rook to drive my bill down ever so far in the hard ground after the worms." He dropped down on a lower bush, and found himself half choked with the heavy scent of the flowering currant when he opened his bill. "Just look here," he gasped, "and the gooseberries are flowering, and the midges and gnats are both in regular swarms along the side of the plantation; and what do you think of the bees, too? you can't say they're stupid! and they were very busy yesterday; the snowdrops are quite over, and the primroses are as beautiful and plentiful as ever was on a bridal morn." "But the frost always comes, you know, Robin, and my toes were so awfully cold last year, and everybody says it's sure to be cold yet, and they'll all laugh at us," she whispered, as a crowning argument against the proposed folly. "Do you know dear," he said, "that I saw two gowans to-day growing in a ditch, and all the world knows they are sensible, reliable flowers, and not to be humbugged." Just then he flew across to her other side, and ruffled his plumes, and strutted manfully; it was clear there was another arrival, and here he is with a skip and a hop.

"Ha! Jenny, my darling," sings the new-comer, "the pear trees are blooming at Ardchattan, and the apple trees in Glen Creran; and, what do you think? As I came across the hill I saw a nice soft place, left by the water going down, and thought the worms must be easily got at, and so went flop down without looking, for I was very tired; and it nearly turned my stomach." "What did!" said Jenny, looking interested just to spite the first comer. "What did?" repeated he. "My dear, I was actually up to the knees in frog spawn! the awfulest lot of it, and there I was right in the middle; so you see——," he whispered. "No; I dont see at all," said Jenny; "a nice lot of fools. What were the frogs doing throwing their spawn on the water when they ought to have known it would only be there for a day or two, and pretty fellows to tell whether it was really spring, when they didn't know a day's puddle from a regular bog. The cold-blooded wretches, too, what can they care about weather, or know about a mother's cares—I mean 'a lady's considerations?'" she corrected, with a little toss of her head.

All this time No. 1 was edging round the new comer, and now asked him if he saw the bat last evening, and noted how busy he was? "Spoke to him some nights ago before going to bed," he replied haughtily; "wasn't looking strong," he added carelessly, "said he had been confined to his bed for some time." "Hungry enough, I'm sure," said Jenny, mischievously, "and he will be 'confined to his bed' for a while yet before the new moon's old." "Has a very nice time of it," said the first Robin, "always takes to his bed in hard times, and says he never felt last winter at all." "Blinking fool," said No. 2, "didn't recognise me although I had on my new waistcoat," and he smoothed it with an air of conquest; "and never thanked me, although I told him where the nicest lot of gnats were to be had. But he *has* a nice easy time of it."

"Better go and keep him company if you like that style of thing so much," said Jenny in a fret; "neither of you will have a 'nice easy time of it' with me." And with a flick she was off, and the two others were left to settle the dispute that arose in the orthodox Robin Redbreast fashion, and with a vehemence that sadly spoiled the serenity of their new waistcoats.

You don't believe it, perhaps, but it's all quite true.

We can't exactly make out the rooks. We have always been under the impression that rooks paired, that the pair built a nest, that the said nest was a private affair, and that no others interfered with it. Like the apparent simplicity and real complexity of some savage tribes, however, it is quite possible a rookery is more a "commune" than in the mere fact of their living in community. For it is certain that more than two rooks are constantly found *building* at the same nest, whatever further arrangements may be made. Do the different pairs find it facilitate progress to combine in the manipulation of the large sticks they use in their building operations?

Wednesday the 22d was a pet day, with a sharp north wind blowing over the white carpet of snow, and teaching Miss Redbreast how wise it was of her to delay the event. So we put "our best foot foremost" and hurried off to examine a part of the shore we had persistently neglected.

Look at this rocky corner now, thrust out into the midst of the great bay, and well grown with sea-wrack. This is a great nursery, and seems as much a haunt of dog-fish *(Squale Roussette)* as the cairn at the upper part of the loch is a haunt of skate-fish. They have apparently agreed to keep each to their own ground. For rarely do we find a dog-fish egg at the cairn, and we have not seen a skate egg here. The dog-fish seeem to be of a most cautious, unbelieving character, as well as to have a powerful instinct to provide for the secure hatching of their young, as the way these eggs have their long tendrils wound round and round the seaware is most remarkable. It would take some minutes to unwind the tendrils of one egg, so as to free it from its hold ; and we have no doubt the ware is much more frequently thrown ashore to which it is attached than the egg itself thrown loose from its hold. The seaweed chosen is usually a short, tough, strong species, and not the long-fronded, weak-stemmed classes that are commonly found among the gathering on shore.

We came at length to a grand sweep of the fine bay, which has now been so left by the sea that a graceful curve of green *Zostera marina* borders it, tying the sandy stretch together, and making a pleasant path to-day. Here and there scattered along it are to be seen bunches sticking up out of the grass, as if a small branch had been washed ashore and caught in the mud and grass. These turn out to be bunches of serpulæ tubes, from six inches to near a foot in height, growing straight up, or with but a slight curve from the stone or shell to which they have attached themselves. They have clearly taken possession of this locality, and monopolise it to the exclusion of most other life, as we find to be so commonly the case with every class of creatures. We must have a nice bunch to watch its progress, so we gather bunch after bunch, only to discard them in succession as a finer one comes in view. Their footholds being sunk in the mud, we do not see them until dragged forth, and several of the finest bunches prove to be affixed to well-buried *modiolæ*, or large horse mussels, which decline to leave the beds they have made for themselves, and anchored themselves to with their strong byssus; and so the tubes are removed in isolated patches. The whole green sloping bank where the grass has emerged from the deep is, for several hundred yards, specially occupied by this most interesting "crop," and at length we observe a finer specimen than any we have yet procured thrusting its head above the waves at the water's edge. This we catch hold of with care, and draw slowly towards us, in hopes that the foothold is of a movable character. A stone! no, a mussel! no, well yes, it is actually an oyster, face down as we should say, for it is lying on its flat, with this huge bunch of living creatures, in their homes, standing on its back. They are very delicately affixed to the shell; and no wonder, standing thus upright with a weak grip, these bundles of separate tubes are so frequently found lying on shore broken up. But they have so many points by which to catch hold, and are so incapable of rolling, that only fragmentary patches are usually obtainable. We carry our capture home gently, and set it in one of the ponds, where it soon expands into the wonderful little community that is quite past our comprehension ashore. Just come along and look at it. Gently, now! for the creatures may not see, but they either feel the concussion or notice a difference in the light, and—there they go! The crimson corollas of the serpulæ were all ablaze, a second ago, but one after another they shut up like a flash, and leave the sober-tinted tubes on the sober-tinted oyster as dull as a room with the fire out.

But we had more than that to carry homeward, as any one who had met us on the way would have seen. Oysters on stones, oysters on mussels, and of all shapes and peculiarities; gathered for their droll modes of hanging on to their little world. Crabs in all sorts of wonderfully ornamented shells; and, poor fellow, are you on your way to the comfortable rascal near you to beg for enough to take you across the ferry? A hermit crab in a whelk shell, but such a shell! Far too big for the occupant, to start with, it is worn through in many places, and covered with barnacles and serpulæ. Its uncovered tail shows clearly through the end, an equally indecent and dangerous exposure, and its claws in vain try to stop a rent half-way up towards the proper aperture. You are busy! we suppose, and object to walk home with us! Well! if you were similarly laden, we would be busy somewhere else too!

With the rain in absolute sheets for days, and the gales continuous for weeks, the world is desperately busy in spite of it all. The enemy is upon us with a rush, and soon scarce a portion of the lower foreshore, and the sea bottom (to a depth of one or two fathoms) but will be covered with the slobbery annual melanospermous seaware that we have long voted an intolerable nuisance, except when expanding its filaments in a dish of water. A few days has done it all, and now the foreshores are rapidly covering with it, hiding everything of interest in its slimy embrace. The hardest and finest ground gets covered with it as surely as the muddiest, and even more certainly; so that no spat of oyster could possibly find room for attachment. It is at least six weeks sooner than one naturally anticipates, and so will account for the non-increase of certain classes of shell fish, whose embryos demand hard ground on which to attach themselves. For the growth is so rapid, and the consistence so soft, of this seaweed, that no attempt to form an attachment could be made. What purpose does this growth serve in the economy of the foreshores, or rather how does it influence the balance of life on the shallower seas?

Let us walk across by this bit of wooding while we consider the subject, for to-day the north wind has come unexpectedly, and although yesterday we could scarcely have moved across the grass, much less over the moss, without going over the boots, to-day has dried the country marvellously. What a deluge has fallen, to be sure, and see what a large pond has gathered in the hole left by that overturned tree-root! We step behind the moss-clad mass that towers above us, while we shelter from the driving sleet and hail that still comes at intervals. Peering around at the pool of water, we watch the active water beetles flash as they traverse the home they have already discovered. That one has disappeared in a moment under—under—why! a lot of bright "slobbery stuff!" Here is, indeed, a fresh-water alga of a cognate character to the black-spored shore weed, and it, too, has suddenly made its appearance, and is making rapid progress under the warm southerly winds, despite the almost entire absence of sunlight. Have we not thus a means of judging of the utility to ocean life, as well as fresh water life, of this easily *penetrated*, but with difficulty *traversed*, alga? May it not, indeed must it not, be a source of security and a readily-reached asylum for the multitudinous embryos of all classes of life thrown during the spring and summer; into which they can slip, and under which they may remain hidden, until with the autumn it departs and leaves them of sufficient vigour and growth to fight the battle for themselves. We are satisfied that whatever safety a tangle forest, with its magnificent fronds, may secure to certain classes of life, the extraordinary growth of these masses of fine filaments that cover the foreshores in summer, must ensure far greater security to masses of fish spawn, and still more delicate organisms, that could scarcely otherwise escape the onslaught of crabs and starfish, &c. For although it is certain that a proportion of fish spawn floats on the surface of the water, it is equally certain that other classes of fish deposit their eggs in gelatinous masses on stones and stems of seaware on the foreshores.

As we crossed the softer ground, we found the iris shooting up strongly, and spring sitting up, after rubbing its eyes, all along the hillside. Next week he will bestir himself with a rush, unless this somewhat keen norther from the Bens should benumb his awakening faculties.

Seed! certainly, scattered among the moss, but such as never grew on a Scottish hillside, nor was stored in a Scottish stackyard. We lift the Indian corn that has been thrown here and there, and the truth flashes across us. The squirrels! for only their teeth could have punctured each corn *with a clean hole through the germinating end* so as to prevent their growth when stowed away. The little rascals have been robbing the pheasants of the winter provinder put down in netted enclosures for them, and storing it away among the trees, for the evil day that has not yet come this year. Good teeth and good heads to guide them, ere they could show so much intelligence as well as foresight!

APRIL, 1882.

Although we have had the north and north-east winds for most of this week, drying up the country most thoroughly, they have not had their usual effect in giving us low tides, so we conclude there is some south in the wind elsewhere, and this we find is the case from the weather report. Walking around the shore therefore produced little of interest, and it is just too early on the whole to find much novelty on land. We turn away from the little bay and cross the bit of moor, when something light and bright and lively flicks across before us and alights on the bordering fence. This is the first wheatear we have seen this season, and it continues to flit about as restlessly as if it had already something to conceal. What is that overhead, asks our companion, and we scarcely wonder at the question, as the twitter of the descending skylark is not sufficiently distinctive to enable us naturally to compare it with its summer self. Still it is the skylark, and it has been soaring heavenward, evidently as a sort of preliminary canter. Left in the lurch, you are! we mutter, as we come upon a stretch of iris, shooting vigourously from what has been a muggy spot for months; but now it is as dry and solid as could be desired, and the chances are that the gay flowers of the "fleur de lis" will never reach maturity. A very remarkable change this spell of easterly wind has produced upon the country after the long duration of leaden skies and constant downpour. Everything that could carry a lichen or a fungus was laden with them. The very small branches of the young larch, in damp, sheltered localities, were covered with a species resembling blobs of half-cold glue; every paling-stob had circling rows of frills, or other class of fungus, and a new vegetation of this description seemed to have sprung into life in order to take advantage of the new and suitable conditions. Now these are curling everywhere into tinder, and what was really a charming botanic garden to the mycologist has in a few days become a *hortus siccus* without either beauty or interest, for the innermost juices have been dried up, and scarce a semblance of their former selves left.

You can't do much on the water in a succession of gales, but we did make an attempt to lower a dredge these last two days, and the result was more agreeable to the naturalist than to the "gourmet." Following upon this we had swarms of specimens in odd dishes endeavouring to examine them singly, and careful that no inveterate enemies should come together. In one small dish was a specimen of *Adamsia*, sea anemone, in a shell inhabited by a fine *(Pagurus Prideauxii)* hermit crab. This we were carefully keeping for the anemone, looking upon crabby as a very subsidiary party. At the last moment we picked up another rare prize with us, in the shape of a *Fissurella Graeca*, a limpet shaped shell with a hole in the apex, and the whole creature much more exposed to assault than the shore limpet, as the shell does not properly cover the animal, whose curtain stands up a good quarter of an inch all round clear of it. It so happened that this was dropped hurriedly into the dish with the sea anemone, and other cares occupied the minds of those interested. Later in the evening we were passing, candle in hand, and took a view of the scattered creatures in their various domains, so that we might catch them at their more natural movements in the dark. The natural movement of the hermit crab was at least apparent, as the poor limpet was clinging despairingly to the side of the dish, and the great claw of the crab had already made a deep hole in the curtain as he tore the creature from its hold. These fissured limpets are beautifully shaped, but they have, of course, no security against depredators like the common limpet, and although the curtain can cling strongly to the article on which it may be at the time, the presence of the hole in the apex and distance of the verge of the shell from the edge of the foot prevents its house being its castle. This is the first we have taken in our own loch.

"One more draw of the dredge on the scallop ground," asks a companion; and over it goes, while we glance roughly at the spider crabs, starfish, and other ordinary products of a haul, with here and there a little *cypraea*, always so interesting, or a *milligrana* (Trochus); and there, sliddering in among the larger specimens, is a small *Ophiocoma neglecta*, a specimen of which diminutive brittle starfish we have not yet been successful in preserving. But the iron is again upon the stern of the boat, and as the contents are turned into the tub we hurry shoreward; for little do we expect, beyond these lively scallops from the grounds frequented by them, some six or eight fathoms deep. Ere we cease rowing, however, it is plain that another of these large scallops, *Pecten maximus*, is among the crowd of shells of *P. opercularis*, similarly adorned to the last we took on the same ground. So there are a few about alive, but what a crowd of freshly-opened shells of the smaller pecten! When they are dredged in quantity we generally find little else, but here are regular piles of starfish, and they have evidently been at work, and busy too, among these delicious bivalves. For although a *P. maximus* can close his shell tight, there are always two unarmed holes at each side of the hinge of *P. opercularis* into which a strong limb of the wriggling wretches can be readily inserted.

But we turned our eyes from the tub too soon. What is that brilliant gleam of crimson fringe? A rude glance took the shell for a mussel, but there is a fine specimen of *lima*, with its splendid show of crimson ciliae, the first of its kind also we have ever had the opportunity of dragging to light from Loch Creran. What a mass of colour, and what an interesting creature it is, but we should think its means of defence are few, and chances of injury numerous, for the hand brushing lightly against it brought away the touched ciliae clinging like little suckers to the skin. We have not yet exhausted that last tub, but could we exhaust even a *lima* itself in a pámphlet much less a letter?

From the first of the month the sheep are returning from their wintering grounds to their companions left among the hills; and very loath they are, even in this mild season, to go back to hard rambling among the rocks in place of being able to gain a comfortable livelihood in the richer nooks lower down. So now commences the troubles of the shepherds and the various Highland railways. It is an interesting fact that for six months after the opening of the Callander and Oban Railway the damage to fencing by sheep, and the number of sheep killed by the trains, was very great, but thereafter kept constantly decreasing with the increasing knowledge of the various flocks. Periodically, however, with the return of the young sheep from the Lowlands, an excess of the average destruction follows, until the damage by the trains to unsettled sheep with visions of recent plenty is lost sight of in a new danger of even a more pressing and less easily obviated character. This is the inquiring nature of the playful lambs now appearing, who soon discover the sweeter qualities of the forbidden fruit inside the wires, and wriggle through accordingly. This is bad; but if the mothers remained outside, their youngsters would answer to the warning call of the alarmed mammas, and skip with ungainly haste out of danger. Nothing of the sort, of course; for what mother will not seek to follow the reckless and frivolous children that delude them so playfully, and so the frantic parents follow the little brats on to the line, to the deep regret of all concerned. The ewes won't go of their own accord, for they know the danger and are aware of the difficulty, but nothing will keep them out from their youngsters. The question is whether the season of comparative freedom from accidents of this class is the result of education, so that the flocks have acquired a real knowledge; or is merely a sort of settling down and general sobriety, so frequently the result of a routine existence, and aided as it would be by the early discovery that the game was not worth the candle. At present the ground that is best worth feeding on is exceedingly dirty with the regular winter's stock, and it is not to be wondered at that the returning hoggs are willing to risk a good deal in order to "better their position in life."

Whether is a hare or a rabbit the most intelligent? is one of those questions readily asked, and as a general rule most difficult to answer. Yet we think we have obtained some data that will help towards a solution of this query, and at any rate they are still more interesting simply as facts. Unlike the sheep, that seem to gain a kind of acquaintance with the trains, the hares are always more or less getting in the way, and don't seem to have their wits about them sufficiently to enable them to get out of it. In the early morning, along the line, dead hares are by no means uncommon, and in certain quarters are numerous occasionally. This is quite what one would expect from a hare. It looks by no means bright of intellect, with its great eyes; and although an adept at doubling, and able to make the best of a mountain or country-life, must feel like a country lad in Glasgow when it comes within range of the iron horse. Who has not seen a shrewd country farmer able to hold his own at kirk or market when within range of the breeze from Ben Nevis, yet behave like a cow before a conveyance on a public road so soon as he finds himself obliged to cross the street at the Trongate or the Jamaica Street Bridge. He is not sharp enough for the city-bred inhabitant. The same seems to be the case with the hare and rabbit. The hare cannot make up its mind to advance or retire, and probably ends in that "middle course" in which we are told is safety, but which before an express train means disaster. The rabbit, on the other hand, is rarely killed on the line, and this might seem the more remarkable, as they throng the stony and sandy embankments along the railway, and slip through the confining wires to their matutinal and vesper meals among the railway grazings. But they have their wits about them, and no doubt have always the one clear, definite idea to their minds in danger, to make if possible a bee-line to their holes. Certain it is they manage to exist in multitudes on the verge of the destroyer's path, while the hares seem to be unable to visit the same grazings without imminent danger. So that the question of intellect after all is one between the occasional visitor and the habituè, who has been bred with greater experience if not with greater intelligence. We suspect the rabbits have both.

Under a rocky scaur in the Pass of Brander, we observe one little lamb lying, with its mother grazing near, on ground where scarce one would expect conies to find pasture and provender; and if there is any excuse for the formation of deer-forests, it is surely to be found in such districts, where many acres of scarce traversable land are required to feed a single blackface. The great distance between the dwellings and the wild nature of the intervening ground, must make these quarters very isolated; and the inhabitants must gradually acquire some of the self-dependence and shrewd hardihood of the blackfaces and the collies with whom they mainly associate. Many of these farmers, in the wildest districts, have wrestled in the thickest of the fight in the struggling mercantile world; and consequently appreciate the advantages, while they are greatly saved from the manifest disadvantages, of the situation; and when this is considered, and it is known how many purely Teutonic names yearly seek a calm haven "out of the hurly-burly," it appears more and more absurd to talk of the Highlands as peopled by Celts, and subjected to the domination of the "brutal Saxon," as we have been so often told of late. This constant intermixture has gone on at all times, and many of the most thoroughly Highland families are Scandinavian, Saxon, and Norman by descent as thoroughly as they are in appearance. Many of these outsiders have been partially baffled in their contests with their compeers ere they retire to these solitudes, where they recuperate their exhausted nervous systems, and, if not in their own persons, at least in their descendants, are better fitted, physically and mentally, through their struggle with wild nature, to return and once more enter the too-often fatal lists with human nature and civilisation. Such stern solitudes are therefore training schools for the nation; and it is almost a pity to see them steadily narrowing. Yet as we look at the stalwart shepherds ascending the rugged hill-faces on the way, the consolation remains with us that the hills are not to be levelled, and that the heart strengthens as the knee-joints stiffen, and the mountains in all ages are justified of their children.

The bushy-tailed collies, with the easy step and graceful carriage bred of the hills, are skirting the slopes and scouring the corries; and there, although it is so far away, you can see the expression of delinquency on that lowered countenance, as with depressed tail it skulks down the bottom of the ravine. Have you been on the rampage, you rascal, or have you been sent home in disgrace for incompetence? There it goes at a hard gallop, leaving its master standing a solitary figure on the distant hill! Every hundred yards of those apparently barren hills is a picture, every hut and homestead a living novel of intense interest; and we pass them all with a yawn of *ennui* at the lagging train, and with the nerves of the brain made callous by custom, the sensitive plates spoiled by exposure, and the photographic "artist"—there are no photographers nowadays—dozing under his black hood inside, and incapable of taking cognisance of the myriad-minded creation, telling its complicated story, with its ever-varying features.

MAY, 1882.

The cuckoo was calling bravely this day week as we passed southward; and still more willingly should it call to-day, with Loch Etive a sheet of silver, and the splendour of sunlight over all—not hazy, but crisp, bright, life-stirring sunlight, such as we have not seen for a twelvemonth. How gay is the scene as we sit under the ear-splitting rookery, and peer through the many-tinted trees at the loch beneath us; while we listen to the tales of the doings of rooks, under the peculiar circumstances of the late season. These birds had completed their nests under the natural impression that the mild, early spring was to continue, and they were conducting themselves with sobriety, and with the peculiar solemnity and decorum that approaching " paterfamiliarity " seems to give to the most undignified of beings, and that sits so well upon his sable rookship. But suddenly there came a change, and the bitter east wind swept down upon them, and the snow fell thickly for a day or two, and all the vicinity looked as if Nature had made a mistake, and sent the spring first, to be now followed by the bitter season. The rooks at first were thoroughly demoralised, for were not their nests built open, and of the rudest sticks, without a fraction of warmth, or the smallest claim to comfort and snugness! How were their young, just on the point of emerging, ever to sit in such exposed quarters, without an effort by the parents to hap them from the wind? Now, rooks have built their nests of sticks since ever a rookery was established, we suppose, and it is so commonly understood that birds act from " instinct," and are incapable of introducing a new style of architecture or a new mode of construction, that any change at this time of day is absurd to expect! Yet what do those sable birds do under the unusual circumstances? Do they sit close in the nests in a half-frozen condition, and endeavour to impart their own vitality to the coming young, regardless of the personal cost, or fly about in a disconsolate condition, bewailing in guttural accents the untoward weather? No! The first morning after the storm the lawn is covered with active multitudes all in a state of determined activity; whether the result of a council of peace, or led by an inventive genius that had risen to the occasion, we know not; and the birds were tearing great bunches of moss up through the snow and flying off with it, in order to render their nurseries better suited to the strange freak of a season they had hitherto found so kind. Now, we do not suppose these birds will continue to use moss in future any more than they have done in the past, as their simple style of structure—skilful as it is in a way—is quite sufficient for their purpose in ordinary circumstances; but it is a remarkable proof of the capacity of birds to rise up to the occasion when they could thus promptly augment the chilly nests in the tree-tops with a warmer and hitherto unemployed material. It seems to us, indeed, that for a rook to thus suddenly make use of moss is on a par with the American weaver bird that sewed its nest with *wire* from a blacksmith's shop. It is certain that birds are as capable of suiting themselves to circumstances in the matter of material and form as most savage nations, and we know how almost impossible it is to get an orthodox African savage to build his hut other than circular.

We have been wandering this morning in a land of wonders until the time has slipped through our fingers, and we found it most difficult to return from the labyrinthine mazes. Here are glorious trees of strange cactus form reaching across the mouths of the mammoth cave-like entrances. Carefully we descend into the abysses and get lost in the dark recesses, down which stretch beautifully formed greenish branches, turning brown in the drier winds we have had. We are threading our careful way over an apparently-burned grey stem when our heart fails us, and we creep slowly backward afraid of the rotten footing. So we turn into this great limestone-like cave, like a bit of Derbyshire, almost feeling as if we slipped on the white marble-like footing, and were suddenly arrested by the gleam of sunlight on an iridescent surface. This proves to be a rich film spread across the inner mouth of the cavern, and reflecting the rays in rainbow tints; while all around are the huge cottony tufts of —of what? Well, you see we have been in fairyland—a land anyone can enter at the very smallest cost, and where they will find such endless sources of amazement and interest that they may employ themselves for weeks without moving very far, and not only add to their own knowledge, but the knowledge of the world. For there are explorers in all departments of nature, and all we have done is to bring our lens to bear on a few big tree trunks, and the great cotton tufts are the cocoons of a small insect on the trunks of the spruce, and the same in character with the blight we have observed so frequently on the branches of the larch in the summer. The brilliant opalescence, stretching from mouth to mouth of the cavernous depths of the cracked bark, is simply the shiny track of a small mollusc, that little knew of the beauty and wonder it had left behind to tell of its progress. The whitish marble pavements are smooth lichens, and the burnt branches are grey lichens, while the lovely greenish ones are those of the more feathery mosses, covering the wrinkled hides of the vegetable giants. You cannot walk far, my friend, to enjoy nature and you grieve over your deprivation! You, my little fellow, are too poor to travel into far lands; and our gentle sister there cannot handle the geologist's hammer, or tug at the rope of a heavy dredge! Then sit down for an hour or two per day under the shadow of a great tree—or even a little one—and tell us one-half the wonders a pocket lens will bring before you, and study the ways of one-half the creatures whose world goes little beyond the one "planet" comprised in an oak-tree, or a larch, and you will never weary for want of a subject to think about, or an object to examine. We are obliged to turn away startled at the *embarrass des richesses*, and unable properly to appreciate the immensity of our ignorance.

Quietly now! just come up this garden walk to the side of the sparsely clad beech hedge. Never mind the bee-hive; pass it quietly, gently, and confidently, for there is nothing like haste or excitement to alarm any living creature, wild or tame. Here, now! just behind the hive in the hedge, and don't be exuberant. Her eye glints up at you so deprecatingly as she sits there "hoping, fearing," with a look as if to say "I'm only a weak, little she-blackie, very foolish, and only too confiding; please don't!" Of course we "please to don't" and slip away, for we know there are three callow nestlings under her, and an unhatched egg still an object of hope. Just about three feet from the ground, three feet from a bee-hive, in an open hedge and a fine fruit garden! Such a tempting of Providence, and yet she escapes with her young brood. The redbreast at Ledaig garden, too, has already added to the bird life of the district, and the cosy nests of the chaffinches have for some time been seen in snug situations on bush and tree. We have already come upon two wren's nests about finished. One is very badly concealed in an upturned root of a tree, and will probably never be occupied if the shrewd little bird takes note of its surroundings; while the other is on the top of a furze bush, scarcely distinguishable from the thorny accretions that gather on the forks. We should think this one of their most successful situations, as, although we know their favourite corners, we but seldom manage to find them there. Year after year a pair of coletits build in a hole under the roof of a cottage at Barcaldine, and already this year they are hard at work; but whether it is exactly the same pair or some of their progeny, would require a lengthened experiment to discover. There seems little reason to doubt that the same pair exactly will return for a considerable time to a suitable nesting situation, and we have no doubt that, in the event of misfortune overtaking them, others will be ready promptly to take advantage of the vacancy.

The last dredge has been taken, and we are rowing quietly in the vicinity of the "Cairn," with unexpectedly calm water around it. Just one glance to see if the skates are coming in, although a skate-spear is no part of our dredging armament. The boat drifts slowly back and forward above the waving *laminaria*, and we peer through the water for the dusky forms above the still darker seaweed. We are about to leave, when a dark grey figure floats across the field of view, and an unfailing hand has sent the handle of a graip well through it before the others are properly aware of its presence. "Catch it by the tail!" says the captor eagerly; but our acquaintance with skates is of ancient date, and our hands are not sufficiently horny to handle a thornback with impunity. Even the scales of the skin are sharp enough to score the hands of an ordinary person severely, and a knife is the only implement we can improvise with which to gaff them. Another and another now come within sight, evidently coming in cairn-wards as the evening advances; and most exciting does the pursuit become, carried on as it is at a disadvantage from want of a barb to hold on the fish, even when it is transfixed with the tapering graip handle. More than one drops an egg as it finds itself struck, and we have only to examine the bottom carefully to see how numerous are those eggs already deposited in this favourite spawning ground. Five fine thornbacks are soon in the boat; and as we have an interesting tubful brought up by the dredge still to examine, we hie away home with our varied plunder. In almost every case these skates are on the point of depositing eggs, having just arrived from deeper water for this purpose. Down each Fallopian tube an egg is on the way, with the tough gelatinous coating complete, and the end horns curved towards each other to enable the egg to pass. No other egg was coated even partially, and it seemed as if the fish deposited two eggs, one after the other, about the same time, before it commenced to secrete the coating for the next pair. The undeveloped eggs lie alongside the kidneys in two groups, from whence they pass into the Fallopian tubes in pairs. In no case did we find a *single egg* ready to be deposited, except when we had seen the other dropped as the fish was struck. We always find the eggs of the skate of all sizes, like those in a laying hen, and the period over which the spawning extends must be many months; a great security against any sudden destruction that might overtake a spawning-bed through a specially low tide, a shifting sandbank, or other eventuality. It is somewhat remarkable to find a highly organised fish like the skate so prolific of eggs, and these so strongly protected by a coating as tough as leather, and not nearly so readily penetrated as a hen's. Yet there must be some reason for this prolific production of eggs, and it may probably be found in the lower class life of the sea, such as predatory mollusca, which will penetrate to the embryo and devour it.

He is "in chancery," and no doubt about it! But whatever was he doing in that gulley? We had been trampling the mossy tree trunks and enjoying to the full the charming weather, to which we have been so long unused, when our eyes caught sight of the wizened head bones of a departed woodcock, which we lifted and glanced at. This was the prison-house and here was the prisoner. But what, we again ask, was he doing there? A small mollusc with a whorled shell—a species of *clausilia*—had endeavoured to pass from the large eye orbit through the opening into the brain, and again from the brain cavity through to the other orbit. Had it gone wholly into the brain cavity first and then out at the other side this might readily have been managed; but the shell would not take the necessary bend, and the deep suture above the aperture of the shell kept it from returning, the slight osseous band that divides the entrance to the brain catching and retaining it. We learn from Jeffreys that these molluscs are vegetable feeders; and the brain of a woodcock is not commonly chosen to lay out a kitchen garden in! Was it merely taking a short cut to a choice bit of greenery, and thought that when its head got through it was all right, like a schoolboy with his head between iron railings? Appearances are against him, and if he was really a brain sucker, like so many others in higher walks of life, he has been born "to be made an example of," and we had better all take warning in time.

Less than a yard off the road the earthy side of an upturned tree root met our view, and struck us as a likely spot for a robin or a wren to build; so we took the one step necessary to glance under it, and as we stooped our most prominent feature nearly met the point of a redbreast's bill, as it sat solemnly and immovably on its little nest. We remained stooping and looking at it for some time, and at length left without it moving. A fact explained, as we again peeped in an hour afterwards, and found that the poor thing was in the same circumstances as the old women that lived in a shoe. We would never have observed it had the mother not been on the nest; and, indeed, redbreast's nests are rarely discovered until the demands of the offspring make the place more frequented.

Nests of all kinds are now more numerous, and we saw other two this week that were as boldly placed close to a frequented path as the nests of the redbreast itself. These two were in trees, against which passers-by were brushing their shoulders daily, and both were so low that a glance aside enabled the snuggery with its speckled contents to be readily noted. The one was that of the large tit *(Parus major)*, the other that of *P. cærulius* or smaller tit, and the nests were placed in the hollows made by the bifurcation of the tree stems near the root. *P. major* was most plucky and determined, and swore at us lustily while we were removing a sample egg, by means of a toddy ladle at the end of a stick. The little blue tit was in a narrower cavity, and we had to substitute an "egg spoon" for the ladle ere obtaining the desired specimen. We stood for some time looking down at the sitting mother in the deeper hole, but the tit is a bold and fearless bird, be it large or small, and although we could see the palpitations of the little bosom the eye met ours unflinchingly. Leaving the nest of the larger tit we stroll through the neighbouring garden, and stop short in our walk, for beautifully placed in an espalier apple tree is the compact nest of a chaffinch, so dexterously worked into the gnarled branch with grey lichen that only a practised eye can detect it. We have lately had our attention called to the alleged fact that there is always a chaffinch's nest in the vicinity of a missel thrush's, but this we are not aware of; and this year nor last have we seen a missel thrush's nest anywhere in the district. What can have become of this daring and predatory bird, so unlike in character to our gentle mavis; and what possible "paction" could it make with the little "shilfa?"

The seals have once more become common in both Creran and Etive, and their splashing and dashing may be heard these still evenings as they play upon the row of boulders off the Cairn Rocks. They are both numerous and fearless at present, and are no doubt able to feed luxuriously without much labour, as our lochs are all full of saithe. One boat caught upwards of 300 with the rods in less than two hours, and one fisherman with the rod caught 160 in less than an hour at Connel. So the seals are lolloping about in playful companies, and gambolling close inshore to our delectation. We were amused with the movements of some mergansers in Loch Etive, that had not completed their summer arrangements last week. The duck was swimming quietly and unconcernedly in the water near the shore, while two drakes were careering around, making strenuous efforts, the one to retain, the other to gain, possession of the coveted fair one. Whether she had any partiality or no could not be discovered, although she may have cast occasional glances of encouragement at the new comer, who stuck so persistently to his purpose of superseding the previous *engagé*. No doubt she enjoyed the idea of being contended for, and would despise, even if she did pity, the beaten admirer, and welcome the conqueror, as a product of "natural selection" should.

Every one knows the little pools between the hillocks of the lug worms on the sandy shores at low ebb. Walking across the sands just now, little flitting shadows may be seen in these pools, that only their own movements would enable the eye to perceive. Examine the pools closely, and you will find that they are thronged with small flat fish about the size of elongated threepenny bits; a proportion being still smaller, and so very gelatinous as to be transparent. We fill a test-tube with about a dozen of them and examine them closely, when most of the specimens bear unmistakable signs of being young plaice, the spots even in most cases being apparent. Every ray of the delicate fins, every bone of the transparent body, is clearly visible, and beautifully delicate objects they appear against the light. Here is a youngster you can only see when it moves, and its movement is most irregular. Watch it closely, and you will observe that, as it lies flat against the glass, you can only see one eye, while it almost swims on its edge, and its mouth has not the twisted look that the ordinary fish has. The fact is that in the earliest stage the eyes of the flat fish are normal like other fishes, and only become twisted round to suit their existence on their sides as they mature. Here they are, however, in plenty not half an inch in length, and yet regular chips off the old block— twisted mouths, spots, goggle eyes, and all. Every stomach, too, is filled to the full, the only gross, worldly, untransparent portion of the tender little shavings.

We described the young plaice as being numerous in the little pools of the foreshore, and remarked upon the extreme difficulty of discovering them except from their own movements. They sink into the mud until nothing but the two minute eyes are out, with the contour of the head shown, just as in the case of the full-grown flounder kind; and even in their case it demands an experienced eye to note the whereabouts of a flounder when spearing them from a boat overhead. It has often been a source of wonder to us how any of the very young of certain fishes escape their many enemies; but we suspect even heavier gaps are made in their ranks further on, when they are more worthy the attention of the water-fowl, for it is really wonderful what large flat fish a duck itself will swallow with apparent satisfaction. At the same time we do not doubt that our ducks are making havoc among these little fellows even now, as they seem to have the faculty of scooping along with their bills among the mud, allowing the mud and water to escape at the sides, and swallowing what is appetising, in place of having to pick up each minute article separately, like a common fowl. It was clear that, despite their number, they had been sadly thinned in the still earlier stages, and yet no other fish were about at that time; so we resolved to hunt further out, if perchance among the boulders of the rougher bordering ground their enemies had found shelter. As the edge of the furthest ebb was reached, we kept a sharper look-out, and were repaid by glimpses of little black specs, like very minute tadpoles, that cut into the seaweed at the approach of our shadow. Soon one, then another, delicately-transparent gobies appeared, as they flitted to another portion of the ground, where they were almost equally hidden with the young plaice, so closely did they resemble the ground in hue. We have no doubt these gobies, so numerous in our little bay, would account for a considerable percentage of the eggs and young. The ground roughens meanwhile, and we roll over a large stone, under which we observed a brilliantly-coloured object to glide. Not to be seen! As we gently turn to the one next it, a flop in the water tells of something dropping off the upturned stone, and we have just time to catch a glimpse of a reddish-yellow fellow that we recognise and appreciate; for he has been lifted up along with the stone, while we expected to find him cutting from under it. In fact, it is a pretty and interesting specimen of a *Cornish Sucker Fish* (Couch); and we have not gone far when we meet a companion to it, equally bright, and with beautiful eyes; but not nearly so active in its movements or difficult to capture as the *Two-spotted Sucker Fish* that also frequents our loch. But these are mature specimens, of two to three inches long, and stout build, and what we are seeking are fry; for other fishes must of a certainty be spawning already this season. Stone after stone is carefully upturned, and nothing shows but the ordinary Butter Fish (*Gunellus*), so we decide that our eyesight, and not the season, is at fault. Lower we drop, and gently move the smaller stones and gravel we have uncovered, and soon we are in the midst of the little world we are seeking. Not under the large stones, but under the little ones beneath them, are numbers of little black and grey specs, not to be mistaken for anything but the young of the two species of *Cottus*, those big-headed, thorny customers that frequent the rocky foreshores. Plaice are there, too, and little slips of yellow, half transparent, that prove the gunnel fish has been some time spawning; and there, jerking into view as we continue our inquiries, come the minute imitations of the two-spot goby; while that quaint little crustacean, the *Mysis*, is in myriads in the brackish water, and a proportion have strayed in here among the sea-weed protected boulders. Suddenly, as we lift this other stone, there is a gleam of purple and silver, and a beautiful creature, covered with opalescent plates that work across each other strangely as it progresses, crosses our field of view. Gently! gently! or the plates will all come off, and leave it nothing but a gelatinous worm. You have shrunk from it, my friend, and so, because it is an annelid or seaworm, you will lose the wondrous beauty with which it is endowed. No doubt it too is a factor in keeping down the over-swarming of the smaller fishes. We have nothing on land, unless it is the caterpillars of the different moths, that can vie in beauty of colouring and wonderful organisation with these various marine annelids. They are almost all possessed likewise of properties that produce phosphorescence in a very high degree; indeed, higher than any class of marine or land creature with which we are acquainted, excepting the glow-worm itself.

Will the same pair of birds produce a nest of young twice in a season? This is a question we have frequently asked ourselves respecting the common hedge-row birds, and although satisfied that they might occasionally, under favourable circumstances, we could never positively assert that they did. Now we have an admirable opportunity of seeing this at Ledaig, where the poet's tame redbreast produced a brood of nestlings early this season, and is now busy with a new nest, which it will no doubt fill in due season. The weather has been especially favourable for nesting purposes, and we hope to find that this season has filled up the serious gaps made in our community of small birds of recent years. We have not known so many nests since we came to this part, about our own place; and it is a curious fact that the most shy birds will crowd about the immediate vicinity of a dwelling to nest—probably from protection against hawks and weasels—while the redbreast, our most familiar bird, is the shyest when nesting, and the most secretive!

JUNE, 1882.

The sandy bottom we have been rowing over is covered with a forest of a peculiar character. This is composed of the leathery tubes of annelids with their waving tufted crowns, and yet the character seems strangely changed! We peer down at them once or twice ere we understand the transformation; for the annual seaweeds have attached themselves by their spores to the tubes, and are now waving their dark olive fringes above and around the obtruded inmates. Anything that will permit of a spore settling, in strong salt water, is in danger of having a great growth to carry, beyond its own individuality, and the tough noses of *Mya truncata*—the burrowing shell-fish whose siphon tube does not get properly accommodated inside the shell—frequently carry a tough frond of some of the fuci. This, although apparently inconvenient, is yet a distinct security, and makes the bearer more difficult to be discerned on the foreshore.

We are pushing off the boat with the skate-spear on board, when the water alongside is rippled and dimpled by many little noses, and it is obvious we have again been visited by the little atherines or "sand smelts" that we have noted once or twice previously in our bay. But our little net is not in order, and we are otherwise resolved, so we leave them until "to-morrow," and set off for the cairn. While the boat progresses over a sandy stretch, a dark object is observed at the bottom, but before the boat is checked and the spot reached the skate has escaped our sight. How lazily we skirt the rocky shore with one eye on the algæ-covered bottom! for although the sun is fast sinking behind the Kingairloch hills, the sinking tide is shoaling the water on our fishing ground, so that the bottom will be nearer us and not more difficult to examine, although the light may be less.

It is not so easy to hit the cairn with a fathom and a half of water still over it, but we ought to know every inch of ground here, and we don't go far off it. At last the boat is over the top stone, all covered with mussels as it is, and we continue to circle about it, awaiting the advent of skates from the deep. Here is a dark form among the algæ, and see, as it is covered by the shadow of the boat it turns and hastens into deeper water. A few yards and it will be beyond us, for the cairn rises suddenly and with little slope, so the long spear is thrown at it, there is a white gleam as the belly shews, and then the handle comes up to the surface and enables us to hoist it on board—a nice thornback of a nice size. Hold! now, steady! and the boat halts as another comes in from the deep straight towards us, and with a desperate protest is at once in the boat. Between times the boat circles about a moderate space of ground, covered with a great growth of fuci, and these again wearing a yellow beard of more delicate annuals. Now and again a saithe or lythe crosses under the boat unregarded, and we are too intent on skate even to note that the sun has disappeared, until the diminished radiance warns us that the time must be made the most of. Ha! he has crossed our bows and is off. The spear is launched after him with apparent success, for as the handle bobs to the surface some yards away, the wriggling, and struggling, white figure shows the skate is pinned below. But it has had just a second too long to itself, and when we again secure the handle one last jerk frees it. For a skate, by folding itself back, and giving a great jerk, will manage to chuck itself off the end of even the barbed prongs of a spear. Eyes require to be sharp, and the thruster skilful now, as the bottom is but very faintly illuminated, but—there is a dark form hurrying into deep water in advance of the boat. The spear is flung vigorously after it, and for a minute disappears. What has happened? Has the fish gone away with it, or has it stuck among tangle fronds and stems at the bottom? Suddenly, as we sit looking about us, the handle bobs up several yards away in an unexpected direction, and a desperately struggling skate still at the end of it. By this time the sharpest eyes are getting overstrained, and the dissipated looking moon, half ashamed of itself, is peering over the fir tops behind us, so we slip past the varied foliage of beech and silver, and seek our own beach in the moonlight, with eight fine thornbacks on board, "as much as any one ought to take at a time," says every one, although we had taken advantage of every moment of daylight to increase the slaughter.

We are often surprised at the impunity with which certain classes of marine life support existence in fresh water, which is yet certain poison to the great majority of marine creatures. When passing over the little bridge across the neighbouring stream, at high water, during which time the tide comes a good way up the stream towards it, we observed a profusion of life in the fresh water pool below, and great activity among a few small trout that usually inhabit it. It turned out that these were the little crustaceans (*Mysis*), that so swarm in the sea outside as well as in the brackish water, but this was the first time we had observed them to have penetrated to the pure fresh-water pools of the burn. Walking further down, examining the teeming multitudes of large-eyed, curved-backed creatures, we suddenly met a lively party evidently in a most unaccustomed element. Working assiduously, and with all its ciliæ, fringing the curtain, in active motion, a medusa was advancing up the perfectly fresh water with apparently as much vigour as if in the sea outside. Its every effort, too, was being made to advance against the current up the stream, and it must have been for some hours in nearly fresh water ere we noticed it. It does not at all depend upon simplicity of structure or lowness of organisation whether a creature can endure the transfer from sea water to fresh, and *vice versa*, as the starfish succumb at once to a fresh water bath, which acts like a dose of prussic acid to these simple organisms. On the other hand, the very beautiful, intelligent, and highly-structured little gobies, even those species taken in pure sea water, are apparently indifferent as to the change ; and the same to an extent, and for a time, may be said of the fifteen-spined stickleback, that clever nest-building little fish that dodges you among the more luxuriant seaware on a rocky shore. The simplest way to procure these delightful objects for an aquarium is one we have frequently made use of with success. A little hand-net with a long handle is swept through the sea-weed in a likely place, and if the spot is properly chosen and the net rightly held a prisoner will be found in it of the character desired, besides the multitudes of small shrimp-like crustaceans—mostly *Palæmonidæ* and *Mysis*—that are sure to throng the bottom of your muslin or cheese-cloth net after such performances. A fish that is occasionally to be found in similar localities to the above is the pipe-fish *(Syngnathus Acus)*—one of a class fully more interesting than the nest-builder, if that is possible. We found one lying stranded in a little pool, and looking foolishly conscious, when out at farthest low water some days ago. On lifting it, the reason for its uncomfortable position and want of energy appeared in the shape of the swollen sides, that extended towards the tail from the vent for about four inches, looking like two wings in a small way when seen from behind. Aware of the tenacity of life of the race generally, we sought to carry it home in a basket we had, well wrapped in damp seaware and constantly dipped in water for some minutes at a time, while we continued our search for another class of objects. But whether its condition rendered it more necessitous of water, or whether it had been poisoned by the brackish water near which we found it, is uncertain: at any rate, we could not take it the few hundred yards alive. These fish are said to be very readily affected by fresh water, and this being a *male* "in the family way," must have been more especially susceptible, for, the interesting part of the history of these fish is, that the female lays the eggs and the male hatches them out in his marsupial pouch, where he is said to give them asylum from enemies, even after they have been sufficiently matured to swim about alongside. It would be most interesting to learn what constitutes the peculiarity of any organism that can endure the transfer from salt water to fresh, or the reverse, with equanimity; and what it is that causes it to act almost as a poison upon creatures apparently closely allied to those that are invulnerable.

The land that was greatly washed by the sea last severe winter is now blooming under a crop of ryegrass, and showing very well indeed already, despite the salting the soil received. But there is a line curving along, occasionally in the middle and sometimes on the verge, that looks as if the track of a fiery dragon has passed along and left all barren behind it. Its irregularity and peculiar appearance prevented us at one discovering the cause, which, however, was simple enough. At the highest swing of the tide during the November gale the storm left a line of straw and seaware and other floating *debris* at the highest point reached, and this had acted as a complete destroyer of vegetation, nothing whatever coming up where it had lain. No doubt it had "burned" the soil; whereas, had it been distributed, the result would have been advantageous.

We have had bursts of severe weather and storms of hail, with "glimpses that have made us less forlorn" between. As we return laden with mollusca from a seaward ramble, a shout from our comrade informs us that a "flounder" was in one of our ponds; so, armed with our 18in. "spatula," we approached, in hope of securing a nice fresh supper. The captive turned out to be a plaice in wretched condition, and quite covered with a whitish fungus; and the poor fish had evidently retired to the quiet of the pond to ponder over the great question of how to recuperate, leaving the more important consideration of whether the fungus had been induced by its low physical condition being incapable of throwing off the disease, or whether the low state of body was primarily caused by the fungus, to be discussed by those less immediately interested. We have little doubt ourselves that vigorous fish, with plenty of nourishment and well oxygenated water, will not yield to the assault of any fungus as a rule; and certainly in the case of this plaice the system must have been lethargic and incapable of secreting sufficient mucous, or else the spores would have been thrown off from its back in the ordinary slimy secretion usually so plentiful in the flat fishes.

The hail was dashing violently in our face, and the waves rolling with a rush and a roar up to our feet, as we skirted Ardmucknish Bay, wondering if aught of the secrets of the deep were to be thrown in our path. The elegant white, almost circular, shells of *Venus exoleta* were plentifully strewn along the gravel, so common that their exquisite symmetry was almost lost sight of; and many elegant sea-weeds were tossed in from the deeper water outside. But only one vegetable product of the deep could attract our attention to-day. It was no use for the tangle to throw its smooth leaves of richest and darkest brown in complicated heaps upon the beach when close at hand those magnificent fronds of *Saccharina*, the Icelandic sugar ware, were spreading themselves full along the water's edge. Our thoughts were otherwise engaged, but even the absent eye is brought suddenly home in the presence of such luxuriance. Here is one by itself, so we stretch it out and pace its length, good 15 feet, although a considerable portion of the ribbon-like end has been broken off, while for a large proportion of its length it is from a foot to 18 inches wide. Verily, no such leaf can we produce from the soil of Benderloch, and we must go to the Banana-decked tropics to find any comparable frond, washed by an *air* in place of a *water* sea. Now we are at the sea verge, we diligently dig out towards the end of the seaward tending promontory, now turning up a razor shell, now a cockle, a *venus*, or a *tapes*, until we come to the region of the mushkin *(Mya truncata)*, which is considered one of the best of our edible shellfish, and is readily distinguished by its long, black, leathery nose, that is promptly withdrawn on the approach of danger. All these shellfish are to be found at this time of all sizes, small by degrees and beautifully less, as a rule, the nearer we dig to the shore. They have consequently been spawning for some time, as we find them so graduated up to maturity. The question suggests itself how these seemingly sedentary shellfish, living in the gravel or mud, can progress seaward as they mature; for this they must do, or otherwise the full-grown specimens would be found among the small fry inshore! Although we seldom see them in motion, yet these shellfish, provided with strong "feet," can push themselves along vigorously, and no doubt will take advantage of the reflux of the tide to remove to more suitable premises. This is a very difficult matter to understand in the case of *Myæ*, with their large shells so deep in the ground; but it seems as if we could come to no other conclusion to account for their distribution. It is with many of these shellfish as with other common creatures, their very multitude and universality has prevented their receiving that attention less interesting but rarer forms receive. And so it is that their spawning seasons and mode of increase is so little understood, although thousands of tons of cockles, those most delightful of the edible bivalves—scarcely excepting the oyster—are annually consumed. The only distinct statement the inspectors could elicit concerning them from the fishermen was that very minute specimens of cockles made their appearance in June, and yet the livelihood of thousands of the coast population mainly depended upon understanding them and their ways. We are satisfied that although certain seasons find the larger proportion of shellfish, as of true fish, spawning, yet they spawn in our warm seas almost all the year, and so are independent of any sudden untoward occurrence at the spawning season of the majority. The quantity of "food" we dug up in a foot or two was most remarkable, and how a cockle manages not only to get so fat but deposits such a quantity of lime in the short time at its disposal is a mystery. The *Myæ* also are most vigorous, and form large and strong shells, each valve occasionally reaching 5 inches by 3, in favourable positions with us; although this is much beyond their customary dimensions elsewhere. These latter shellfish, although rarely taken by the people about, do not consequently increase the more; but the cockles that are steadily hunted more or less the year through before our door, are as numerous and as large as we have ever seen them! This itself would point to regular relays of sizes growing up to take the place of those removed, and at the same time shows the advantage to a species to have the larger individuals regularly removed, just as the Fijians "clubbed" their fathers!

The sea-farer and sea-labourer have not found the days so kind, but you did steal one happy day, my friend, to probe the sea-bottom, and endeavour to decipher more of its story than you previously knew; and all, too, were lucky enough to tumble on board at the right time, as the strong-winded launch puffed across to the deepest water to be had inside the Atlantic. We know that if the land were to rise or the sea recede a hundred fathoms, all the German Ocean, the English Channel, the sea far to the West of Ireland and the outer Hebrides, as well as around the Orkney and Shetland Islands, would become dry land; but even then there would be a few lakes left, and some of the very few deeper spots within the sea-line mentioned are in our neighbouring Linnhe Loch. What will the water swirl into such pits, or what purely pelagic forms will take up their permanent residence in these deeper quarters? we ask ourselves as the dredge is already over a hundred fathoms from the deck. We have found from experience in our own loch that the deepest pit is mostly a receptacle for the dead shells of the ordinary mollusca of the loch, or at least it has rarely yielded us anything else—but we are hopeful of something more interesting here. The little capstan creaks as the line strains around it bringing up an evident burden, for the dredge has been biting well, and its "pulse" has been favourable, as our hearty friend remarks, and the wildest enthusiasm animates the hunters as its contents are tumbled out for investigation. Keep it quite clear of the stuff from paltry sixty fathoms, although we did dive with delighted alacrity at the splendid keyhole limpets and Hungarian's caps that came up from that depth.

Well! well! and what have we got? Did you ever see such clumps of *Sertularia*, those beautiful plant-like zoophytes, as we have here; and the masses of *Terebratula* of the most splendid proportions will force us to talk of these interesting shells in future with regal indifference. Here are two beauties, almost white, with their serpent heads (*Caput-serpentis*), seated on the living shells of *Modiola* or horse-mussels. Set them in water and you will observe that, although fixed to the shell of the mussel by a strong muscular attachment, beyond their power of voluntary removal, yet they revolve upon it in the most curious fashion, half forcing one to look for eyes, so serpent-head like do they appear as they revolve. These are really finely-grown specimens, far beyond anything we have in our own loch, yet they are affixed to and have reached maturity upon living *Modiolæ* of a very moderate size compared with those to be found at a fathom or two in the laminarian zone. This is surely proof enough that the large mussel is better suited for shallow water, while the *Terebratulæ* are clearly better grown in the depths. This is evidently the case with various other species, and we go on passing the material through our hands, now tumbling two varieties of *Holothuriæ* into water, now chucking little bits of sticks, with remote resemblance to crustaceans, into other receptacles, until what with hermit crabs with beautiful green eyes and jackets like boiled partans, and large *Porcellani* crabs, *Munida rugosa*, mixed up with fragments of mutilated Norwegian lobsters, *Nephrops Norvegicus*, our receptacles are getting filled with a motley collection. The sea urchins are represented by large fellows, bigger than the fist, but still inferior to those we have taken in shallow water; and the little curious flat creatures, scarcely larger round than peas, with mouth and vent on same side and the spines only observable with the lens, *Echinocyamus pusillus*, are they not called, with the customary contrariness of naturalists, whose nomenclature increases at an inverse ratio to the size of the creature named.

As we come to examine the contents of our jars, we find that the little stick-like, or rather straw-like, crustaceans are really the quaint looking *Arcturus*, with claws at the end of two feet-like antennæ; but whether they chose such a deep quarter to reside in from dread of that 100 fathom rise in the land, or because their attenuated bodies were little affected by depth or consequent pressure, we do not mean to decide. Here is a shell of *Venus casina* so covered with a growth as to be of as brilliant green as a copper salt, and sitting in the middle thereof, turning about its droll head, is a small *terebratula*, wondering into what inhospitable world it had been dragged from its home more than 100 fathoms deep. The dredge has meantime been jumping along a rocky bottom at a lesser depth, and when it appears over the gunwale the principal product is a cluster of barnacles. You have all seen our barnacle-covered sea coast with the myriad ciliæ of the owners waving in the water, and no doubt suppose that double or triple the size would be a reasonable increase for a deep water barnacle to reach. But what do you say to them when they would contain as good a dram as the most exacting Highland throat could desire?

Slowly our nervous system gets settled from the excitement of expectant Columbus's, and settles back into the more sober tone of mind represented by gloating over and arranging our garnered riches. And our friend dispenses his treasures with most uncollector-like generosity, and we promise to search the deepest pits in fraternal association, and we look forward to a new species of mermaid and a particular variety of sea-serpent; but alas! for our wayward clime, the wind blew and the waters rose, and the dredge and its owner have once more changed positions, the latter to labour and the former to play! But, perhaps, it is scarcely to be called play bringing in a dredge from a hundred fathoms even by the partial aid of a steam winch, laden with the spoil of a course along a gravelly bottom, travelled with a "good pulse."

The sun has just sunk behind the Kingairloch hills, and the loch is richly bathed in cross lights as the moon swings lazily over the summit of Ben Breac. We are turning homeward with but one skate to reward our long watch around the cairn, and as we tug at the oar our attention is once more attracted to what—a shower of rain or of flies? One glance at the serene heavens dispels any idea of rain drops, and neither midges nor flies are troubling us, so we are forced to seek in the water itself for an explanation of the peculiar appearance—as if sharp drops were striking the surface and spreading a multitude of wave lines all around. On closer examination the explanation is sufficiently simple. The water is teeming with sea-blubbers *(Medusæ)* just on a level with the surface, and at each pulsation the centre is lifted over the surface so as to cause a break, in the very same way as any object, be it rain drop or insect, that struck the surface from above would do. The great multitude of these jelly-fishes all breaking the surface gave a most remarkable appearance to the water, and as we passed through them with the boat, the infinity of waving ciliæ invested the sea with new interest, these creatures being as beautiful in the water as they appear slobbery, uninteresting masses, when out of it.

Suddenly, as we proceed, "there is a sound of revelry by night," and hundreds of sable musicians of the most dismal character commence "We won't go home till morning," or its equivalent among dissipated rooks. These birds have all been roosting on a low tree by the sea-shore, and indeed, almost on the sea-beach, for it over-hangs the gravel. Whether they had chosen this particular spot as the most suitable one near to their hunting ground, and so as to be able to commence operations after the few hours of semi-darkness had dispersed, or because it was more comfortable than if it had overhung the grass, we know not. It is probable that the radiation from the gravel would keep them warmer than if they were sitting over the dew-distilling grass, and rooks are sufficiently intelligent to know how to make themselves snug.

We have not seen many skates these nights, and our most dexterous spearman has only struck small ones, so he asks the pertinent question whether they may not be coming by relays, and the older fish having deposited their eggs are now followed by younger brethren? We do not profess to understand the spawning of skate nor properly to appreciate the length of time required for the maturity of the egg either inside the fish or after deposition. We have already called attention to the fact that thornbacks caught in November or December are found supplied with well-developed eggs, although they do not make their appearance at the spawning-grounds until May or June. After this they disappear from these grounds, and yet they are at this time full of eggs at all stages of development. This would mean either that these eggs take a long time to be covered with their final capsule, or that the fish go elsewhere to spawn as the season advances.

We this week secured in shallow water a species that we have not hitherto met in our loch—namely, the cuckoo-skate *(Raia miraletus)*, of Couch. The pale yellow colour and large darkly marked spot or eye on each wing are quite distinctive, more especially when accompanied by the numberless minute hooked prickles on the surface of the skin. Now, this species is said to throw its eggs in December, and yet this specimen was supplied with eggs in various stages, the larger being wholly developed, with the exception of the enveloping capsule of tough fibrous gelatine that apparently takes so long to form. We have never succeeded in hatching out skate eggs, probably from impatience of results being so long delayed, but when removing several for experiment the other day, we were surprised at the marked difference between the eggs as removed from the fish and the same egg as it appears when a short time out of water.* The fish seems to throw out a stringy mucous of the most tenacious character, with which the egg attaches itself to whatever it is deposited upon, and so far from being thrown at random as some naturalists assert, we believe the spawning ground to be carefully chosen, and the eggs that are thrown ashore are the victims of the turbulence of the sea and not of the stupidity of the fishes. If these carefully protected eggs are never found in the stomachs of fishes, they are certainly punctured by some borer, notably the dog whelk, so that they do not escape the dangers that await all embryos. The cuckoo ray, whether from its small size or intrinsic quality, proved to be the most delicate of the class we have ever tasted, and certainly superior to the thornback in its present condition. Only once have we procured a small fish fry from the stomach of a skate

---

* We succeeded at various times in hatching out the thornback, six months being about the time required to absorb the umbilical sac.

here, the usual contents being crustacea and mollusca, no doubt a good proof of the dearth of fishes in the loch.

We had recently sent us the contents of the stomachs of a number of sea-trout taken in salt water, away from rivers, and these proved to consist mainly of small cuttle-fish *(Loligo media ?)* with a few annelids and half-digested fry. The presence of these small cuttles in such numbers on our coast was unknown to us, as we have rarely captured them, but no doubt they frequent the laminarian zone more than the deeper water usually traversed by our dredges.

When examining a number of large ascidians lately in order to extract the *Modiolaria* or delicate mussel-like shells that take up their abode in the thick surrounding integument, and live upon the juices of this low-class pseudo-vertebrate, we were surprised on two several occasions to find a crustacean quite three-eighths of an inch long make its appearance, upon pressure, from the entrance orifice. These proved to belong to the family of *Gammaridæ*, not unlike in general appearance to the familiar shore-flea. The sluggish organisation of the ascidians seems to present especial facilities to unwelcome guests to quarter themselves upon it.

The familiar green lintie of the south *(Coccothraustes chloris)* is by no means a common bird here, but we were sorry when we lately came upon a nest in our garden most skilfully concealed, and with the five dainty eggs we know so well, to find them cold and evidently deserted. We hope the little mother was more successful elsewhere, and that it had not paid the penalty of over-familiarity, and fallen a victim—for we keep no cold-blooded assassin in feline shape about our premises. In consequence of this all birds are friendly, and we had the pleasure this week of watching a gold-crest, our smallest British bird, performing its antics on the hedge two yards from our window for several minutes, regardless of our presence. Its movements were more like those of a tit, as it passed along the hedge sprouts, and the plumage spoke of immaturity, but the brilliant crest of *Regulus cristatus* was its unquestionable patent of nobility.

JULY, 1882.

We peered in vain into the hole in the shed in which our factotum had placed the rat trap, but at length a ray of light enabled us to observe that the trap was sprung, and yet nothing observable in it. We had just come to this sage conclusion, and decided to let other hands withdraw and re-set it when shortly thereafter the trap was pulled out with an empty rat-skin in it! Clearly its brethren had declared in favour of rat pie, and "drew the line" at the skin and tail. "The horrid cannibals," said everybody, "the brutes will eat anything!" But they would not, you see, and left the skin; being in this far superior to the Irish savage who used to exhibit himself before a delighted audience of roughs, in the charming occupation of eating up a raw live rat. Why should we scoff at rats because in the absence of other savoury food they should inter their benighted companion in friendly and sympathetic sepulchres? Is it not, indeed, a further instance of their exceptional intelligence thus to rise above all paltry sentiment and utilise the body of their defunct comrade; perhaps even led thereto by the humane desire to put an end to its sufferings? Certain it is that the rat is one of the most intelligent of living animals, while the cannibal races of the old and new worlds, whether Fijians or Maoris, Niam-Niam or Caribs, have been the most vigorous, intellectual, and respectable savages that our advanced civilisation has come in contact with. So that we are forced to conclude there must be some connection between intelligence and cannibalism, and that as we ascend in the scale of being as a rule we feed upon still higher class organisms than the order beneath us, and consequently it might be advisable to consider whether—whether—we seem to have lost the thread of the argument!

A lobster! said one, as we stood by the shore in the dusk. A beast that bites! remarked another in explanation. But there are quite a lot of them flopping about, so we soon gather them together and ascertain that we have got a lot of cuttle-fish. These are the largest we have seen in the loch, for although we have met the eggs of the creature in a forward state of development, we have never yet obtained full-grown samples of *Loligo vulgaris*. These fellows are about a foot long, without their tentacles. Ere we manage to transport them to our domicile, the receptacle in which they are placed is swimming in the black ink which they throw, in place of the brown liquid of the *Sepiæ*. So the youngsters gather round to see the Sea-Clerk dissected, and its ink-bottle taken out, followed by the quill pen of a back bone, so delicately transparent, and such an exact reproduction in its way of the old goose-quill. The mandibles of the parrot beak, too, so characteristic of the octopi, are keen enough to prove that they are really "beasts that bite," even if we had not been foolish enough to prove the ability of the tribe, and be sharply bitten by little creatures two or three inches long. Their stomachs are well filled, and the contents at once show the difference between them and ordinary vertebrate fishes. The fry in the stomachs of sea trout are nearly whole, and but little bruised, showing enough to satisfy us that they consist at present of small herring fry and sandlaunces; while those in the cuttle are so finely comminuted with their parrot beaks that only the crushed bones and scales are evidence of their fishy character. Here, then, are Nature's paths crossing. The low-class mollusc (for, although highly developed, the cuttles are mollusca) eats the vertebrate fishes on the one hand, while the larger vertebrates, in the shape of the sea trout, are eating the smaller cuttles alongside.

We recently procured a lot of small fishes that are rarely caught on the Scottish coast, simply because they do not take the ordinary baits employed, or come within the ordinary engines of destruction. We refer to the Wrass family, which frequent rocky coasts or algæ-covered boulders, and have very small mouths, that no usual haddock hook could enter. It is very rarely that any one fishes them with fine hooks, as they are of little value for the table, and give little sport to the angler unless he uses extremely fine tackle, and in consequence, they are little known among us. The common Wrass, or Ballan Wrass *(Labrus maculatus)*, is a very brilliantly marked fish, red and blue streaks and marking covering him all over, more especially vivid about the head. The soft lips, which are a special characteristic of the family, no doubt enable them to feel their food among the dark fronds of the laminaria, where little light can penetrate at times. Among the more brilliant specimens, an example of the Green Wrass *(Labrus lineatus)*, came ashore. This fish is scarcely acknowledged as a species by Couch, and is considered a variety, owing its colour to the difference of ground; but here we have both caught within a few yards, a fact which distinctly militates against the ground theory in this case. There seems as good reason to make it a species, notwithstanding structural similarity, as there is for many others which have been separated out. Several specimens of the little Corkwing (*Crenilabrus cornubicus*), one of the commonest of the family on our coast, were captured along with the above, so that we do not seem to be deficient in species, if we only devoted a little attention to their elucidation and capture. In fact, the abundance of seaware on our coast ought to be a surety that these rock and luxuriant algæ haunters are not uncommon.

We have several times amused ourselves by endeavouring to secure various wrasses and sea perch that frequent a rocky islet out off the shore, employing a hand-net with a long handle, but they are much too knowing to be enticed therein, and, when disturbed from among the seaweed fronds, they at once bolt seawards. The fifteen-spined stickleback and various gobies, may, with patience, be thus taken, but a crick in the neck and benumbed hands are our usual reward whenever we seek thus to add to our knowledge of the wrasses. That the green wrass may well be a modified ballan wrass we must not, however, deny, as we have always held that colour is greatly influenced by the ground, and although captured close together it is quite possible they may have grown up in conterminous haunts of sufficiently distinct character.

Scrambling up the front of our dwelling, and twining across the top of the door, a vigorous *Tropæolum* has established itself by the help of a stout cord. Although starting annually from the ground, it has already traversed an extensive range, and the show of blossom of a brilliant red hue is something startling. In the short space across the top of the doorway the flowers are to be counted by hundreds, to the complete exclusion of any green—and all these, it must be remembered, have to be supplied with vigor, and life, and beauty through a stem like a piece of small cordage. It is difficult to realise the speed with which the sap must course upwards, in order to feed such a magnificent display; not to speak of the fresh progress made daily and the daily new supply of flowers. We look upwards with an idea that there is a secret to be unravelled here, and that a dexterous experimenter might arrange an experiment by which the speed of the flow of sap would be measured. This beautiful and graceful plant grows with the utmost luxuriance with us, and yet it is exceedingly difficult to establish in a new quarter. Many plants have been sent to the warm south without success, and the more anxious the recipients have been to secure it, the more obstinately has it declined to be coddled. It especially affects a gravelly soil, and whenever it takes a fancy to a district *and it is left alone,* it will spread with marvellous rapidity, and threaten to choke all other vegetation about it.

Surely there is no other plant like this American exotic, to send the sap scudding upwards through a minimum of stem, we mutter, as we traverse the burn side with the blue harebells in dainty groups nodding at us from the wall on our dexter hand, and the white *digitalis* in studied groups close alongside. We are at the garden gate under a 20-foot wall, and our attention is called to something on the top of a tree, by the side of the stream a hundred yards away. Quite a gay group on the tip top of the tree, and the tree well nigh 50ft. over the stream. Your favourite flower, my dear, but we're not going there to pluck them, so you must e'en sniff the evening air, and fancy the odours from the wild honey-suckle are wafted hitherwards, and that you are better to leave the daring flowers in their point of vantage, where the dwellers in the woodland can enjoy their fragrance. Yon are suggesting stiffened joints and youth departed; but we are only contemplative, we assure you, and are startled at thus discovering our simple, hardy, native plant, with its wrinkled, cordage stem, feeding its honey-laden head at a height to which the bright stranger we have been discoursing about cannot yet aspire, with us.

The deer eat the *Tropæolum*, as they eat almost every other green thing, and what they do not eat the rascals destroy with their feet and horns, out of apparent mischief. Not always do they come by a righteous retribution; but that black fellow that hopped so lightly over that wire fence, and waxed so fat on forbidden turnips, and seemed to flourish, in despite the direst anathemas, what became of him that he ceased to "lard the lean earth" as he sped along to his daily meal? Perhaps the dogs that enjoyed the venison know best, as the "black fellow" hung with his heels on the wires and his nose in the little swamp alongside, out of which position he could not extricate his fat carcase. How he must have bemoaned his weakness for cultivation and turnips, and wished he had stuck to the hillside and the heather! We turn from the stream, with the *lycopodium* growing far up the stems of the trees on its banks, and revel in the rich hay crop, with as much on one acre as last year showed on three. For if the year has been uncertain and backward in the eyes of pleasure-loving humanity, the crops as a whole look remarkably well, and all vegetation flourishes, even the bunches of hazels having caught what sun was about and tinted their cheeks therewith.

A plague in the shape of midges, so we did not stop to examine the results of our dredging, but fled ignominiously from the field. That is the reason that little fish happened to be left stranded on the bottom of the boat, without the slightest attention being paid to it, although a glance is sufficient to assure us we have not taken any of his kind hitherto in Loch Creran. We have often wondered at the absence of weever fish, and here at last is a young specimen, about 2in. long, of the larger weever, *Trachinus draco*, with long dorsal and anal fins, and the black fin over the head in which the dangerous weapon is concealed that procures for it the name of sting-bull. These fishes, when more mature, are really most venomous customers, and the wound they inflict is very poisonous. As they bury themselves in the sand with the sting out, naked feet most frequently are apprised of their truculent presence. Although said to be not uncommon on the Scottish coast, we have only once known of their capture before, over a lengthened experience of Scottish sea-fishing. Does any reader know of their frequenting the coast elsewhere?

AUGUST, 1882.

That we behaved like a fool we acknowledge, but we have been quite unable to decide wherein our excessive folly lay! To stand, hat in hand, at a corner of Buchanan Street, in the busiest part of the day, and make half-furtive and consequently abortive attempts with this instrument to capture the object of our attention, is so self-evidently foolish to you that you cannot understand our difficulty.

Well, the fact is, we scarcely agree that the act in question was so foolish as was our weakly refraining from following up the attempt until it had been a success. For the first time in our experience, amid the throng of business, a really magnificent dragon-fly was jerking its unaccustomed way up our principal street. Now it swerved aside from a tram only to meet the danger of a highly-poised hansom-cabman. Here it almost fled into the face of a policeman, only to rebound under the nose of a cab horse. Up it soared, to remove from the turmoil, but the din and bustle seemed to disorganise its intelligence, and once more it is only avoiding by rebounding movements the trams, cabs, and hurrying foot-passengers of our most thronged of thoroughfares. We pretend to be absorbed in ruminating whether or not to remove our various deposits from the Limited Scotch banks to the Bank of England, and assume the sternly contemplative expression of a great financier, as we conceive him to be, while we follow the flight of the stranger from the country up and down, round and across, in its wayward wanderings.

No one else in all that crowd could find an eye for the beautiful interloper, and we amused ourselves for a time watching whether any of the faces into which it nearly popped over and over again, took any notice of it. But not one seemed even to note its presence, or surely the eye would have changed expression, and the swamp with the groves of iris, and the pond with the water lilies of their boyhood, been tossed for one vivid moment before their mental sight. Whence and how could this brilliant son of a water-nymph arrive in the centre of a great city, to pursue his excited, jerky existence? Our only explanation pointed to the vegetable and fruit shops of the vicinity, to which it must have been brought when at rest in the early morning, the heat of the day and the city sending it forth on its fruitless errand among the flowers of the ladies bonnets. It could not have come in embryo, as the dragon-fly is matured as it issues from the water, and so in all likelihood it had simply passed the night in some vegetable, to find itself in a new world in the morning. A friend informs us of a very fine specimen having been captured in Buchanan Street some years ago.

We lately observed a decision that has impressed us with a high opinion of the general knowledge of natural history in the North. A man caught *in flagrante delictu* with a poached salmon in his possession, declared he did not know a trout from a salmon, and thereupon drew down upon his head the stern rebuke of the judge, promptly followed by his committal. We should much like to know how many in Glasgow can tell a salmon when they see it; ay! even how many in the country can tell a salmon from a grilse and a sea trout, all, say, about 7lb. weight? And then, if by *salmon* the speaker talks comprehensively of all the *salmonidae*, we could confront him with members of the family only to be acknowledged by a thorough specialist. We have no doubt that roughly speaking the judge was right, but it is also quite possible that, technically speaking, the poacher was also right, and that he could not tell a trout from a salmon. What relationship is there between a brown trout and a sea trout? and if brown trout took to salt water, would they become silvered like the parr when it becomes a smelt? Many such questions that would once have appeared absurd are now put most seriously by men well qualified to judge whether they are serious or no. We have taken brown trout in very brackish water, and off all our small streams local shoals of small sea-trout are to be found; sea-trout that have bred in these same streams. These shoals are quite distinct from the quantities of large sea-trout, strongly marked occasionally, and at other times with quite delicate markings, that throng towards the larger rivers from the deeper sea, in time to make havoc among the smolts and younger salmon fry. It will one of these days become a grave question whether sea-trout should not be confined to these smaller streams, leaving the larger rivers to the salmon, as we look upon the voracious sea-trout as a great enemy to its nobler congenor, and to attempt to stock a river with both appears to us very like the conduct of the boy that wished both to eat his cake and keep it.

We have had occasion before to refer to the growth on the shells of univalves (*Hydractina echinata*, is it not, my friend?) and one of these shells we were keeping by us to watch the movements of the associated *Polyzoae* in the water. A pretty little grove they appeared, and we were wondering what the creature could assimilate, and whether any but the lowest life would ever be brought within their power. Into the dish we popped a beautiful annelid, its many segments iridescent in the light, and the creature itself moving like a railway train round a curve. In its excitement it traversed the dish over and over again, until at length in a thoughtless moment it ran over the hydractina-covered shell. It had not gone far, however, despite its activity of movement, until the end of its tail got seized among the creatures, and after the most desperate struggles and efforts to relieve itself it was forced to sacrifice a portion of its extremity in order to secure the safety of the remainder, only escaping with its life from these determined communists, whose union was strength. Had the community been a little more extensive, and the creature had delayed in ridding itself of the portion seized, it would have all gone to form a meal to these strange coralline-like growths.

It is interesting to learn from "W. L. H." that instances of dragon-flies in cities are more common than we imagine; at the same time we cannot bring ourselves to believe that these insects willingly traverse the smoke-freighted city of their own accord. Still it must be recollected that these larger species of *Libellula* are more like swallows, for power and speed of flight, and their carnivorous character might induce them to follow, say, a butcher's cart even into what must appear to them an African desert of city. We in vain endeavoured to follow a fine specimen to-day in its swift progress over a stretch of mossy ground, its large eyes scanning the neighbourhood for living prey; for these predacious insects may be called the *Raptores* of the insect world. The neighbourhood or immediate surface of water is their customary hunting-ground, water being the element in which their eggs are laid, and in which their nymphs emerge from the pupa case and develop their wings. It is therefore impossible to believe them developed in the city, and we are forced to suppose them carried thither accidentally rather than traversing the streets like insect Livingstones. Their life history is a strange one, well worthy the attention of youthful naturalists, who might "choke" them with a drop of paraffin on the complicated tail, through the end of which they breathe!

In passing along the highway these last days every step has been accompanied by the most reckless slaughter, for it was quite impossible to proceed without destruction, owing to the myriads of ants traversing the path. On Tuesday, however, we came upon a variation of this spectacle, for these ants, wingless, busy, purpose-like as they appeared, had given place to vast multitudes of winged specimens, fushionless, helpless, purposeless, and that seemed to flop about in the dazed fashion of young birds too early driven from the nest. On examination they were the well known winged ants of our boyhood that we so well knew to be destitute of stings or power of inflicting vengeance, and that came and went like a visitation. They are the gentlemen ants, whose services are no longer required by the community, with a sprinkling of pregnant females, not yet captured by the working ants to continue the life of the ant hill. The males very soon die, being as unfit to feed and support themselves as they are unable to defend themselves; and the females soon rid themselves of their useless glittering appendages, as a young mother throws aside her frippery and settles down to maternal cares. The season seems to have been most suitable for the propagation of the insect world, and, certainly, if "every lad had his lass" among the ants, there should be no lack of ant hillocks in the neighbourhood, nor need the barren workers have gone far to secure the certainty of the continued existence of their community.

Scarcely have we left the bright winged insects behind us when we come upon a prettily marked reptile basking in the sun in the middle of the road, evidently enjoying the change from a muggy vegetation to the dry and warm dust of the highway. We soon secure the fine specimen of a blind adder, the only snake-like reptile we have yet found in Benderloch, despite the stories of "adders" that, when investigated, generally prove to be examples of this timid and harmless member of the family. It seemed so thoroughly overcome with the *dolce far niente* of the hot afternoon that it made no effort to escape, although fully alive and uninjured.

The eaves of our cottage can be reached with the hand, and yet, although close to the road and dotted with windows, so confident are some of our native birds that nests are actually built in the *Cottonia* that hugs the front of the dwelling. A foot or two from the windows, a few feet from the ground, and in the way of being almost rubbed by the passing shoulder, the wren *(troglodytes)* had commenced one nest and finished two others, all within a radius of a yard or so. The charming little domiciles had apparently never been occupied, whether from her mate declining to entrust his precious existence so close to humanity, or from her ladyship being herself dissatisfied with her workmanship or site. It is quite possible she was only practising house-building, and that last having been quite a little masterpiece, she may have removed herself and her skill to more suitable quarters. Yet the plentiful greenery of the neighbourhood of our doorway must provide a sufficiency of insect food, and we yesterday observed a little blue tit clambering among the *escalonia* and *cottonia*, and devouring the insects, as it hung, all ends up, within a foot or two of our door and ourselves; whilst a redbreast in the pursuit of flies entered the open window of our sanctum, and getting between the two panes, had to remain imprisoned securely until we liberated its panting bosom.

Some one has been endeavouring to explain on Darwinian principles why the greater proportion of flowers are yellow, although we can scarcely consider the effort successful. On similar lines, can it be explained why the greater proportion of individual butterflies are white? At present it is quite an exception to see a dark-coloured one, while the white of various species are legion. That a white butterfly is as readily observed by a bird as any other, we are as satisfied as we are that it is *more* readily noted by the human eye; so it cannot be to escape its enemies. Is it really from a wholly opposite necessity—that of being observed by its fellows? This is, perhaps, more than probable; and as they jerk along over the heath, or flutter so jauntily and aberrantly over the fields of oats until they recognise their "affinity," you conclude, as they tumble together into the vegetation, that it is more important for the race, with us, to be readily recognised, than to be specially fitted to escape observation.

Very frequently we have brought up in the dredge, a smooth species of sponge, in which a hermit crab is ensconced, and we have wondered how and why it should have selected such a situation. The peculiar shape of the sponge at length satisfied us that it must have originally started from a shell, but again and again no shell has been found inside. We find, however, that it does seemingly start as a growth upon a miniature shell, in which the crab has placed itself, and gradually the sponge has eaten away the shell, but had no effect upon the movable body of the crab. Nothing could better prove the effect of sponges upon shells than this case, in which it ends by entirely removing all evideuce of there ever having been a shell at all. Other sponges seem to act more slowly, as those upon oyster and scallop shells, but even these puncture holes all over the shell, and gradually disintegrate as they continue to penetrate.

The evening is remarkable still, the tide very high, and

the slightest sound is carried readily across the water. Suddenly we are startled by regular splashing from the direction of the sea-surrounded cairn, and conclude that the seals are at their games again, although we have seen but few of them about recently, since rifle balls from youngsters "on the rampage" have been ricochetting too freely over the waters. But the steady regularity of the sound demands another explanation, when we discover that the cattle, usually browsing on the little rocky islet in front, have remained so long at their posts that they are obliged to walk along the narrow ridge towards the shore, quite shoulder high in the water, while the accompanying calves have little but their uplifted heads out of the water. Had the water been rough the feat would have been almost impossible to the calves, and only habit could have bred the confidence and self-reliance necessary to induce them to attempt such a passage homewards unbidden. A strange, weird, and picturesque sight did they appear as they passed in single file shoreward through the water.

The islands of Loch Linnhe are now quite cleared of their vociferous inhabitants, with the exception of a scattering of lesser black-backed gulls. These have still a few young, half or three-quarters grown, and, as the boat approaches, the young birds start swimming seawards in another direction. The terns, nesting latest of all, were last week nearly over with their summer labours, although a young one still fluttered into the water from the rocks on our approach, while overhead the screeching parents circled, except when their silence was enforced by the mouthful they were bearing to their young. This provender proved as usual to be herring sile, about 2 inches long, showing that these fish must spawn in the neighbouring waters, as we scarcely ever find these birds without such food at this season in Loch Linnhe. Herring have been taken in the above loch of late, but in no great numbers, while mackerel in shoals have also been visiting their occasional haunts in Ardmucknish Bay. These latter fish are small but are still large enough to prove a great boon to the locality. Sea trout are still appearing in Oban in considerable quantities, the result of the poaching raids of the Oban trawlers; but the fish are not nearly so large as they were early in the season, and are no doubt local products from the various smaller streams.

As the rowers toiled against the stream, that curiously interesting phenomenon, the combinations of the dookers and the gulls—voluntary or accidental—to make an assault upon a shoal of fish, again came under our notice—the dookers below keeping the fish towards the surface, and together, while the gulls and terns had a chance at them above. On these occasions the frightened fish crowd together like sheep, so that the whole tragedy is confined within very narrow limits. Doubtless the dookers merely look to their own convenience, keeping the fish from sinking too deep for them, and the screaming, gobbling sea fowl are accidental jackals.

At the islands we hear a sudden reverberation, and shortly thereafter we are surprised to find it was a shot from one of the party, the nature of the sound and the real distance wholly concealed by the peculiar state of the atmosphere, which must have now all the character of a light fog from the quantity of moisture in suspension, although the day was otherwise clear, warm, and fine. Long before darkness, however, a heavy rainfall of long-continued duration partly explained the atmospheric conditions. The result of this shot was a large cormorant (*phalacrocorax carbo*), still alive and not greatly injured. Had we possessed facilities for a regular supply of fish in our poorly-inhabited loch, we should have sought to keep his lordship, for they will live and recover from most severe wounds, and are by no means delicate in any way. The eye is bold and piercing, and the head has a somewhat fierce and aquiline appearance. But there is another shot, and a blue rock pigeon is dashing Lismorewards from the island. As it reaches the water edge it decides not to attempt the crossing, but turning, makes a valiant effort to regain the cliff whence it started. It is wonderful that it did not fall at once, considering how badly it was hit, and as it comes down with a sudden thud it is clear no great suffering could have been endured, all the nervous energy of the poor bird having been perforce concentrated into that final effort.

You would rather have had that blue hawk, my friend, which has so often just escaped your gun. How it must scoff at slinking humanity skirting the cliff on careful feet, while it sweeps outward from an unexpected corner and soars seawards, the monarch still of the little domain! Rarely is the Black Island without a pair of these ever beautiful and now comparatively rare, peregrine falcons. Here we are on the bare summit, the hard rock for a yard protruding through the heath-clad hill top—blown bare, or worn bare; for here is the gathering ground of black-backed gull and other seafowl, where they sit and devour their tidbits, and yet can keep an eye on the hunting-grounds around for anything else that may turn up. Around the summit are numberless bleached limbs of small crabs, and these must surely have been borne hither by the gulls; although our friend mentions that where the cormorant was perched a dozen small crabs were lying with the carapaces broken through. We are not aware that cormorants are eaters of crustacea, and are more inclined meantime to suppose that some gull or other had borne the crabs thither.

The wild bees were very numerous on the island, but we did not see a byke, and believe these to have come from the island of Lismore, as no sooner did they suck around a little than they dashed off at a tremendous speed to some other distant ground, a mode of proceeding that no local bees with a limited pasturage would ever adopt. Those we saw were the white-ended bees—the strongest of the wild bees, and we should think the most capable of flight. Grasshoppers were quite plentiful, and must have been local, while butterflies were represented by one white that we could not capture, and a great number of a small yellow, that found abundant facilities for hiding among the heath. The caterpillars of the tiger moths were numerous all over the island, but of the moth itself we saw no example. The most common of our coloured butterflies at present is the northern brown *(Erebia Media)*, with the meadow brown *(Epinephele Janira)* among the grassy hills and pastures. These are very sober-tinted, and when they drop to rest with their wings together, are scarcely observable, nor will the sun throw much light upon them, the rays being absorbed, and not reflected.

"A story of partridges!" said the veteran keeper; "the strangest I have ever known! We had brought partridge eggs from the South, and hatched out a young brood under a hen, and these were doing well, and looking flourishing. Well, just the night before the 12th what should appear at the hen's crate but a pair of old partridges, and there they took up their abode with the youngsters. When anyone approaches they retire to some little distance, but at once return as soon as the intruder leaves." In fact, they have recognised the kinship of the little ones, their want of parents to properly understand their feelings and sympathise with their wilder yearnings, and these birds of the wilderness have consequently felt it their duty to take upon themselves the serious responsibility of introducing the young strangers from a far country among their brethren of the hillside. Descending to dull prose, the chances are that these are barren birds, or a pair that have lost their brood; but the remarkable fact remains that they have recognised their kinship with the little strangers, and overcome their fear of and repugnance to human vicinage in their determination to father them. When we consider the readiness with which a hen will charge herself with ducks—there is even a turkey at South Connel with about a score of young ducks—small birds with cuckoos, and other still stranger connections, it is a most valuable *per contra* fact to have such a remarkable instance of acknowledgment of relationship.

Were it not that birds, as a rule, are rather oblivious of distinctions, whether in a wild or domesticated state, neither the cuckoo nor the henwife could play so many pranks. A young nephew of ours, with a dry humour and a shrewd turn for natural history, carried out a series of rather novel experiments upon the credulity of birds this year, and as they have a distinct bearing upon the question before us, as well as helping to solve another problem which seems still to require proof for some observers, we will note them here. Having discovered a sparrow-hawk's nest with two eggs, he removed one of them, and turning a piece of wood in imitation thereof, he painted it so as roughly to resemble the real egg. This he put back in the nest, and by means of it induced the bird to continue laying until she had placed six eggs at his disposal. This was more than her complement, and she must have matured and laid one or two eggs more than she would have done had she been permitted to follow the natural course of incubation. About the same time he discovered another hawk's nest, and one belonging to a wild pigeon. Painting the pigeon's eggs in imitation of the hawk's he took away the originals from the nest of the hawk and replaced them with the hypocrites, leaving them to be hatched out by the bird of prey, should it not discover the deception. In due time the youngster repaired to the hawk's nest on which the poor, deceived mother was sitting so closely that he was enabled to ensconce himself among the branches and watch her conduct. She was pecking sharply at something under her, which turned out to be the eggs just chipping, the occupants of which she was assisting to make their exit. Unfortunately he was not able to see the finale, as, although the young birds were there next day, they had entirely disappeared the following again. The disgust of the rapacious birds must have been extreme to find their choicest morsels rejected by the little seed-eaters, and they may have ended by devouring the ungrateful creatures that could not accommodate themselves to their altered circumstances, and pined under the "burden of an honour unto which they were not born."

Here were these wild, keen-witted birds deceived like barn-door fowls by a bit of painted wood, and the rudely painted eggs of their faint-hearted neighbours!

When out with our boat the other evening the sea was calm as glass, for a marvel this summer: and all about, even in the course of the swift current, patches of slaty gravel were floating on the surface of the water! The slightest splash at once sent them to the bottom, but the small stones of which they were composed were sometimes as large as the thumb nail, and the patches from the size of a hand to that of a hat. The tide was rising, and they must have been floated off the beach by the gently rising water, so quietly that the layer of air between the gravel and the water would not be moved. The phenomenon was a most interesting, and to us quite a novel, one on such a scale. The water would be about ten fathoms deep at the place, and our best scallop ground just under, so we left off agitating the water to see the sudden descent of the unwonted sailors, and turned to the dredge. When the first haul had been thrown into the tub, what was our astonishment to find what appeared to be an actual spider *(Arachnida)*, caught by a leg, in the mouth of a sea-urchin. How a land spider could have got into such a corner defied us to conjecture, and a sea-spider was a thing to us unknown. The specimen was evidently defunct, however, and we turned to other interesting contents of the dredge. Thus engaged we discovered a second specimen of the same species, with the soft sac-like body of the spider, quite different from the plate-clad body of the small spider-crab, that is so unmistakably a crustacean. This second specimen proved to be alive, and we thus were apparently furnished with data to show it lived at the bottom of the sea! Had it not been at the bottom, how could the urchin have obtained it, and did not one come up from the bottom alive? We were greatly interested, and much exercised, over our captures, and endeavoured to prove to our satisfaction that they were really spider-like crustaceans; but it would not do. Sitting on shore pondering over the problem, we noted the vicinity of a veritable spider of a class that is common about the beach, and its very distinct markings being exactly similar to those obtained in the dredge, we secured it and carried it home with us. The most natural thing to do under the circumstances was to place it in sea-water and see if it would retain its life and activity; but so soon as it was put under water it displayed the utmost helplessness, and soon ceased from troubling or being troubled. Clearly these spiders could not accommodate themselves to an ocean career, and we came at last to the conclusion that a number had been carried off the beach along with the floating gravel, and by a strange coincidence one had been captured as the prey of a sea-urchin, and another perhaps taken from the surface as the dredge came on board! an instance of the readiness with which we may deceive ourselves by accepting as facts appearances that are capable of being otherwise explained. Have we not all heard of the authentic case of the learned Glasgow Professor, who had discovered a new mullusc of a remarkable character, until a shrewd observer and thorough naturalist, still to be found in the vicinity of Gilmorehill, suggested that a common Limnœa had tumbled into a ditch!

We have lately been watching a set of key-hole limpets, *Fissurella Graeca*, in a dish of sea water, but have failed to see that they are other than very lazy and unenterprising. If turned on their backs or sides they are incapable of regaining their feet, nor have they shown any capacity for withdrawing entirely into their shells, as stated by

Jeffreys. The elegantly-fringed mantle becomes inflated like the delicate texture of a sea-anemone, and they mostly remain with their shell perched on the top, their foot firmly pressed upon the dish, and their inflated mantle spreading around them. One we placed on the edge of the dish actually crept out, apparently in search of water, and too stupid to find it, although within an inch or two. Another crept down until its head alone was in the water, where it remained for a day or two, seemingly quite satisfied for a time with its breathing tube in the air. This fringed-tube emerges from the hole in the apex of the shell, but does not communicate with the foot, and so presents no difficulty to the mollusc in the way of preventing the sucker action of the foot; for these creatures stick as firmly as a common limpet *(Patella)*. Although commonest on our coast in ten fathoms, they exist at low water mark in some districts, which seems quite in keeping with their power of living comfortably half out of the water.

Two feet from our study window the sweet peas are growing luxuriantly on the hither side of a rustic, wattled fence, and on this fence all the day long the birds come and go. Are they, too, lovers of the beautiful flowers, or do they fancy the papilionaceous plants are carrying butterflies? Is it an æsthetic development, as in the case of the Bower bird, or do very earthly considerations mix themselves up with the various feathered visitors that come to nod, and hop, and go again from the many-coloured flowers? Do not various flies and bees linger about them, and form a point of attraction to these shrewd entomologists, who all know well the customary habitats of moth and fly! Here is a little wren "sewing" its way along the fence, for it dodges along first on one side then on the other, nipping an occasional insect in its passage. Jenny has scarcely left when Cock Robin takes her place, his bosom no longer aglow with the passions of the spring, but with sober breast, as he thinks of the troubles of paternity. He lands on the fence full face to the window, then hopping up turns round with his back to view, performing this simple piece of gymnastics again and again, as he passes the sweet pea region, now diving at a fly or a gnat, but always with a bright eye fixed upon the window. Chaffinch after chaffinch comes, for they are legion, and the way they cling to the swaying heads of oats, and strip the grains therefrom, is most interesting to the onlooker across the little fence, although scarcely so amusing to the farmer. The gay wing seems to flash as it comes and goes, for although so extremely common and familiar, it is much more suspicious and restless than our next visitor, Mr. Sparrow, who feels really at home, his nest being among the ivy overhead, and who simply rests his well-filled corporation in a quiet, sedate, self-satisfied manner, as he contemplates the ripening grain, upon which he has been levying blackmail these weeks past, to his great comfort and consolation. He actually looks in with an expression of curiosity, seems to take a sniff at the sweet peas, turns lazily round his back to the window without hopping, and without the constant backward glance of the bright eye, as in the case of the redbreast! and then with confidence in human magnanimity, and consciousness of special immunity from the ordinary cares of bird life, ruffles his feathers, and settles himself down to an after-dinner dose on the fence. Bang comes a bigger fellow, as if he were thrown at the fence from a distance, and stares in stupidly for a moment, like a country bumpkin, as he is. He is fresh from the moor above—a common, sober-suited, well-fed bunting—and, after shifting from one foot to the other, goes off in a series of rainbow curves. For he is one of the jerky fliers, as if his body were too heavy for his power of flight, and obliged him to progress by spurts.

Suddenly our observations are interrupted by our name being called, while our attention is directed to the cackling of a hen on the little wooded knoll, and we are implored to discover the nest of the errant fowl. Now this is one of the penalties of greatness, we sigh, as we emerge from our den and seek the hillside. Were it not that some one of a shrewd, sensible turn of mind could turn *dilettante* qualities to practical use, what value would they be to the world? And so a sound head, having discovered that we are not unskilful bird-nesters, sends us forth to utilise our faculty in a manner directly advantageous to the breakfast table! The voice of the voluble bird soon gives us a general direction as to the whereabouts of the nest, but the moment we are observed approaching the hen stops its music and skulks silently through the brushwood. You silly creature, if your instincts have led you to such a natural and sequestered nook for your nest, what purpose can your cackling serve but to undo your otherwise secretive tendency? Or is the secretive instinct derived from wild ancestors, and the proud proclamation of having delivered an egg the result of human intercourse, and an evidence of domestic slavery? We are not aware whether any wild gallinaceous fowls cackle under similar circumstances, but, from the silence observed by all wild birds on the nest, we should scarcely expect the peculiarity to be other than the result of love of admiration, and a self-satisfied declaration of success. At any rate, to us the two instincts seem wholly antagonistic, although some birds more cunning than others reconcile them so far as to skulk off some distance from the nest ere starting their announcement. The nest we find well filled and cunningly hidden, or in all likelihood the grey crows would not have left an egg in it; and a day after our discovery another wanderer appears with a brood of ten, that she has successfully hatched out under trying conditions. We think there is here an interesting direction in which the earlier and later acquired instincts might be studied to advantage, as well as the extent to which the intelligence of the individual bird may reconcile them when opposed. This question of individual intelligence, compared with the average intellect of the mass of a species, is too frequently overlooked in experiments upon the lower creation, and this we note even in such careful observers as Sir John Lubbock and other workers in the school of ants, bees, and wasps. The bulk of the lower class of men act in accustomed grooves, and display singular lack of capacity when moved out of them, quite as much in a way as the ants experimented upon by Lubbock. We must observe specially intelligent fowls, as well as the ordinary silly creatures, in order to do justice to our inquiries.

SEPTEMBER, 1882.

We saw the northern lights last week, and although the sword of the Frost King has not yet swept along the hillsides of Benderloch, he has flung his javelin freely—here leaving its track marked by gay bunches of dead leaves on the birch, or bronzed bunches on the oaks. Elsewhere the hillsides have been more severely handled, and as we yesterday traversed the shores of Lochiel and the road up Glen Nevis, the sharp winds from the King of Bens had spread a golden hue over the bracken-covered slopes, and everywhere a wealth of gold and bronze on the sward and amid the tree tops evinced the immediate vicinity of royalty.

Not a sloe in our district, says one observer, and the hazel nuts are *nil*. But we shortly come upon a blackthorn-covered bank, and to our delight, in spite of the seasonal dearth of wild fruits, we discover this to be covered with the richest clusters of sloes we remember to have seen. The delicious bloom on the sloe berries, with their rich blue ground, contrasts beautifully with the dark-green leaves, not too numerously spread, and the fine, almost black, stems, of the bushes; so, as we gaze our eye-hunger increases, and a prickly bough is carefully detached and borne to "our special artist," with the request to transfer it as it stands to an imperishable canvas. Once inside the door it still looks lovely, but no longer has it the glory of the hillside, and we soon "accept the situation," and acknowledge that no art can give the surroundings, with the sun playing bo-peep among the bushes, and the young oak-trees nodding overhead, and the lowly brambles underneath (whose coherts are even now "gleaming in purple and gold," like the levelled hosts of the Assyrians). In our hands, also, the treasures of the waning year have been fast accumulating. The seedling birches have yielded delicious lemon-colour leaves without a speck upon them; the young oaks are liberal with their treasures of delicate bronze, running into a sober yellow; while before and beyond all the brambles are resplendent in the richest array of colours, from the deepest chocolate, through all the variations, to the tenderest hues of yellow, and mingled yellow, pink, and green. The sweet-peas, still gay and vigorous, are not more really brilliant than these leaves, and they so readily lend themselves to make a trophy, in which the tints are retained with success, that those who are not too much oppressed with the feeling of decay, that seems to make autumn and its miracles of colour a source of deep sadness to many, ought to cull and arrange autumn leafery that they may recollect how great is the power of Nature to confer pleasure on the eye. It will lead them to look forward to the "fall of the leaf" as an artistic revel, in which the bracken on the hill, the ferns in the nooks, and the trees by stream and fell don their ball dresses for one glorious "gathering in Brussels" before their Waterloo.

"I am glad to hear that you have sloes on your side," remarked our friend, "for I feared that they would be a complete failure this year, and we should get none at all. Now I mean to have a hunt after them the first opportunity." A hunt after sloes, we thought, as we looked at the grave and reverend seignior, who had bellies to fill with more substantial viands ; and so you have preserved a boyish love for a woodland ramble, or a particular fancy for sloe jelly! There was a knowing smile of satisfaction on the face, however, as the word "bitters" escaped him, and we were fully prepared to accept his statement that sloes made an admirable tonic with a due proportion of whisky, with a snap "that cleaned the mouth." Hitherto we have had pleasant memories of a famous teapot, with a dexterous admixture of camomile and gentian, and a suspicion of Turkey rhubarb, concocted by means of a minimum of boiling water and a maximum of Islay, that gave a ravenous appetite to many wanderers in the remoter north; but here is a much simpler recipe for those inexcusable people, whose appetites fail them in the vicinity of sloe bushes!

Came to us from our poet's corner a little paper parcel, and on opening it, appeared two finely preserved specimens of the larger sand launce or sand eel *(Ammodytes tobianus)* about eight inches long, in their beautiful blue and silver livery. These are the first of this species we have met with here; but the population do not know how to capture them, nor are our sands quite extensive enough to harbour more than a few small shoals; although Balure and Ardmucknish Bays may be considered to offer plenty of favourable ground at low water. In our own Loch Creran we have not seen this large species, but so late as yesterday we observed quite a shoal dip and pass under our boat near the Sound of Eriska. Yesterday was indeed one of the finest days of the year, and the water for a time was calm and clear, so that we could hang over the gunwale of the boat and watch the young lythe and saithe, the various species of gobies, and an occasional wrass or rock perch circle around the more luxuriant seaware, and play with the scraps of cheese and biscuits we dropped enticingly into the gaping mouth of the dredge hanging below. There is a magnificent specimen of the 15-spined stickleback *(Gasterosteus)*, the largest we have ever met with, but we sweep the dredge through its thickly-matted seaweed lair in vain. We have had some interesting experience while dredging these days, as we drew up from deep water a Gunnel fish or Butter fish *(Gunnellus)*, which is plentiful under stones at half tide and low water. This was very near the same place that we once obtained a similar fish from the mouth of a guillemot, and is additional evidence to prove that these birds really dive down 10 fathoms in search of prey. A 15-spined stickleback likewise came up from 10 or 12 fathoms, but did not long survive its transfer to the tub. We have always found these to be most sensitive, nervous fishes, and unable, either from fear or a demand for excessive aeration, to stand carrying about. A peculiarity of this fish that we do not recollect noting in any other is the facility with which it can swim straight back. You will constantly see them advancing inquiringly, and then, as if alarmed or dissatisfied, shoot straight back. This is performed mainly by a peculiar circular movement of the pectorals, always a marked peculiarity of this fish, which "handles" them with seeming dexterity. The nervous-like jerk with which they dart back or shoot forward, their intelligent skill as nestbuilders, and their watchful care of their young, as well as the large eyes and head, all point to this as a fish whose intelligence is worthy of more attention, and one well qualified to be experimented upon in respect of natural capacity, capability of education, and comparative constitution of the principal nervous ganglia as against terrestrial and aerial creatures. Still another fishy inhabitant of our tub appears in the amusing shape of a small lump-sucker (*Cyclopterus lumpus*), the first of the kind we have met with us, and a very small specimen he is—exactly one inch in length, but with all the unmistakable peculiarities of the parents, even to the general rich blue tint, the eyes being quite remarkably bright.

Most of those who have visited the sea-shore are well acquainted with the pretty little cowrie, perhaps the most favourite shell with children. The animal contained in it is most active; with a mantle that comes out and covers the whole shell, or rather, might we not more justly say, a shell into which it draws its otherwise encircling body! This little mollusc has a congener, with a shell as smooth as glass, and in fact of quite a vitreous appearance, and it also, when scrambling about, has its shell inclosed within its mantle. Two of these clear little shells, *(Marginella laevis)*, have recently fallen into our hands, and one is now actively scrambling out of the water in the basin and up the sides. Let us examine it, and we will be surprised to find that the *mantle* is all barred exactly as the *shell* is in the cowrie, and under the lens, even the clear glassy surface has wave-like indications, as if our delicate little friend were making an effort to reach the simpler, stronger, more durable formation of *Cypraea*. This may well have been the intermediate development of the cowrie, whose shell, by being ribbed or corrugated externally, is thereby indefinitely strengthened, and fitted to cope with the very varied positions in which this widely-spread shell is found.

We have not hitherto met with such fine specimens of the web-footed starfish, *(Palmipes)*, as in our loch here. We recently procured a brilliantly tinted specimen, $4\frac{3}{4}$ inches in diameter; the upper surface not only nicely marked with pink, but a beautiful pink border extending for a quarter of an inch along the edge of the lower side! We so seldom find colour on the under side of flat mud frequenters, that this exception appears to us worthy of attention.

A tale of starfish! a long tail too, for they are spread along the whole way we have been traversing to-day, of extraordinary dimensions and in equally remarkable numbers. At low tide, occasionally on shore, among the seaware, but more commonly a yard or two out, they were so remarkably comfortable and well grown, as well as numerous, that our curiosity was aroused, and we wondered where and how they obtained the required nourishment to sustain their important-looking corporations. Here is one doubled up like a sea-urchin, brilliant of hue, and when spread out quite 16 inches in diameter; where, and oh where, can you obtain a prey? The hoe we carry is thrust out and the mass dragged shorewards, when the rascal disgorges two large dogwhilks he has been in the process of devouring. We feel a comfortable glow of satisfaction to think that this enemy of our oyster-beds is also the enemy of our other enemy, this carnivorous borer. Here, quite close alongside, is another, only inferior in size, and we drag him ashore likewise, to find that the fellow has actually had the courage and audacity to suck the contents out of a large horse mussel *(modiola)* the strong muscle alone remaining undevoured. We proceed along but a short way when we meet with still another in the curled up condition in which they gorge themselves, and as we drag it shorewards the shell of a *tapes pulastra* drops from the relaxing grasp of the ogre. Slowly the extended stomach returns to its place, and the monster settles back to an uncomfortable after-dinner siesta on a large exposed boulder; for the star-fish wraps its turned out stomach around the prey it has secured, in place of attempting to devour the limey covering in which most of its game is protected. Once the mouth of the shell is enclosed in the stomach of the star-fish, the creature soon sickens, the hinge spring relaxes its hold, and the shell opening permits the star-fish to suck out the gelatinous contents, and cast free the calcarious skeleton. No wonder the star-fish are many and corpulent on this stretch of sea-weed covered shore, for the shell-fish are numerous and fat, the tide ever bringing them a plentiful supply of nourishment. As we toss monster after monster shoreward we are apt to look contemptuously at any under a foot as poor wretched creatures, until at length we are constrained to examine a moderate seven-inch fellow, who has the temerity to endeavour to aggrandise himself with only four rays to aid him, in place of the orthodox five. It is bad enough to differ from your fellows among mankind, but to attempt idiosyncrasies among animals is certain annihilation, if you come within cognisance of the higher animal. So we take possession of the novelty only to find it is a cripple from its birth, not a proper abnormality, for there is the embryonic indication of a fifth limb one-eighth inch long, that from some unexplained reason has been arrested in development, leaving the other four to carry on the sub-division of the disc among them.

Not with starfish alone have we met on our shoreward ramble, however, for this is the district in which the famous white scallop dwells, and the tide is low enough to have stranded quite a number of small ones; and if you use your eyes well you will note a number of mature size among them. These latter have no connection in colour with the little white beauties, perhaps you conclude, as you observe the deep green colour; indeed, almost black, it is so deep. A closer examination will satisfy you that the number of ribs, the general contour, and the whole character of the dark shell is similar to the white, and the fact that no small dark shells are found will enable you to divine the reason of the difference. The white pectens are almost invariably discovered affixed by a byssus to the tangle fronds, which are rich in tone and smooth and bright in surface, so as to reflect the light, and altogether suited to promote the purity and brilliance of the white covering. The young retain their whiteness for a time anywhere; but after a long sojourn on the fronds of the black seaware, such as *fucus serratus*, dark in hue and dull in surface, they gradually assume richer tones and lose their pristine purity. Further out, among the tangles all will be found white !

Stumbling along over the stones and seaware we met a fresh-looking crab, that is, nevertheless, quite empty as to shell. It has been thoroughly cleaned out by some skilful operators; and, concluding that some small crustaceans have done the work, from the neat manner in which the membranes of the joints have been penetrated, we take possession of the specimen and carry it along with us. During the evening we resolve to complete the preparation by soaking in fresh water, so as to remove the corrosive salts, but no sooner had we placed it in the tub than a great commotion ensued, and soon from joint after joint there issued quite a multitude of small crustacea—white, grey, and pink—whose energies had been up till then absorbed in cleaning the specimen, until they were forced to enter a protest against the fresh-water invasion. Just as we anticipated, the sea ants whose labours we so rudely interrupted were the small sand-hoppers, of several species, so active among the stranded seaweed, so we will know of a certainty again to apply to them for well-picked marine skeletons. When we consider the trouble involved in properly preparing a specimen of the smaller crustaceans, the value of these still minuter species in cleaning out the limbs is apparent.

Wagtails are more or less constant residents with us the year through, but we rarely see more than one pair at a time. Last week, however, as we stood gazing forth of our doorway leading into our sanctum, we observed a pair of grey wagtails alight near our back door and show a disposition to quarrel over the treasure trove still left by the fowls. They were in the midst of a mild altercation when another arrived, and ere long we actually counted *seven* together at a time. They were not long of quarrelling savagely over the easily gathered store, and we soon lost sight of them as they tumbled pugilistically over the roof.

OCTOBER, 1882.

"I don't like the rooks congregating on the shore like that," says the many-wintered observer, whose eyes have scanned the drift of the cloud over the deer in the corrie more than half a century ago. We, too, object to the movements of the sable meteorologists, but seek to know the reasons of our friend for the faith that is in him. "They should take to the hill, but it is too wet, and there is too much moisture in the air." It was clear from their movements throughout the day, never getting higher than the scrubby knoll, where they hung about and loafed ignominiously, that they were in no humour for an important flight. Was the atmosphere too heavy for them, were they depressed in spirit despite the high barometer, or were they waiting until the enormous rainfall of these latter days and nights should drain somewhat, and permit the half-drowned worms to throw their earths once more on the terraced slopes of the hills?

The day is really strangely mild, close, and oppressive,

notwithstanding the barometer, and as we climb the hills towards the distant wooded gullies our companion protests against the exertion and the heat! Yes! positive heat in October. And there is a butterfly busily employed about mid-day on the hillside, and the blackberries only blackening in places; while what are ripe are either tasteless from the continuous soaking or else from the recent touch of frost. All the same, it is a summer day, and even the grasshoppers are chirruping merrily, yet with a subdued mirth, as if their souls were oppressed with the thought that they had no whisky to counteract the continual soak. We have heard them but seldom this season, and the exceptional rainfall must have most seriously discomposed them. Not one have we seen leap, so suppose that they are merely airing their damp bed-clothes at the mouths of their holes, for we watch for them in vain to-day. The sun has at length come forth bravely, and that rocky, mossy corner of the broken hill, with the patch of well-grown timber, looks quite gay. Stop a bit, and glance along the surface, and you will be surprised to find the sun glinting on bright streaks of silver here and there amid the moss. What a time they have been having! a carnival of the mollusca! and why should they not have their turn? The bank is strewn with fungi of all shades, from the deepest, deadliest crimson, to black, yellow, and white; and over and about every one of them, of whatever hue, the snails have been crawling and feasting, leaving a slimy, silvery film to tell the story of their morning's labours. They seem to have no preference, but have attacked all alike, and that bank alone is proof positive that no reliance can be placed upon the snail tribe as prior tasters of the banquet prepared for humanity.

We have got up among the birches, and the dancing streams with their courses filled to overflowing, the steep banks heavily clothed with lichens, the ferns decked in yellow and gold, and the bracken lying in rusty masses. Here a solitary *digitalis* lurks in a quiet corner, a few gowans meet us on the green slope above; and no sooner do we emerge from the darkness of the gorge than the eye sweeps outward over placid lochs and isles of beauty, with the dreamy clouds drifting across the sun, and turning the whole wondrous scene into a giant kaleidoscope, as the play of light and shade alters the diversified landscape, and plays bo-peep with a thousand nooks and crannies, slopes and gullies, from Morven to the peaks of Ballachulish. The ground is soppy, indeed, or we would willingly have reclined under the rosy-leaved birches in the blinking sun, and seen whether the "beauty born of the murmuring sounds" about us would "pass into our face," even for the passing hour. But visions of rheumatism dispel any such illusion, and the "old fool" of our more youthful companion, anxious about temporal requirements, warns us that, like "every dog," we have had our day; and the "murmuring sounds" of those waiting for dinner are not conducive to human beauty or felicity.

Wednesday night was exceptionally dark, and we chose it, perversely, in which to traverse the wood for a couple of miles or more. As we stumble along, starting the fallow deer and the roebuck, to send them plunging madly through the night, and occasionally startled ourselves by the shriek of a belated heron on its way home over the tree tops, we were again interested in noting a very brilliant light in the moss under the trees, so bright that we were led by it about 50 yards to where it shone, and then picked up what proved to be a piece of fir bark, the inside lining of which displayed the phosphorescent gleam in question. It was damp, which may have added to the brilliance of the effect; but this is only another example of what we observed previously in the case of a fresh cut piece of fir wood. This time it was the inner lining of the bark that shone as brilliantly as a fresh herring, or even as a basket of herring. What is the cause of this peculiar effect, which is by no means evanescent, for we carried it some miles, showing brilliantly like a small lantern all the way?

"Did you observe the gossamer threads the other morning?" asks our artist friend, whose eye had caught the beauty and delicacy of the myriad lines as they floated in the morning air. We had not been so early afoot on the moors, but in the forenoon we had found the unfrequented paths crossed and intercrossed to an exceptional extent with these airy creations, whose whereabouts were only observable by the sunlight glancing from the fairy fabrics. There tenacity is most remarkable, and as the wind puffs them with a graceful curve from the heath to the bramble, or from the grass stem to the bog myrtle, the little spinner hangs on to the end and is borne along by the breeze. Here is one hanging from the roof of a shed to the end of a very delicate line, with no perceptible line beneath it. We breathe heavily upon it from a little distance, and the creature instantaneously drops to the ground. Our first conclusion is that the spider loosened its hold and dropped clean away; but very soon it reappears, coming up the thread "hand over hand." Just where it loosened its hold a white little puff is observable on the line, and as it once more approaches this we again breathe upon the thread and spider. The proceeding is repeated, the spider dropping like a flash, and the spot where it left being again represented by a little white puff. The creature evidently is quite aware of the effect of wind to send its web floating through the air, but being resolved on this occasion to remain where it was, it at once went down to the ground and held the line taut. The light was such that we saw every strain upon the line as the spider ascended, for these little puffs bobbed up and down as if the line were india-rubber, exemplifying the very elastic character of the thread. We have generally found these webs most numerous on those mornings when the air was calm and the atmosphere somewhat heavy—just such weather as precedes rain and wind. The reason for this may be that gnats and flies are all low among the grass and amid the vegetation at such times, and also because the light "airs" that are then abroad float the threads gently, while stronger or more severe whiffs of wind would blow them to fragments.

We find a tangle with the bottom cupped away, and in the very centre of the depression a specimen of the peculiar variety of Helcion called *lævis*. This is the first we have obtained, and we had been informed it was mainly an East Coast variety, although Jeffrey says it is composed of the older individuals who had descended the tangle and given themselves up to a life of laziness and gormandising. Clearly, it was a lazy vagabond, and— ho! of course it is, and here is the result, for has it not proved an asylum for a parasite who has at least shared its "mantle," if it has not sucked its juices? A little crustacean of the sandhopper class comes reluctantly forth, and has apparently also degenerated terribly through a life of luxurious ease.

Why does that interesting shell, covered with wrinkled protuberances *(Murex erinaceus)*, only appear in dead specimens? One of these we have obtained in Loch Linnhe, and Northern specimens are said to be invariably dead. We may conclude that they are alive somewhere about, and are only difficult to obtain from their rocky habitats, like some other mollusca; we subsequently obtained various live specimens under stones at low water.

In front of the newly-extended pier at Port Appin the black ware has already grown several feet long, although but a few months have the piles been down.

We were rowing down towards Eriska when we observed two very large herons coming hurriedly along, evidently on very bad terms with each other. In a minute or two they became engaged in a fratricidal struggle, and, interlocking, came down all of a heap with a splash into the water, as no doubt "the nations' airy navies" of the future will do, when they presume to grapple "in the central blue." "I saw two herons off Eriska diving for fish into the sea the other day," remarks our observant companion, and we all agree that the circumstance was most remarkable; for these waders are seldom seen to emulate the divers or swimmers, although they can swim well when they fall wounded into the water.

Having landed at low water on a small islet to hunt the finely grown and coloured specimens of *Zisiphiuus* shell, and the many specimens of the striped variety of *Littorina*, we have again returned to the boat, and, while sitting waiting for our companions to enter, glance carelessly into the waving tangle fronds now gradually being lifted higher and higher by the rising tide. On the top of a rich frond a little creature is nestling, and we call attention to his successful imitation of the colour of the sea ware, supposing the visitor to be a specimen of the two-spotted sucker fish, so common about our shores. But their eyes have not caught the little fellow, and we slip our hand-net under it and bring it on board, when to our surprise it proves to be a female of the Montague Sucker Fish *(Liparis Montagui)*. This fish has the dorsal and anal fins and tail prettily marked with dark spots, in lines, in the female; while the sucker on the breast is much smaller than and of a different, character from, those of our other little sucker fishes. It proves extremely active and restless in captivity. Still, when it might have escaped into the waters of Loch Linnhe, it trusted to its resemblance to the marine vegetation around it, and made no effort to elude capture. Although we have not met with an example hitherto— and it is said to be very rare in Scotland—we yet may only be unaware of its presence through want of attention to the minuter frequenters of our coasts. We afterwards found them not uncommon at certain seasons.

If "circumstances alter cases," similar circumstances produce remarkably similar results in widely different "elements." We all know how the *Sygnathus* or Pipe-fish has pouches like a Kangaroo for the reception of its young, and we find here, amid these fronds from the deeper waters, the homes of annelids, exactly similar in character to those of many terrestrial caterpillars. Here they are with nests made of the seaweed fronds curled round, and bound, or agglutinated together with tough gelatinous threads. They might be caterpillars on the leaves of a tree, only they are beautifully organised marine worms from 10 or 12 fathoms. Veritable silk worms in their way, for their threads are very tenacious, but, like most of such marine productions, so soon as they dry they become brittle, having little of a fibrous nature. But for this we might some day have met with a marine annelid to enable us to compete with the dexterous spinners of the south and east. What a delightful industry it would be to cover our shores with seaweed gardens, full of busy multitudes of thread manufacturers, like a long-drawn-out Paisley!

Who first invented india-rubber? What a remarkable idea it was, and how clever we were to find out its use! Indeed; you lay the flattering unction to your soul that you belong to the terrestrial race of superior intelligence because you draw it from a plant and employ it, when there before our eyes in that bucket are scores of manufacturers, who know its value and use it continually. No paltry rubber to rot and decay for a little damp, but capable of preserving all its snap and spring under the trying ordeal of a continuous marine immersion. You are incredulous; but lift that *Pecten* and look at the hinge. Ho! you try to drop it, as you have carelessly and stupidly lifted it by placing your finger inside the half-open valves, and they have closed with a snap that enables you now to raise it with one finger. Dip the whole into this cup of boiling water, and the wondrous diamond eyes are extinguished for ever, and gradually the strong muscle that held the valves close relaxes, and you have but to wait a minute or two more and the poor animal, now completely apart from the shells, comes out in a contracted little blob of matter. You lift the empty valves, now wide apart, and mechanically press them together; when, the moment your pressure is removed, they spring apart, for the hinge that binds the valves together is a perfectly composed and exceedingly strong elastic spring of black india-rubber, or at least something that serves the same purpose and has the same appearance. It is arranged for the water, however, like the worms' thread; and, dried, becomes as brittle as the elastic spiral anchors of a dog-fish egg. You affix your india-rubber spring to keep your door shut, the *Pecten* has it placed to keep the valves open, the natural position, and the one assumed the moment the strong muscle, that closes the valves against an enemy, is relaxed.

Here is the seaweed growing luxuriantly about some stones in the midst of the muddy expanse, well out on the foreshores; so we stoop to sweep it away and expose the scuttling dwellers under its shade. As we do so, our face comes in contact with—yes, with!—we rise and draw carefully from our beard the unwonted object, and scarce believe our eyes when we find it to be the gossamer web of a spider! "Blown out to sea," we mutter, "but no doubt the little spinner secured a safe retreat long ere the fated thread was carried hitherwards by the breath of the frosty morn." We turn once again to the eel, seeking to escape by burrowing dexterously and rapidly under the nearest stone—where has it gone? A moment more, and the least movement in the world is perceptible at the other corner of the imbedded stone from that on which it entered! An eel must breathe, and just as a seal must come to the surface for air, an eel must have its snout out of the mud or else it would be choked, so the poor eely has betrayed itself, notwithstanding its cunning. Cunning indeed, for it chose a corner under the shadow of the stone, and only brought its nostrils to the edge of the surface, the gentle displacement of the sand alone betraying it. As we scan the environs of the eel's hiding-place carefully, we catch sight of a little fellow in a tremendous hurry. A novel crustacean? we would once have observed, but, as burned children dread the fire, our experience with the dredged spider has rendered us cautious. Clearly another spider, we will pass it by! Just then we recollected of the negro who passed a guinea contemptuously because he had lost some shillings on a light one he found before; and, stooping, we captured the wanderer with difficulty. Here is actually the little gossamer spider itself to which the web belonged that we have just destroyed! It was racing full speed on a bee line for the shore, swimming the pools of water even more rapidly than it traversed the intervening muddy hillocks thrown up by the lug worms. We place it upon our hand, and blow it sharply through the air for some yards into the centre of a pool of water, when it at once starts without being the least disconcerted, and hurries shorewards once more. Whether it ever arrived at the goal, which was several hundred yards off, or how it behaved if overtaken by the tide, we could not wait to see.

On a solitary hunt a few yards off the shore at low water we had an excellent opportunity of examining the inhabitants of what is ordinarily several fathoms under medium tide, and while thus wandering along in the bright sun and the clear water of a crisp frosty day, we came unexpectedly upon a colony of scallops, *pecten opercularis*. We had never seen them "on their native heath" before, and looked down upon them with especial interest. The ground they affect is a mixture of stones and mud, in the latter of which they lie with open mouth upwards. Although active enough when stirred, they seemed very lethargic, and required to be roused with the long pole ere they commenced their droll peregrinations; while many allowed themselves to be dragged into the boat with the long graip without an effort at escape. This will account for their becoming a prey to star-fish, which otherwise could scarcely pretend to follow them through the water. We have so frequently examined them in buckets of water, and seen their mode of progression, that we never had a doubt but what we knew all about it. They have so frequently squirted the water in our faces from the bucket, that they might thereby shunt themselves *backward*, that we had concluded this was their customary mode of motion, and, like the historic crab, they "advanced backwards." Yet here in their native element, with plenty of searoom, at a depth of 2½ fathoms, their proceedings were quite the reverse. In fact, they shot themselves *forward*, evidently by gulping the water and expelling it through the two orifices, one at each side of the hinge! This was quite a new revelation to us, and accounted to an extent for the presence of these openings, which were otherwise inexplicable.

NOVEMBER, 1882.

What peculiar fancy could have taken possession of those birds, we wonder, as we pass down the avenue under the finely-grown trees with any number of good roosting places around. Trees to right of them, trees to left of them, palings and outhouses behind them, and yet there are two good fat turkeys, actually squatting for the night on the wire fencing. As we approach in the dusk we think to set them swaying, like a clumsy boy walking on a paling, but they sit with perfect steadiness and composure, only flying off a little way after we have repeatedly tried to startle them. We cannot account for such a position being chosen, as these birds require plenty of footing, and even hens do not like small foot spars, which cause their feet to become contorted.

Wading at lowest tide among beds of *Zostera marina*, amid bouldery and ware-grown surroundings, we had a particularly good opportunity for observing a class of life we have not hitherto noted much "at home." As we advanced, a little fish apparently would skim or skip along the surface of the water with great dexterity, and we had some difficulty in procuring a specimen. It then proved to be a species of palæmon, a crustacean with a prawn-like bend in its back, and these were plentiful and most active. While amusing ourselves stirring them up and watching their active movements, we suddenly came upon a gleam of purple and silver, and looking up at us through the water were a pair of brilliant eyes at the end of footstalks, which appertained to an Æsop prawn, that large, brilliantly-marked species, with long barred antennæ, whose humped back and intelligent appearance have procured for them the name of the old fabulist. They not unfrequently come up in the dredge, but here were a few "at home," and the rapidity and dexterity with which they escaped through the Zostera fronds was most amusing. It was quite clear that these same sea-wrack beds were favourite haunts of crustacea, so, going seaward with a large hand-net, we swept it rapidly towards the shore through the grass. A few palæmons and many mysis, and nothing more. Nothing more!

say all the sharp-eyed ones around; and yet there is a number of bits broken off the sea-grass. We are about to empty it, when these startle us by leaping hither and thither as we sink the net in the water, and soon it dawns upon us that we have about a score of exquisite green crustacea, exactly the tint of the Zostera itself. The wonderful transparency of the delicate tint, and the extreme activity of the creature in the water, wholly hid it from our eyes; and, although we have been wading through long stretches of grass, with here and there a tail-spot goby flashing off before us, and myriads of little mysidæ skipping around, 'we had not really caught sight of a single one ot these living chips of *Zostera marina.*

" Weather " enough and to spare, indeed, we have had of late, and the provoking part of it all is that the season is exceptionally mild, and no excuse for complaining of ordinary severity of weather. We have been repeatedly assured that the season is not severe, but with a gale blowing two days out of three, and rain in such floods as can scarcely be credited in a temperate clime, what more " severe " weather could be forthcoming? On the 9th we sought to traverse Glen Salloch, and view the land through as cheerful spectacles as we could muster, for the hillsides had still a subdued beauty on the now gently intermingling tints of the sobering deciduous leaves, great portion of which yet hung upon the trees, even under the shadow of Ben Breac, down whose misty shoulders the snow was creeping for the first time this season. If the tints in the woods were so subdued, those around the dull-hued loch were still more so— Appin and Eriska, drenched and sulky, bounding a commonly boundless view, and Loch Creran resembling nothing so much as those mirror ponds our grandmothers loved to insert in the model landscapes that delighted the wondering eyes of our youth. Near at hand the masses of rushes are black on the soaking reaches of the shoulders of the hills, and the new black heads and stems of gay "Highlanders' bonnets" stand starkly out against the grey and yellow ochre, picked out with silver, of the rain-wearied meadow hay. Nearer still the cup-mosses and hepaticæ are exceptionally green, and scarce a post by path or stream but carries a gracefully curving arrangement of delicate edged fungi, that declare as boldly as any meteorological register that the season has been most unquestionably "moist," to say the very least of it. Along the hillsides the most distinguished figures are the holly trees, richly green, and having apparently repaired the breach made in their costumes in the early spring, when so many lost their leaves. All evergreens, indeed, are unusually fresh; and, with no northern visitors to speak of among the bays of Loch Creran or Etive, we fear the winter will be again "open," which means stormy and wet.

"Hope springs eternal in the human breast," and although we have again and again failed to enjoy a quiet time with the dredge on Loch Etive, we last week made a further attempt in the midst of the usual wind and rain, which we have come to consider especially Loch Etive weather. We cannot return empty-handed again, and say that the Demon from Cruachan Ben presides over the waters, and guards them from prying eyes; else we would much rather sit in the charming home amid the pines, far above and yet alongside the waters, with art striving to surpass in perfection the natural beauty around, and ——

Steam is up! the little vessel at our service, and we

are soon in the rush of Etive's tide, with mud coming in up to our elbows, and fresh water above and salt water below sorely trying our enthusiasm. Suddenly we dive into the argilaceous mass, and no longer fear the "bit shower," for has not a *Pecten Septemradiatus* come up, one of those strong-ribbed, handsome scallops, not one of which has hitherto met us in the surrounding waters of Benderloch? The tentacles are shorter and the ocelli smaller than in our other pectens, but it is a handsome, finely marked, and finely coloured shell, and the only important British species we had hitherto looked upon as absent from our waters.

Now we feel the strong beat, beat, as the iron travels over rough ground, and when the contents are once more emptied we are again rewarded with notable shells. Those who seek the wonders of the deep are ever anxious to obtain the strong-shelled limpet, with a rich nacreous lining and a deep silt in the margin, known as *Emarginula crassa*. This beautiful and interesting mollusc frequents rocky or rough ground, on which it is difficult to work any instrument that would bring up the inhabitants, without great risk of said instrument of whatever kind being broken or lost. So a creature that may be common enough on natural ground is rarely captured, and consequently becomes the more eagerly sought after. Living on the same ground and coming up along with him, we find several fine specimens of that Cornucopia-shaped shell the "Hungarian's Cap," which reaches such size and beauty on the South Coast of England; while numerous specimens of *Astarte*, that richly toned, finely marked, northern shell, come up to reconcile us to our own fauna.

The sea bottom after all is just like our woods and

moors, on which special classes of animals have a wide range, while others are wholly local and strangely limited in habitat. A small species of this same *Astarte*, *A. compressa*, with numerous very graceful lines upon it, is so comparatively rare that we have only procured two specimens in our extensive dredging in our own loch. Suddenly we come upon their haunt, and a dozen or two are procured in Loch Etive in a single haul!

As we gather our treasures in the evening in our snug retreat on the hill, amid sympathetic and all-enduring onlookers, we find the fragments of a *pennatula*, or sea pea, with its myriad polyps still capable of expansion, although the stem has been broken into fragments. Into the porcelain dish that the sun artist has graciously loaned we toss a few sea slugs or sea cucumbers, whose uncouth, snail-like form is sufficiently forbidding. When morning dawns, what a contrast they form to their evening appearance! The one has thrown out a splendid set of crimson suckers, beautiful in colour, arrangement, and form; the other large fellow has spread his delicate, almost transparent, tentacles—tastefully divided at the extremities—far across the dish in search of food; while the little hermit crab that had chosen the summit of the sluggish creature as a point of vantage the evening before, had evidently thought better of it, and was racing with incessant and by no means intelligent activity around the dish again and again. These *Holothuroids* are very interesting marine forms, and will repay any one who can overcome his repugnance to their slug-like appearance, which is soon lost sight of in the beauty of their expanded crowns.

About 6.15 on Sunday the 12th we witnessed a really remarkable display of aurora borealis. Not only were the streamers of the most brilliant character, but the auroral bow was quite complete, and bounded the lights that streamed upwards from the north. This was the first really satisfactory auroral bow we remember to have seen in this latitude, and although the light was of the pure silvery character peculiar to our "Northern Lights," without any of the colour we see figured in Arctic displays, the general effect was similar. As we rose betimes on Monday morning to find the tail of the comet streaming in a brilliant curve over the southern sky, it distracted our attention from the north and monopolised our eyes for a time. It was now almost exactly twelve hours since we had gazed on the Aurora, and when we again turned from the comet to the opposite point of the compass, what was our delight to find the streamers now reaching almost to the zenith, and where the lights crossed the arc of the Aurora, the fine delicate blues and reds were most distinctly visible. Only the blue and red of the lunar rainbow, however, was anywhere displayed, and we could not satisfy ourselves that there was any regularity or certainty in their distribution. The most notable fact in these displays was that the auroral arc was pure in colour when uncrossed by the lights streaming from the horizon; but when these streamed through the arc the result of the cross lights was the production of the red and blue bands we have referred to. As may be imagined, it is not often that our sober skies are at one and the same time lighted up at opposite quarters by such a brilliant pair of strugglers for popular admiration, and the lines of Blanco White appeared exceptionally applicable to the night in question :—

> "Who could have thought such glory lay concealed
> Beneath thy beams, oh sun !"

And yet what numbers of magnificent night landscapes there must be, "while you and I and all of us" fall down, and wretched gaslight triumphs over us !

So thought we on the previous evening, as our boat rippled through the darkening water under the daintily copse-clad rocks, near Cregan Ferry, and we watched the woods of Barcaldine in the growing evening haze. "There are the three smokes all close together !" some one remarks; and sure enough they are close enough from here, and only a mile or two apart in reality. What are the three smokes, you ask ! and how can they be distinguished? Just look up there over all those woods to the hillside above, and the clear grey smoke of the wood fires streams dreamily over towards Glen Salloch. Quite a poetical, hazy smoke, just such a misty, ghostly enveloping of the habitation as might have gathered over the Bower of Deirdre, by Etive shore. There, again, in the centre of the woods, rises the harsh black smoke of our higher civilization, gathered at the cost of our lower civilization, that so painfully drags out the bowels of the earth to toast the benumbed souls of a thankless generation. It drifts across the pine tops to the shoulders of Ben Breac like an underbred ghost that thought it unnecessary to wash itself or purge its neglected raiment. Down near the shore, again, with a humble deferential air about it, hangs the skin of the Benderloch soil, unwilling to rise too far above it. The smoke of the dissipated turf has a homely blueish-brown hue of comfort, and one feels as if it alone could be reasonably called "reek," and allowed to cover the sanitary sins of the people with a disinfectant mantle of kindly security.

But here we are at Cregan, and we may land in the gloaming at the little bay, and stroll up by the Ferry House. The mountains are now as if close beside us. Those of Glencoe are virgin snow-capped, with etherial blue sides shading into delicate pink above in the afterglow. Nearer, the white tops glide downwards into deep black, thence into rusty yellow or russet brown. The shadow of the shapely Craig beside us is shivering in the loch, and every birch stands out clearly on its well-defined ridge. But how describe the innumerable shades and indefinable shading of the yellows and browns upon its sides, with little gullies of deeper tints that slip from the gold-tipped summit to the solemn-visaged base? We turn aside hopeless of speech, and only receptive of beauty, and gaze towards the sun, now far beneath the horizon. A single cormorant sits like a sentinel on the little rocky islet whose top is just above the waves; and the gleam of brilliant yellow above the rich blue-grey banks of cloud throws the little peninsula, with its birchen knolls, into delicate relief against the Appin background.

A breeze has stolen down the hillside, and is curdling the waters seaward; with a sharp bite in it too from the snows of Glencoe, that bids us hie away home. The night was so bright that we lost sight of the heavens in the new lights thrown by them upon our little bit of earth. There is the smoke curling from Barcaldine Gardens, where they recently trapped a buck in a novel manner. These animals frequent the garden environs in numbers in the winter, and one had made frequent invasions of the bulb house, where it had regaled itself with the choicest flower bulbs, being carefully gathered and stored for the winter. To prevent the door being open so as to invite entrance, a spring had been fastened upon it lately, and next morning a buck was captured; having pushed its way in to find an invisible enemy close the door behind it! It had created quite a shindy in its endeavours to get out, and had even sought to escape through the window! A buck in a bulb-house, with the door shut, must be a close approximation to a bull in a china shop.

There is the light of the cottage blinking over the port-bow, so we slip over the seaware bordering our little stream, and soon beach our craft before our door, satisfied that a cruise by moonlight is not at all a bad substitute for a day excursion, and that beauties unimagined crowd upon the sight, and filter into the soul, under the light of a frosty sky.

DECEMBER, 1882.

We had traversed the neighbouring stream a week ago without seeing a single finny inhabitant, and again yesterday we met our shrewdly-observing friend, and asked him where the trout went to from our streams in the winter? To the sea! was the reply; and still unconvinced we followed his stream from the seaweed verge, poking under every stone, progging every bank where, in the "merry, merry sunshine," the spotties would flash and go in twos and threes. Not a fin shows from bank or boulder, from rippling shallow or quiet pool, and our search to-day corroborates our previous hunt in the other stream, where equally the absence of fish was remarkable in lower and upper courses. Are the fish in these uncertain, short-coursed mountain streams, with a sea exit, afraid of being frozen up towards the upper course of the stream in the winter, and, having no important pools or ponds to congregate in for security, do they really seek the warm, deep water of the contiguous sea for the winter months! If this is so, it greatly complicates our ideas of the ways of *Salmo fario*, and may account for certain appearances among local shoals of sea trout that greatly exercise us, and demand further elucidation.

Do squirrels throw down their nests? we are asked, as we turn from the stream towards the road, and pass under the trees lately tenanted by unmistakable nests of the squirrel, built under the watchful eye of our friend. There on the sward lies the complete nest of a squirrel, not a summer nursery, it appears to us, but a lately re-lined winter snuggery. It had been tumbled holus-bolus out of the tree, whence it could not have been blown, and where no boy about, had there been any, would have disturbed it. Only built originally this summer, it could not have become intolerable through the increase of parasites, and the lining was fresh! Are any others down! is the natural query, and we examine the tree but a few yards away, where another nest is still standing. Is it? look again; it is really almost out, having been clearly dragged from its position in the fork of the fir. Other two nests further along, but apparently not interfering with the hunting grounds of each other, or stepping beyond the unwritten forest code of Mr. Squirrel, remain as they were. The natural conclusion is that there has been a little jealousy, or a great deal of ill-feeling; and that, remembering the shrewd remark of the Indian to be "near to the far, and far to the near," they of the two closely contiguous nests have been a little too "distant" to one another, and ended by having a battle-royal among the tree-tops; endeavouring to topple each other's domiciles out of their secure positions, and forcing the shivering wretches these last nights to wish they had listened to Watts's hymns. How else to account for the destruction of two nests so close together, and safe from gales?

How differently did the two cows underneath behave last year, and what a lesson might you not have taken from your bucolic neighbours, you sillikins! Did not "Maggie" make her appearance at the gate at an unreasonable hour, in an excited condition, butting at the gate and bellowing plaintively, while refusing to be driven away until aid was brought to her companion in the ditch hard by, into which it had tumbled helplessly. And did not the wise Maggie restrain her annoyance at the stupidity of her comrade, and disgust at the snubbing her first efforts met with, until her sympathy was no longer required; when she gave her liberated comrade a proper butting, to relieve her mind and tail-off her exhausted sympathies! A most sympathetic, wise, and considerate animal Maggie, when she might have so quietly punished the other for all the stolen mouthfuls, and had a quiet half-hour by herself among the titbits. One almost fancies that such an incident could only occur among well-fed animals, where there was plenty of everything, and that it is a homologous growth to the amazing sympathy for everyone suffering, be they knave or fool, evinced by the well-fed comfortable classes in England to-day.

We have been getting up our Christmas pantomimes in the neighbourhood, and the private view we obtained on the 14th was quite delightful, with promise of greater things to come. Special invitation to the members of the press on condition that the public should know nothing whatever of what is going on, of course! So we rambled up the little stream, and past the ruined dwellings, and under the cluster of beeches hiding the ivy-clad cliff and moss-covered rocks. That fallen tree makes a capital bridge across the now gullying course of the stream, but it is covered with a slight coating of rime, and we decline to trust ourselves along it to-day. Here in force the stream jumps over a few feet, before which an apron of ice is spread, and we only hear the murmur of the water as it trundles along underneath the new white dimity. We clamber up the little fall, and find the banks of the stream deepening into moss-covered walls, with rocky projections. Slow music! gently ushering us into the front seats close to the maundering orchestra. Silver icicles are hanging in gleaming masses from the rocks all around, and the lilting stream now and again popping its head out of its covering like a clown through a trap-door, the crimping mosses and clustering ivy scrambling along the little slopes over the silvered faces of the rocks, all deck the approach to the stage. The shivering lady birches in the scantiest of costumes occupy every point of vantage, and right in front of us we find our progress barred with the splendid drop scene! never more to be painted by Sam Bough, but still a wondrous scene.

The beautiful fall has been completely covered with a heavy coating of ice, and at its foot a mass of frozen foam, several feet high, hides the dark pool where the "leading lady" now sings gaily as the waters dance down from the ledge above. What has the dexterous draughtsman meant to represent? A portly alderman with a resplendent white waistcoat and napkin devouring a large ice-cream! Alas! what a degrading comparison, when this might be the gate into the Nevada silver land or the diamond mines of Golconda. A fringe of brown leaves on the young oaks up among "the gods," and scanty discoloured napkins here and there waving hurrahs for the opening scene from the side galleries occupied by the copsewood, represents the audience.

Where is the genius of the still-life picture? is there really nothing else animate around to move the scenery?

A pair of mild eyes look down upon us from the slope above, and a lamb browsing on the scanty herbage must be the transformed Fairy Queen. Our eyes turn half sadly to the dead tree lying, with its roots in the pool and its poor head buried in the mossy bank where the last winter had tossed it from the summit, when the clip of a wing catches our eyes and a blackie skips over the bank above, only to disappear in a moment with another flick when it finds a strange intruder on the scene. By-and-by a "tweet, tweet" directs us towards a flock of coletits, restlessly busy among the mosses, hunting for insects with the most preternatural rapidity; but they too pass rapidly on and leave us alone, when we recollect that the scene-shifters may be kept waiting, and we slip quietly back again into the outer world, where we can peep through tree stems to the quiet loch and the snow-clad hills on the one hand, and the white-crusted mosses on the other, like the curly fleeces of whitefaced sheep.

Down by the shore the high tides have left our long foreshores black, that during the neaps were covered with plates of crackling ice. As the tide rose to the highest it met a keen temperature, and, although but a short time stationary, when it fell it left the grasses on the seaturf with little icy tablets, beautifully engraved, sitting on their summits. Such lots of them too, like the little groups of white marble-topped tables on a Parisian boulevard; the fairies will no doubt be coming there for a cold "chop" as they emerge from the pantomime. For there are *such* preparations for Christmas festivities, and so many wonderful drop-scenes. A beautifully delicate rose-pink slid over the mountains all around this afternoon, with a winking haze over the purplish shoulders of the hills. The foreground is lightly dusted with snow, with now a black foreshore shading into purple, and then breaking suddenly into grayish blue on the further waters.

Mussels have been very frequent on the hills of late, and we wondered whether future naturalists would consider them as evidence of the recent elevation of the land. Times are bad, and the crow kind have been obliged to take largely to the shore supply of viands, so they frequently carry mussels to the hills to break upon the rocks and devour at their leisure. Potatoes also are not infrequent, showing how important birds are in the spreading of vegetation when such large roots are borne lengthened distances into the wilds.

He is dead! In spite of comfortable quarters and care he has given up the struggle in disgust, and we have just been transferring his remains to the spirit world. And so the question is not yet quite settled to our satisfaction, how long a skate takes to arrive at that condition of maturity represented by the complete absorption of the umbilical sac, and consequent readiness to commence life as an aggressive unit in the animal world.

Our experiment has been a lengthened one, and full of interest. In June last, when the thornback skates came inshore to throw their eggs, we speared several thus ripe, with the pair of matured eggs on the way down the fallopian tubes. These eggs we placed in our ponds, so that the water might have constant play about them; but, at the same time, that the creature when born might not escape our observation. After waiting 70 days we opened one to see if the fish would ever really be ready for exit, and to our surprise found a fine healthy young skate, with the wings just commencing to curve outward from the dog-fish-looking framework. The fish was so evidently immature, with the venous system circulating powerfully around the very large umbilical sac, that we decided to give the next another month before examining its progress. At 100 days we therefore again opened an antiquated-looking hand-barrow, to see if the inhabitant had not reached an age when it might be reasonably expected to go into society, and be introduced to the real cares of life. Again the fish was found with a large umbilical sac, but with the wings fairly developed, so that it measured one inch across and three inches to the end of its very skaty tail. The sac was yet an important factor in its existence, and it could by no possible dodge have hidden its meal-bag under its body. Yet the creature was an unmistakable skate, and as lively as if it had no encumbrance. Only one egg of a satisfactory kind remained to us, and we anxiously awaited the appearance of the fish therefrom, making daily pilgrimages to its shrine and with difficulty keeping our hands from asking the question ever on our lips, is it still alive, we wonder? The months passed, and our patience had gradually filtered away, when after one hundred and fifty days no sign of any youngster was visible. We were aware that young skates frequently make their appearance on the east coast with the sac still attached, evidently as tired of waiting inside as we were of watching outside; so in order to note exactly when the sac was absorbed, we decided to open our remaining skate egg on the 153d day, and see what stage of progress had been reached. The result although most interesting, has on the whole proved unfortunate, as we ought to have displayed still more patience after having waited so long. After 153 days, the youngster was not quite mature, having a considerable sac still to come and go on; but it was in vigorous health, three and a half inches in length, and two broad across the wings. He was now tumbled into a basin of water, where he seemed quite at home, occasionally floundering around, but for the most part remaining quiescent and receptive. In order to prevent the light being too strong we covered over a portion of the basin with brown paper, and here the little fellow lived for three weeks longer, slowly engaged in absorbing what remained of the sac, and apparently quite satisfied with his position in life. By this time he had reached the age of 174 days since the deposition of the egg, and yet it should be well noted that he had still some weeks of existence before him ere he could have absorbed his patrimony, and be said to exist as a breadearner on his own account. By some means his sac got a twist at this time, causing him great uneasiness, and forcing him to lift one wing back as if relieving the sac of undue pressure; and the following day, at the age of 175 days —a few days under six months—he entered his only protest against the cruelty of fate, and ceased the graceful movements of his tapering tail.

There had been no apparent retardation of the process of incubation, and consequently it must be allowed that these cold-blooded sluggish fish are extremely leisurely in all their movements from the beginning, and that as the eggs take so long to incubate when excluded, it is more than probable our conjecture was correct, and that the embryo eggs found in the fish in November are not capsuled and ready for deposition until the usual spawning time in May and June. No wonder neither Couch nor ourselves could incubate them before, seeing we looked upon six or eight weeks as the time probably required, in place of as many months.

When noting the various mosses to-day in their beautifully-luxuriant development, we came upon the smooth face of a rock up which the cushiony sphagnum had set itself to climb. It was quite interesting to observe the complete change in its apparent character, resulting from the changed conditions of the physical problem it had set itself to face. The soft moss had stretched itself out to the utmost, clinging like ivy to the face of the rock, and appearing as if pressed in a scrap book, so closely did it spread itself on the stone. Several species had behaved similarly under similar conditions, and the extreme tenuity of the stems, as they strained upwards, had extended to every filament, with the result that, dusted as they were with a light moisture, they presented a most ethereal appearance, and were in marked contrast to their commonplace fellows pursuing the even tenor of their uneventful, unambitious, gregarious ways. No doubt these lower forms are less readily injured, and more accommodating in their habits, than others of higher organization.

Mankind is steadily developing an extraordinary desire both to eat its cake and have it. Why does the River Awe no longer send shiploads of salmon away, as it used to do in the old days, when a vessel was regularly despatched to Spain with noble kippers? This question is continually asked. There is far more conservation, both in the river and outside, and we know what is annually obtained; and yet the resultant catch approaches not in importance to those "good old times," that were too stupid to know how happy they were. Now, no one can suppose that a salmon hangs about the mouth of its native river until the time for spawning comes round; and the natural question to be asked in this, as in many other instances, is, where is the gauntlet through which they must run on their annual return? That they go to distant feeding grounds is undoubted, and one proof of this is the mistakes they make in returning homeward. Great shoals of salmon coming inwards from the Atlantic strike the south-eastern portion of Mull, and are there met by the usual preparations for their capture. Those escaping proceed north by Kerrera, where fresh fisheries have been established of recent years, and heavy contributions are there paid for permission to pass. In fact, ere they reach the mouth of Loch Etive the shoals have suffered similarly to an East African expedition, and left three-fourths of their number on the danger-lined path. On arriving near Connel they are met by a colony of seals, and another sacrifice has to be offered. About this quarter the salmon of the various rivers must part company—the Loch Awe fish entering the turbulent rapids of Connel, while those for the Garry and intermediate rivers proceed onwards to their destination. It is sufficiently remarkable how well they manage to discover their home rivers without supposing them never to make blunders. Indeed, how the fish for the River Creran succeed in the difficult task of slipping past Eriska Island is an interesting question, and yet we are assured by those who know both fish thoroughly that River Awe fish find their way into *Loch* Creran occasionally along with the native fish. We say into *Loch* Creran, where they have been captured, showing that they have been travelling with the same body of fish as the Creran salmon, and missed the mouth of the loch. But we understand they are never taken in the *River* Creran, so that they must discover their error and return to seek their own river!

This seems to us an interesting fact, if it is as reliable as we believe it to be; going far to prove that this instinct of returning to the native river is largely founded on observation, capable of rectifying blunders when made. Again, the fish of the River Nant, adjoining the Awe, will enter the mouth of the latter river during low water, and await a spate in their own stream; just as a woman would go into her neighbour's lobby and await the return of her absent damsel to open her own door, declining absolutely, however, to go "ben the hoose." Is this not a comparatively sensible movement?

JANUARY, 1883.

We brought in the New-Year, as well as Christmas, by a forenoon's dredging, and, strange to say, the weather was most propitious, and enabled us fully to enjoy the beauty of mountain and loch, the first just sprinkled with snow and the latter speckled with sunlight, with here a lonely sea-bird or passing gull, and there a seal on the look-out for its Christmas or New-Year dinner. Frost to-day, rain to-morrow, and frost to follow, with the wine-cups of the inebriated gods running over the evening skies, shading into watery greys as the glorious-tinted liquors met the tears of the goddesses weeping over the follies of their mad mates. The festive season, unreliable as it ever is socially and physically, has been especially uncertain during the past days, and we quite sympathise with the desperate attempt of two of those in the vicinity to follow the unreliable weather, and combine Good Templarism with "Ne'er's-day." One good-humoured son of Benderloch, who desired us to sacrifice to the presiding genius of the day, and swallow a molten fiery furnace, displayed a blue ribbon in his coat; and upon our suggesting the absurdity of the combination of his offer and his button hole, he coolly explained that he carried the inevitable bottle all the same, but that he and a crony having resolved to meet an hour after, decided that the only security for their doing so was for them to be Good Templars till they met again? We feel as if the novel idea were stolen from the fields and moorlands about. Two days ago they were "soaking," next day after an evening's frost they were firm and secure, but they were only awaiting the southerly breeze that had gone round the corner, and to-day they are again scarce traversible.

But the loch was traversible, and we enjoyed thoroughly the varied hauls that brought new wonders to view. New, that is, absolutely new, no reasonable being expects much of nowadays, but relatively novel gatherings are ever coming to cheer the lover of Nature, for

> "Whenever the way seemed long,
>   Or his heart began to fail,
> She would sing a more beautiful song,
>   Or tell a more marvellous tale."

Aye, even to the humblest of her votaries. We have never hitherto met with a noble shell with large umbones and heart-shaped, hence named *Isocardia cor*, that has been taken about Iona. Two dead valves of a single specimen came up in one draw of the dredge, and seemed to us a most remarkable coincidence, as they had evidently long been separated, growing a huge bunch of barnacles on one edge, large *Anomiæ*, or false oysters, nestling in the snuggest corner of the inner side, with strong serpulæ tubes crossing the hinge-joint, and altogether showing a complete divorce without the least apparent likelihood of ever coming together again. That the small dredge travelling in the middle of the loch should pick up both seemed to be beyond the ordinary laws of chances, but yet "the unexpected," we are told, "always," or at least often, "happens." This most interesting, but apparently rare, shell seems then to have lived in our enclosed loch—if it does not do so now—and there is a prospect of our obtaining some day a perfect specimen. For we need not consider the chances of it having been borne inward from the outer waters, as it is a deep-water and not an active animal; and our waters are wholly out of the track of ocean waifs.

One can scarcely imagine it possible for the open-edged unprotected scallop, *P. opercularis*, to exist amid its numberless enemies, but the tangle fronds dragged up to-day contained large numbers of minute young sticking all over them, showing that the creatures managed to reproduce their kind in safety and abundance. Their very small size, along with the gradations of sizes dredged by us at present, point to a very elastic breeding season, which may extend for many months. The crustacea of the shrimp class (*Palæmou*, &c.), whether rich green or deep crimson, are full of spawn as they arrive on board, and seem also to exhibit far greater vitality under the circumstances than they do usually. Is this a powerful instinct to preserve and continue the species? If so, it is quite at variance with some other species whose muscles relax, and whole physical system shows marked incapacity for the usual struggle for existence, when in spawn!

We have had the usual three-days gale, this time, for the first time this season, commencing from the nor'-east and working very slowly round to the south, whence it now blows stiffly, throwing a fresh coating of snow on the higher hills and scuds of rain on the low lands. But it has been a remarkable dry gale, cold and cutting until to-day, and only adds fresh inducement to the vegetation to continue its vagaries. Three times within the last few months have the mild spells induced the firs alongside to throw out fresh sprouts, only to be nipped ere they had got further than an inch on their journey; while the primroses are struggling to emerge from budhood, and the bunches of rosebuds along our cottage front are in a most uncertain and unsatisfactory frame of mind, as if a "worm i' the bud" were preying on their scorbutic-looking cheeks.

In spite of the excessive severity of the weather last evening, when the gale was at its worst and the ferries on one side were almost, and on the other altogether, impassable, a goodly gathering from all the clachans around met to spend an evening together. Quite a hundred from our sparsely-peopled vicinity arrived, and this although a visit from the "Great King" to an aged neighbour had kept many kindly faces from the throng. Nothing illustrates the extreme sympathy that pervades a Highland district more than such an incident, as death will not only keep the immediate friends of the deceased from the place of mirth, but the immediate neighbours, otherwise wholly unconnected, who consider it unfeeling to enjoy themselves visibly under the circumstances. This sensibility underlies the Highland character, and accounts for much that the sterner temper of the Lowlander finds quite incomprehensible in their everyday existence. It is both a source of strength and weakness, for while it enables a prosperous Highlander to be a gentleman, it is apt to prevent an unsuccessful one from playing the man.

We are far from cities, in a comparatively poor district, a large proportion being crofters, and a stranger naturally expects that the result of a promiscuous gathering from hill and shore will result in a rough-and-tumble sort of meeting. Enter the school-house during the evening, and you first find the whole tastefully decorated by the young men and maidens with admirable effect, and by the aid of the very simplest means. Branches of evergreens from the nearest plantations are tacked on to the walls in simple patterns, while garlands of holly, ivy, and other evergreens are stretched across in front of the rude platform, over which a plaid is spread for a carpet. A Gaelic welcome in leaves of variegated holly gives life to a graceful meeting-place, while a few paper flowers give the needful touch of colour. All a very simple matter, representing a few hours' merry work of the young people, and no expenditure except of willing labour. The entertainment consists of the customary tea and fancy bread of a town soiree, while an hour or two passes pleasantly with the agreeable and gratuitous aid of the ringing wild native airs, sung without affectation by the young men. The simple programme over, the room is cleared, the pipes tuned, and perhaps a score of couples of all degrees join in the vigorous Highland dances. All this may be seen anywhere, but we question if anywhere out of the Highlands can such a well-conducted, kindly, merry, well dressed and well mannered company be drawn together from the same social scale. Certain we are that the poorest and humblest cottars are not less actuated by that good feeling and "sympathy" that breeds good manners than the most well-to-do; and while we sit and scan the pleasant faces and the comely figures as they wind vigorously through the national dances, we wonder if all this must gradually give way before the hard work and prosaic chase of success so much desiderated for the Highlands? Whether it will really be impossible for those classes in the "civilised" condition to be gentle and kindly, as well as "merry and wise," without forfeiting the other necessity of being also "honest and true," is a question. Meantime we cry "parley" with this terrible taskmaster "progress," and would fain for a time be gentle barbarians.

"It is a notable fact the sin of suicide is conspicuous by its absence among the canine race"—thus a last week's leader. The question thus cursorily settled is, nevertheless, one we are by no means willing to admit as capable of being so readily shelved. We have ourselves had recently a considerable controversy on the subject of the suicide of animals with a most redoubtable antagonist, and while unable to crow triumphantly over our success, the impossibility of "proving a negative" in such a case befriends us. A friend and neighbour assures us of the suicide of his terrier at one time when in distemper, the animal simply going off and drowning itself, and we firmly believe that in an extremity of pain and fear, an animal will destroy itself "if it has the means and opportunity." One argument adduced against this is that it pre-supposes a knowledge of death on the part of the animal, and mankind, as a rule, have come to act as if animals could not have any mental fear or anxiety about death, because they could not foresee it or know of it. Now, this is a very simple way of cutting the Gordian knot, and a Gordian knot it is; indeed, it leads to some of the greatest of psychological problems. But, that an animal knows death, may be pre-supposed from the fact that many of them will *simulate* it, and do this with the most marvellous verisimilitude. Perhaps the best-known cases are those of the landrail or corn-craik and the rat, to choose two widely-separated classes of animals; to which we would wish to add the crab, a creature that will on all occasions simulate death admirably, when it cannot see any possible means of escape otherwise. Under these circumstances the animals will permit themselves to be handled like corpses, and we have known a rat almost succeed in deceiving a whole household, where it lay on the dung-hill as it was thrown from the trap, keeping up the deception for hours, as it knew that it was watched. At length one eye was slowly opened, and ere those watching its movements could prevent it, the knowing creature had escaped with a rush. A creature that could thus imitate death so admirably, must perfectly well understand that such a state must exist for it, equally as for its victims, and prefer such an apparent " rest for its banes," rather than torture, or something horribly indefinite. It would be interesting to obtain a well-authenticated series of cases of apparent "suicide by animals."

We have last week dredged our finest specimen of the key-hole Limpet, *Fissurella Graeca*, and thus satisfied ourselves that they attain the ordinary size in our loch. This proved to be a specimen of distinct interest, as both in form and colour it far more approximated to the variety *gibba* than to the ordinary form. As *gibba* is figured of small dimensions, and we have specimens of all intermediate shades of form between these two varieties, we are satisfied that the two forms are merely the customary variations of the one species, which, although not so given to extremes of variation as our common shore limpet, yet alter widely from the ordinary accepted form. This must point to them as much more common than their comparatively rare appearance in the dredge would suggest, because we find that the more numerous a species is the more widely will it vary within certain limits. This is what would also be naturally expected from the data on which the Theory of Evolution of Species is based.

"There is a black sheep in every flock" is an old saying that we have heard variously interpreted. Besides the obvious one that no large body of sheep could be together without a black one, and no large family without a scapegrace, we have been assured that the black sheep meant "the dog" or "the shepherd," and now we have a fresh notion imported into the serious discussion. "What is there about a black sheep," asks our friend, "that makes it not only look exceptionally wicked and mischievous, but also act up to its semi-demoniac appearance?" "Just look at those two fellows!" and we note their peculiar expression of wild intelligence, as the small group to which they are attached run through two gates and traverse two supposed fences, as if they were not. See that fellow as he stops and turns on the summit of the rock—what an "other world" appearance of extra knowingness there is about it—and yet we cannot readily believe there is any real difference except in colour. Just let us suppose, however, that a black fellow arrived in a white family, would he not be looked upon as something uncanny, would he not be inclined to arrogate to himself the claims so willingly accorded, and gradually develop a character which at first might be foreign to him? Are we sure sheep will not act somewhat similarly, and gradually assert a position in a flock that at first was accorded to their abnormal appearance? For it must not be supposed that because sheep, from their naturally defenceless and timid character, are capable of being controlled by sheep dogs, that they are necessarily less intelligent than these most intelligent of dogs. In a recent article on brains, *apropos* of Gambetta's, it was remarked that a sheep's brain being larger comparatively than a dog's brain, was an evidence against the superiority of large brains over small! We cannot recognise the value of such evidence, and are inclined to believe in the high intelligence of our Highland sheep at anyrate, and would not be startled to find that they looked upon dogs as specially designed to protect them against foxes and other carnivora, and to keep them from straying into danger. On our way homeward we pass another little demon black fellow, whose leg was broken when a pet, and so far healed as to enable it to be a most inveterate thief and unconscionable vagabond about the autumn fields and the winter kail-yard. It is a thorough rogue in appearance, and almost forces us to acknowledge the truth of our friend's assertion, that there is something peculiarly mischievous and wicked about a "black sheep."

During the tempestuous weather of last week we observed on several occasions a remarkable effect in cloudland. For several days a great mass of clouds had lain across from Ben Breac to the head of Glen Creran, in an immovable bank, while the storm had been raging both above and below. Suddenly a light cloud, advancing from the south-east, was found to be circling, not vertically but horizontally, as if an irregular roller had been dragged across the sky, the revolutions being frequent, turbulent, and extending to a considerable distance. Later in the day, towards Glenure, we observed what seemed somewhat explanatory of the phenomenon. A stiff gale was blowing from the south-east, *above* the bank of clouds before mentioned, whipping off the edges, and whirling them outward away from the mountain tops, while another gale, more southerly, but apparently blowing *under* the cloud bank, met these cloud patches at an upward-tending angle, given by the mountains it had met and slanted over; and thus they were carried across the sky in the embrace of the horizontally-cyclonic breeze. The sky was very disturbed, and seemed to point to severe gales, turned in different directions from the mountain range stretching from Cruachan to Glencoe; but as to why the great bank of cloud should have so long remained outside their influence we could not satisfy ourselves.

All through the long-continued gale of last week the barometers of the district had kept steadily rising, and at last Monday, 22nd, dawned with a mild, cheerful, promising countenance, and the glass over 30 inches. The boat was taken over to the "Port" ere the sea should leave it half a mile inland these spring tides, and our friend was hailed for a day on the water. Fine morning, high glass —rising, too, through a gale, as if to promise a fine spell —all looked hopeful for a pleasant day. And yet we shook our heads and spoke ominously. The gulls are in a group in front of the cottage, and are evidently "out of their ordinary," and we cannot rid ourselves of the belief that something severe is coming. They have not scattered since the last gale, suggests an authority, and that does not appear unreasonable, for its tail has just brushed the dead leaves into the ditches, and their rustle has scarcely died upon the ear. But we still shake our heads as we step on board and pull across the loch.

We have not been long away when the clouds begin to bank gloomily towards the South, and a strange weight gathers around the sky; while we have no sooner reached the other side than the wind sharpens, and rises with a vicious touch in it that looks as if it meant something. "The glass over 30 inches, and rising, this morning!" we repeat, as we find the widgeon and the mallard, the golden-eye and the cormorant, as excited and restless as the redshank-sandpiper and the oyster-catcher we left on our own shore! But by the time we have been an hour away it is clear that the birds were right and the barometer wrong, and that the spirit of the storm is marshalling his batallions from every side. A great gloom is over the loch as we hurry homeward in the teeth of the now-rising gale, and we scarce dare halt to pick up the poor rotche, whose white breast is lifted on the white breakers, while a torrent of crimson flows into the waters around. As we step chilled on to the beach, we half resolve to burnish the glass face of our barometer so that it may see better, and hang it outside to take a lesson from the seafowl, not one of which, gull or sandpiper, but knew of the coming tempest! That night the wind blew a gale, which continued all Tuesday, the glass in the interval still rising to 30·3—only commencing to fall the next night, when the gale increased to a tempest. "Never prophesy unless you know," exclaims the Yankee humorist, and the barometers in this quarter seem resolved to be "cocksure" before they implicate themselves, leaving all forecasts of value to the seafowl.

We some time ago calculated the quantity of limpets eaten by the oyster-catchers, and looked upon these as the principal food of our seapiets. Although they are constantly and actively at work on sand or mud banks in front of our cottage, we accused them more of driving their bills into the sand after annelids than seeking other shell-fish. Our neighbour, however, found quite a handful of cockles in the stomach of an oyster-catcher the other day, and this led to a discussion as to how they opened them, for we did not suppose that they knew the trick of opening them by placing the umbones of two together and giving them a dextrous twist! The next day after our discussion, our friend, on returning from a stroll, made a rush for his coat pocket in such a state of triumph that we anticipated the production of gold-laden quartz. The production of an opened cockle dispelled this illusion, and we then learned that he had come upon a gull devouring it, and forced the bird to drop it that he might examine it carefully.

No sign of injury appeared on the shell, and the muscular attachments were still sticking to the valves, showing that the animal had been alive and well, and that the shell had not been found empty. Nor could we find that the shell had been mouthed by the gull, so as to sicken the cockle, and force it to leave hold. It seemed most reasonable to suppose that, feeding on the borders of the tide, both gull and oyster-catcher seized their prey when the siphons were exserted, and then cleaned the shell, as no broken shells, such as would lead to the supposition of rough usage, are visible on the beach, which is otherwise thronged with freshly-devoured cockle shells. We could scarcely have believed that cockles could thus be caught in multitudes unprepared.

When traversing an upland farm with a considerable extent of cultivated land we noted one field fast relapsing into sphagnum and lichen. This, we learned, had been the direct result of an extra dose of moisture in our ordinarily "damp" climate. The field had been carefully grass-sown before a very wet summer, and the seeds had been washed into patches, where they had not been altogether swept away, enabling the original hill vegetation to assert itself, while the cultivated grasses contended for bare existence in little grass "forts" scattered here and there. But what is this on the contiguous field? A good-sized stone on which an unmistakable serpula tube, or series of tubes, has been affixed, and has stood the contest of elements almost unimpaired. That mussel and other shells should be borne to the hills by birds; or that crustacea in a ruined condition should strew the elevated neighbourhood of a cormorant's seat, is simple enough; but why should a large stone with the home of a sea-worm upon it appear in such a position? Look carefully around : there are several smaller stones with miniature tree-roots sticking upon them, but in such a manner as no terrestrial plants ever do, and no difficulty need be found in allocating these also to the seashore. Has the ground actually been raised a couple of hundred feet above the present sea-level within a quite recent period, in which the tangle attachments and serpulæ have not been worn off the stones? No! it is Mohammed who has gone to the hill, not the hill to Mohammed; and the cartloads of tangle and other seaware which have been taken from the shore and laid down as manure have borne along with them many goodly stones to which the seaware has been attached; and thus a fresh condition will be imported into the geological problem of the future, as no doubt many a similar uncalculated condition has found its way into the geological formations which are the problems of to-day.

FEBRUARY, 1883.

This last severe weather has set all the small birds flocking again, and brought down to us from the higher grounds, and in from the further moors, flights of buntings of various species. One would naturally expect that for convenience of finding feeding, birds would rather keep separate in severe weather than throng together, as it can be no easy matter to find provender for these large bands of finches and buntings. No doubt safety from birds of prey and other enemies is one cause of their banding together, and they will also cover a larger area in hunting for supplies, which in the case of these seed-eaters will be found in quantity as a rule when found at all. The several species do not necessarily keep together, and we counted four species of bunting in one flock that had perched upon the trees of a small plantation. Unless we were mistaken—and a bird in the tree is not satisfactory to an ornithologist—the only *Cirl Bunting* we have seen here was in this flock. The Black-headed Bunting is represented by one or two pairs, and they are very local in their habitat, principally affecting a short stretch of ground near the Moss of Ledaig. We saw the Whinchat also a few days ago in its district near Culcharran Moss, where it may be met all the year in one or more pairs. A fine flock of Fieldfares is with us, that beautiful thrush that winters throughout the country, and is so constantly mistaken for the Missel Thrush; or rather, properly speaking, the Missel Thrush is mistaken for it. Whenever anyone talks of a Fieldfare's nest, he is scoffed at as having mistaken the Missel Thrush's nest therefor. In colouring they are much alike, but the Missel Thrush is a much more vociferous fellow. Do the Missel Thrushes really leave us when the Fieldfares come, and return as they leave, thus helping to continue the mystification? For the Missel Thrushes that frequent our neighbourhood have not been seen this winter!

What is a deer fence? We used to think we knew, and supposed a 6ft. fence, with wires a foot apart, was quite sufficient. But we have known deer to get *over* such a fence, and we have heard of them going *under* such a fence; and now we know of a two-year-old buck going right *through* a stiff split rail fence *less than 9in. between the spars*. Caught in a garden, it went straight at the fence, slipped its head sideways between the spars, and *went through it like a cat*. A very slight wire fence is frequently sufficient to restrain red deer, but these wild fallow deer seem to have developed that contempt of humanity and its devices born of familiarity.

This is the first evening since Saturday last that we can be said to have anything like calm, and the room, as we light the lamp and draw down the blind, seems deathly still, so accustomed has the ear become to the continuous howl of the tempest. But the gales we have just found relief from, for the time, would be better described as a succession of terrific squalls, with strange unexpected lulls between. We do not suppose they are yet over, as our ducks were flying this evening like wild mallards to and from the stream in front.

Saturday was a reasonable day, and as our dredge had lain idle for exactly a month, we resolved to have an hour on the water at the scallop ground. It seems fairly reasonable to conclude that these pectens are migratory, like the larger *P. Maximus*, for we had been at work but a short time when we had secured a plentiful supply, although of late our success has been by no means satisfactory. We are tossing aside the empty shells with still an eye on possibilities, when we catch sight of a something at the bottom of a half valve of rough scallop *(P. pusio)*. Empty shells, exactly speaking, unless but lately tenanted, are rarely to be found, as mud, sand, or gravel gets silted into them, or a sea annelid will have built its tube of sand or broken shells neatly coiled therein. So, amid a mass of *debris*, it is not peculiar to find a rough, dirty-looking object in a half shell. But the eye becomes educated in a peculiar way, and it is wonderful how little of interest or novelty will escape one even in a hasty glance through a mass of "stuff," and thus it is that a fine *Fissurella Graeca*, or keyhole limpet, is readily pounced upon, however obscured by mud and hidden in a corner.

Having obtained our supply of scallops, we leave their ground and strike across the loch, and as the rope lengthens out to a score of fathoms on softer ground, sly allusions are made to the little *palmipes* that disappeared from the boat on a certain occasion, the first that had met our gaze in our loch. Why! the fairies are about to be sure. The next haul of the dredge in the middle of the loch, and from the depths of another half *pecten pusio* we drag another little web-footed starfish, neatly ensconced, and exactly similar to the former much-mourned individual. A little wobbling fish, too, among the *debris*—so we chuck it carelessly into a dish. Only one or two edible scallops here, and grumbling deep proceeds from the utilitarians; but the dredge is once more at the bottom, and the oarsman toiling slowly for the Appin shore. There is something in it this time, that is certain, but the disgusted expression of the toiler at the rope tells at least of no pectens, and we are greatly amused to find that into the comparatively small-mouthed dredge a large sea-urchin, five inches in diameter, has been entrapped; and a splendid fellow he is. What a delicate morsel he would have proved in the Mediterranean, where the roe is more especially prized. We have only once taken one of similar size at low tide outside in Loch Linnhe, and the splendid set of grinders he has to show explains his facility in filling his capacious body, which will hold quite $21\frac{1}{2}$ oz. of water.

Here are quite a row of little pea crabs that have gradually succumbed since their withdrawal from the water, and if you look at them carefully you will be surprised to find that a proportion of them—indeed a considerable proportion of them—are "humpbacked," the carapace being swollen from the inside. Here and there we find the carapace is being lifted off, and one is apt to conclude that the creature has "burst itself" to an extent. Ha! what is this we have here? Half emerging from under the tilted carapace is a little yellow-bodied scoundrel, backing out like a burglar from a bedroom window; and here, again, is another that has wholly emerged from its stranded host, only to find itself in an equally uncongenial element. Why, those lumps under the carapace are actually parasites, and the burst-open carapaces have been hoisted apart by them in their endeavours to escape from the dwelling that circumstances "over which poor crabby had no control" has rendered inhospitable. Small we have called these fellows, but they are relatively enormous, and if one could fancy a man carrying about a living hare in his stomach he would be somewhat similarly burdened to those weight carrying little crustaceans!

Where is our little fish all this time? Bring forth the fish! The fish was brought, and proved to be of the sucker class. A delicately organised creature compared with its congeners, with extremely fine fibrous fins, resembling those of the gobies more than its own genus, with a brilliant general tone on back and sides, only to be imitated by adding a large dash of rose to Indian red, and of an almost gelatinous consistence, the little stranger of but 1 3-10ths of an inch in length was a source of greater interest than if it had been a salmon of as many yards. The dorsal fin has 6, anal 4, and tail 13 rays, in this closely resembling the two-spotted sucker; but otherwise the appearance of these two fishes is quite distinct, and three beautiful spots of a richer colour adorn the back, the largest and darkest between the pectorals, and the others graduated in size and brilliance towards the tail. It remains to be added that the eyes of this dainty little fish have green pupils and brilliant gold iris, so that, however diminutive, he is quite a little beau in his way, evidently a variety of the two-spot sucker.

The almanacs threatened us with high tides end of last and beginning of this week, and, so far as this particular corner is concerned, they quite come up to the mark. A little after day-break on the 10th, with one of the rare calm seas of the last two months, the tide crept steadily up around and far beyond our overturned boat. Except on the occasion of the great November gale of 1881, we have never seen the water so far up on our own shore, although on that occasion it was several feet higher on the other side of our bay, on which the hurricane was impelling it. For a steady rise of tide, without any wave to prevent the exact measurement, this Saturday morning's tide was therefore the one from which we must judge in future, the sea in our own loch being waveless. This does not at all mean that the great rise was not caused by heavy gales, for the continued severity of the weather for such a lengthened period must have forced a vast body of waters upon our western coasts. Each winter we are subjected to such weather that we forget the severity of those past, and declare the present the worst; but really in this case we must assert that, for incessant continuous assault by air and rain, we have not seen this season beaten. The gales have been only not hurricanes, and we scarcely think this latter term can be withheld from that of Monday night. The accompanying storms of sleet have been of the most violent and bitter character, and these were accompanied last evening by a short but virulent and brilliant thunderstorm. The sky had cleared and looked favourable, deluding weak mortals out after a tempestuous and bitter day; when, with a hop, skip, and jump came a black thunder-cloud round the shoulder of Ben Breac and the heights of Ben Lora; the darkened landscape was lit up with a sheet of lurid flame, and as the hail fell in an almost impenetrable mass, the thunder seemed to shake the hills. Just a hop, skip, and jump, and the storm demon passed over us, sending three blinding flashes at intervals as his heels struck fire from the granite of Ardchattan, the trap of the Scaur, and the white quartz rock of Appin. And to day we feel at peace, although the blast has still a choice selection of Sheffield cutlery, that the rapid extirpation of the African elephant and the consequent advance in ivory has alone prevented it hafting!

We have been visited by a flock of interesting bullfinches these latter days in the little plantation alongside, and most charming fellows they are to watch. We fully sympathise with our friend who wept when he slew his first cock bully, and thought it a wonderful chaffinch. Here they come—one, two, three—flop among the chaffies on the bare larches; but, unlike the chaffies, they are restlessly active, worrying around heads over heels with the spirit of investigation newly awakened within them; and we, too, watch them keenly at a few yards' distance. How gay you are in your beautiful waistcoats as you draw your heads on one side and squint sharply at the under side of the branchlets! Now, what are you after? We have always considered that bullfinches are not so injurious to a garden as they are represented, so we watch them sharply. They are so very busy and so inquiring with their bills that we come to the conclusion they must really be nipping off the buds and devouring them, so we note exactly the branches and twigs that are visited and overhauled by them, with the intention of having our turn of investigation. It is quite a reasonable supposition, as has been suggested to us, that constant nibbling of buds after imprisoned insects might lead the birds to devour the buds themselves, "as a vegetable adjunct to their insect diet," so we go up to see. There were half a dozen bullies, at anyrate, on this small larch, and on three several days have they paid marked attention to it, yet not a bud do we see nipped from the twigs or branches that we "marked down." It is clear that here, at anyrate, the insects have been scarce, and the buds themselves offered no inducement to the bonny birds.

Squirrels have been increasing at a great rate these last few years, and one even streamed across the little trees of the plantation at our door the other day; while they have penetrated up the beautiful glen, of the same name, at the head of our loch. At the same time our wild fruit harvest has been almost *nil*, our fir cone harvest distinctly poor, and all the bellies of these active beauties to be filled. Will they become carnivorous in sheer desperation, is a question we have long asked ourselves, but although we have kept our eyes open for indications in this direction, we have found none. Our friend from the beautiful glen, however, asked us lately the pertinent question, "Why so many young birds were lying dead last year with their heads crushed and the brains devoured, and who were the murderers?" We had not observed the facts, and could vouchsafe no reply.

On the faith of a professional bird-catcher who visits the locality, our querist answered his own question, by stating that the squirrels were the aggressors, that they attacked the young birds in the nests, only biting the tops off their heads and eating the brains! We do not think this at all unreasonable or unlikely; the temptation to these sharp-toothed tree hunters is great and ever present, and it comes, too, at the end of the winter when forest provender is scarce. Last year we were particularly struck with the absence of nests, contemporaneously with the absence of a batch of birdnesters; and if the increase of squirrels is to be bought at the price of a serious decrease in our feathered favourites, the price is too high to pay. This may only be the "tiger's first victim," and if these creatures develop a refined taste for the brains of birds, there is no saying to what extent they may carry it. They are getting very hard pressed at present, for although our primroses are aflower the severe weather since New Year has kept most vegetation from any abnormal advance.

The barometer going up, and now at 30·3, the usual hurricane rushing *ventre a terre* across the country, and fierce squalls spitting bitter showers with hasty fury as they shout at the heels of those before them. A cheerful morning to be abroad among the tree tops or the tree bottoms, even amid the thickest evergreens! There is a flop among the branches of the small larch just over our head, and without observing our presence a squirrel, with really less fuss than a bullfinch, is busy in the bare boughs of the larch within two or three yards of our eyes. What is the little fellow about that he is so desperately busy and pre-occupied as not to perceive us? He passes along the branch almost as lightly and quickly as a bird, and in his case there is no mistake. Quick as thought as he progresses the tips of the little larch buds are nipped off, now on the top, now on the side, and anon round on the bottom. The movements as well as the occupation of the creature are more that of a bird than of a quadruped, and he clears branch after branch of larch with a dexterity and persistence evidently born of long practice. Caught *in flagrante delicto*, that is certain, my dear! and, however unwilling we are to declare your delinquency, we are sorry to acknowledge that before you have filled your stomach with such minute provender, and supplied the requisite caloric to your active limbs, these keen days, you will have retarded and weakened the growth of a considerable number of trees to an appreciable extent. That you made havoc of the fir-cones, and when hard-up ate a few young fir sprouts, we were well aware, but that you made such a wholesale onslaught on the coming vegetation of the firs we were scarcely prepared to find. It is clear in a winter when all fruit is extremely scarce, such a large population of squirrels as now inhabit our woods must do a serious amount of injury.

We formerly discussed the question as to whence the squirrels came, and how they reached our isolated locality, now about five years ago. It seems they have long been located strongly at Inverawe, amid the beautiful woods near the mouth of the river Awe, at the other side of Loch Etive; and it is quite possible that many may have crossed the loch when it was frozen over a few miles above, during some of these severe winters. This seems to us the most likely supposition, as the years they appeared were severe enough to enable them to adopt this mode of emigration, without resorting to the "piece of bark with tail for sail" that is so frequently brought forward to account for their passage across sheets of water.

Our *tropiolum*, that in ordinary seasons dies down to the root to start afresh in the spring, has never really gone to sleep this season, or at least has early awakened, and is now alive far up, and throwing out strong, fresh sprouts, evidently stimulated to unusual exertions by the masses of strong snowdrops below and the primroses blooming under the neighbouring hedge. We should not have considered this almost unprecedented season of storm and rain to have been so mild as this indicates; but let us stroll round to the back garden and we shall find otherwise. The scrambling tendrils of the bramble have wandered within a couple of months or so from the foot of the enclosing dyke, and have reached quite 10 feet in length during the winter! Not sickly, weakly sprouts, but strong, vigorous growths demanding vigorous measures to eradicate. These are sufficiently remarkable evidences of the forcing character of the season.

What is sympathy? and is there really a mental and physical necessity created for the presence of a kindly piece of animated nature to which we are accustomed? Of this class of feeling must be that desperate home-sickness felt so keenly by many, as if even inanimate nature and its associations bound their spirits by an indissoluble bond. An old and kindly crofter, whose old horse has long been his constant companion on the farm and the road, recently fell sick, and after he had been a few days in bed, a friend met the old horse with its head in at the door, neighing a sympathetic query as to the why and wherefore of his master's detention. "Why tarrieth your weary foot, and wherefore is your friendly voice heard no more in the stable?" it seemed to ask. The incident was quite affecting, but we hope the old couple will jog along many a summer day together yet.

MARCH, 1883.

Two belated wanderers on the southern shore of Benderloch have just come in, bringing with them a goodly array of ocean treasure trove. A mass of delicate pink fish spawn belongs to the "Cockpaidle" or Lump Sucker *(Cyclopterus lumpus)*, and another of the contents of the pail they carried proved to be our second specimen of Montague's sucker fish, with its beautifully marked fins, back, belly, and tail. But what a jump our heart gave as we glanced at the companion fish; not for years have we seen a specimen of what was a common shore fish in the further North, so that the sudden appearance of the *Motella quinquecirrhata* or five-bearded Rockling, with its elegant, if somewhat ling-like shape, and rich chocolate-brown, golden-syrupy colouring, was enough to bring before us the bleak cliffs and rolling moorlands of the Long Island. We have once taken a beautiful specimen of its congenor, the three-bearded Rockling, here, but this is the first time of our meeting with this smaller more sober-coloured species.

Under the stones in front of our dwelling, where the ground is muddy, you cannot help meeting with young eels of varied lengths in multitudes; while under the stones along the rocky shore the gunnel fish are just now equally numerous, driven shoreward seemingly for spawning purposes. Under one large stone we found a sickly-looking specimen, and close alongside a large bunch of the delicate ova, opalescent when fresh. These eggs, however, were all "eyed," and evidently deposited for a day or two, so we took them off in hopes of being able to hatch out the slippery fellows. We have always noticed that these fishes are most careful of their spawn, and although they do not show the constructive skill and maternal instincts of the Rocklings and Sticklebacks, they are yet not without great care for the welfare of their ova, which are frequently deposited in knowing corners, in which the mother remains to watch over them for a time.

The tides were so low and good for a foreshore observer, that we determined to see what could be obtained on the outer islands of Loch Linnhe, and set out at near the half tide so as to get through the narrow passage on the south side of Eriska Island, before the ebbing waters should leave the whole passage dry. " If you can get the boat through inside of Sgeir-na-Caillach, it will get down the Doirlinn," says one authority, but we shake our heads dubiously as we look at the racing waters and the narrowing passage. We are sadly tempted to move aside to various objects of interest, but it is now clear that the water will be low enough ere we get through, and we hurry down the shallowing stream of water with an uncomfortable feeling. A warning bump, a long grating sound upon the banking sea-bottom, and we glance at one another and the mile of intervening shoal with an uneasy feeling creeping up our backs. But every moment increases the difficulty, for no ordinary tide is upon us to-day, and we will be left high and dry in a quarter of an hour. There is no help for it; the wind is bitterly cold, the water equally so under a north-east wind on the shallows; and the first out of the boat up to the knees is the first to jump in again with a peculiarly unheroic dexterity. Feet that can scarcely crawl up a gravel beach must struggle along without halt or hesitation over the great shoal, as we drag the boat seawards; and only after half-an-hour at the galley do we thrust our craft on the outer waters, and hop on board shivering for a dram, as we endeavour externally and internally to bring back life and vigour into benumbed extremities. Over this great extent of sandy, muddy, semi-gravelly shoal we did not start a single flat-fish, so that they must have anticipated the rapidly approaching ebb and fled seaward, although until this last week such an ebb tide had not visited the Doirlinn flounders for six months, perhaps not for years.

Quite a demand now arose for the oars in our spin across to the Black Island, where we soon beached our craft and started to explore its nooks and rocky caves at low ebb tide. It proved to be remarkably bare, as if the great and continued gales had swept it as they have swept all other exposed quarters. Just at the verge of lowest ebb, however, we come upon first one then another Montague Sucker Fish, until we have in all about half a dozen, between the island and its outlying reef of rocks. Its congener the Cornish Sucker also supplied a few specimens, but none of the two-spotted Suckers showed themselves; and thus our find proved that this fish (*Liparis Montagui*), so rarely found in the West of Scotland, is comparatively common in its chosen haunts. The scarcity of the Cornish Sucker here was the more remarkable, as the very next day we came upon a pair of these droll suckers, with their great flat heads, under almost every stone we lifted on a stretch of rough boulder-clad foreshore on Loch Creran. Sometimes three or four were under one stone, and we must have seen at least a hundred during a stroll of a couple of hundred yards. But we have not met the active Montague Sucker in our own loch; so that the more sluggish fish frequent our quieter waters, leaving the storm-lashed outer islands to the stronger and more lively species.

In our shore scrambles among the islands of Linnhe this last week we have at least found that the greater proportion of shore fishes are spawning; and our extemporised incubators are now occupied with brilliant-hued ova of various species, among some of which the eyes are already well developed, and displaying interesting peculiarities. Here is a crowd of delicate ova, lately glutinous, closely cemented, and almost a homogeneous mass. Gradually the eggs have moved away from each other, leaving interstices for the entrance of more and more water as the increasing vitality of the occupants has demanded greater oxygenation. Now some of the more forward ova are connected with the mass by the very slightest cementation or agglutination, the eggs perceptibly moving and working away from their neighbours, as if the internal struggles of the embryos produced the same effect as the mother hen does, who daily turns her eggs with her beak. We frequently wondered whether most of such eggs would incubate naturally, or if the interior ones were really debarred from any sufficiency of contact with the life-giving water. Here is a bunch from which scores of youngsters in the pond, now progressing vigorously, have incubated, so we lift it up anticipating that it is wholly exhausted, as it looks dead and dingy, and we break it across. Within a few minutes of this performance we find the hitherto imprisoned youngsters wriggling out into the tablespoon in which we have placed the spawn for convenience of examination, several days after their brethren have been enjoying an energetic existence. But for our aid we do not believe these poor little fellows could ever have emerged from their place of sepulture, so that no doubt in our calculations of the prolific character of certain fishes we do not generally sufficiently allow for those non-vitalised, non-incubated, and perpetually imprisoned.

We have frequently referred to the *Fissurella Græca* as a shell that is not uncommon on certain grounds; but living among rocks like our common limpet they were naturally difficult to procure. When turning over the larger stones on one of the islands, we were agreeably surprised to find quite an number of the younger members of this family, so closely resembling the barnacle-covered stones on which they crept that it was very difficult to observe them. We cannot wonder at the rarity with which this keyhole limpet is captured by the dredge when it occupies such a secure position amid the largest boulders.

We have had a vague feeling of inconstancy hovering about us as we found ourselves first flirting gaily and then gradually sliding into more serious attentions towards the Etive Loch. For ten days we have been seizing every opportunity of peering into her secrets, in spite of the bitter blasts occasionally sweeping over her restless waters; and when our raids were being made from a snug corner alongside the fine old priory, and in company with a most amiable and sympathetic companion, it is natural that "out of sight was out of mind," and our affection was almost alienated from our own Loch Creran. One of the three earliest priories of Scotland, charmingly situated, and with a wealth of story, Ardchattan has given its name to a parish of vast extent, and including every character of scenery, all Benderloch being within its bounds, while it stretches up to Loch Awe.

Any wind in such a loch as Etive must be a dangerous one at times, and it is well remarked that no boat should sail it with any other sail than a plaid on a stick. Those accustomed with ordinary squalls on ordinary waters may laugh at this, but to see it as we did on the 14th would have verified the saying. Over Durnish came the wind with a savage rush, and dropped into the loch opposite Aird's Bay House—where the genial Dr. Norman Macleod used to bathe his weary eyes in Etive —as straight as if it had been a falling block of granite. The squalls struck the waters absolutely perpendicularly at times, and spread out on every side like the ripples from a stone tossed into the water. Those acquainted with the loch are frequently only advised of the coming burster through the sough of the wind among the trees on the hillsides. Under these circumstances, oars were naturally our most usual means of progression; and the marvellous variety of diseases, from lumbago to rheumatism and spinal disorder, were the equally natural result of huge bags of mud dragged unwillingly from the slimy depths of Etive.

This noble stretch of water receives so much fresh water into it, and has to be filled with its quota of salt water through such a narrow entrance, that its specific gravity, as a rule, is much less than that of Creran; while the unsteady temperature caused by the great supply of cold fresh water occasionally, followed by seasons of comparative absence of such supply—as at present—causes it to support a somewhat different fauna from Loch Creran, which has otherwise many points in common. While the oyster flourishes naturally throughout Loch Creran, it seems unable to obtain a foothold in Etive, and we have never succeeded in obtaining a single specimen of the common pecten, *Pecten opercularis*, from it. Indeed, during all our dredging experience in it we have never succeeded in obtaining a single specimen of any of our species of scallops—edible or minute —except the one species, *P. septemradiatus*, which appears to be favourable to lochs with much fresh water, such as Loch Fyne. Even this is rarely taken in the dredge so that it must be a very active species, as we do not believe it to be rare, although to a large extent local. But Etive is great in mud, as all our coadjutors soon discover; and the courtesy of the hospitable manse is strained severely with tubs and buckets full of most non-artistic material.

What is there beautiful there? A rich slime, so tenacious as scarce to pass through the $\frac{1}{8}$in. sieve, may be very good material for the bottom of a loch, but might as well remain there. Gently! gently! "I never knew there were any Razor-fish (*Solen*) in Etive," says someone. No doubt the fine shell-fish of Ardmucknish Bay could find their way up Etive if so desirous, but— Ha! a *Solen;* and here is another, and yet another. We almost hear the smacking of lips at thought of the rich dainty, as the owners hurry over to witness the grateful arrival. How many of these would make a supper, we wonder! The largest about an inch in length *(Solen pellucida)*, the smallest a quarter of an inch; the impudent little imitations of the seven inch by one and a quarter inch we have lately been demolishing seem so afraid of becoming fashionable as a dish, that they conceal themselves in the mud at a score of fathoms deep. Quite right, too. There is a *soupçon* of nightingales' tongue about the dainty little beauties, and one or two for supper would be a fit finish to the day of the delicate beauty who began it with a "shrimp." Little cockles of various species are numerous, and as they find themselves "on land" under the lamplight, they throw out their long foot, several times the length of the shell, until scarce a fraction remains inside, and thus toss themselves about with a great display of muscular vigour. *Nuculae*, with the mother-of-pearl lining and beautiful comb hinges, are numerous and of fine proportions from the bag full of mud here; while *Corbula*, with its unequal-valved shell, and delicate pink-tinted species, are jostling one another in the mass over there. None are too small to have enemies, and some of these little spiral rascals with the rasp tongues have perforated the shells of many, of all kinds, with a neat, well-drilled hole, through which the occupant is reached.

Here, too, come a lot of stupid fellows, dull, slimy, and sluggish, without a redeeming feature apparently. Chuck them into that basin of water and leave them for a time; ay! even those little dusky quarter-inch and eighth-inch slugs, with the rough flat foot on one side of the body. By-and-by, first one and then another of the creatures throws out a beautiful branching set of tentacles; here rich purple, there rich crimson of feathery form and most delicate consistency. You thought to deceive us into tossing you back into the loch, did you! and declined to display your finery until you thought you had escaped. Well, you are indeed dainty slugs, and we expend an infinitude of the patience of our host in our endeavours to transfer you in a proper ostentatious mood to the lovely spirit land, where you now look like peripatetic sea-anemones in full flower.

Loch Etive has actually smiled upon us, and enabled us to probe its secrets peacefully then, you ask. Of course—at least it blew a little, you know, and—you need not tell anybody that the net we sunk with the dredge rope attached to it as a buoy, has heard of Manitoba and the North-West and gone in for emigration! Perhaps we will be able to tell you in our next if there are any fish in Etive, like the farmer from our side who set his herring-net opposite Achnacree and found it a day or two after at Island Ferry. "No herring in the loch," was the sententious remark; "my net has swept the whole of it and did not get a fish!" Loch Etive, you see, is of a lively turn, and its terrific currents have their own ideas as to where a net should be cast!

There has been an exceptionally rich show of marine worms of late on the foreshores, and only those who have the courage to inquire into this peculiar class of life can have any idea of the beauty to which it can attain. Turning up a large stone at low water, we came upon a wriggling mass of iridescence, blue and green struggling for the mastery in the display, and the play of colour of the opal glancing along its shimmering rings, *Polynoe viridis*. Each side showed a row of what could only be termed bangles, resembling nothing so much as the glancing plates so freely employed in a pantomime; and the whole squirming mass would naturally have been taken for a colony of beautifully-coloured marine creatures of an elongate form. A point of a stick inserted into the mass finds a place of support for a portion of the creature, and as we lift it up the extraordinary colony gradually develops before our eyes into one single worm upwards of four feet in length. But it has been slightly injured from bearing its whole weight on one part of its slippery body, and when placed in a tumbler in order to display its wonders, the water at once becomes dyed a rich dark-green from the "blood" of the wounded creature. Three or four waters are in turn dyed in a similar manner, without at all destroying the rich appearance of the body of the worm. Such a quantity of colouring matter from one slight annelid seemed extraordinary, and we could only wonder at the æsthetic development of this low class life, if this exquisite creature has been evolved out of the admiration of its progenitors for heavenly colours and spangled forms! There are few more interesting classes of marine life than the worms with their many novel tubes; and one of the commonest of these tubes, made of beautifully cemented silicious sand, is lying in quantities on the sandy foreshores, so tenacious are they, although their constructors and late occupiers are no longer there to care for them.

A correspondent at Ness, in the Lews, sends us an interesting account of a number of stranded herring of small size, found upwards of 300 yards from the sea, during recent stormy weather, near the Butt of Lewis. These fish have been caught up in a sort of whirlwind and carried inland, as so frequently happens in tropical regions, but why the youngsters were so near the surface in such weather is the question. We have heard of a similar fall in Sutherland being taken for a thunderbolt, and no one daring to go near the spot for some days, until one bolder than the rest discovered the unfortunate waifs. During our recent visit to the Black Island we obtained both a young haddock and a diminutive whiting, of sizes rarely procured, about two inches, that had been flung up on the rocks high and dry, no doubt during the previous very stormy weather.

We have had a very striking onslaught of measles in Benderloch, so peculiar as to be worthy of note. On the Saturday, the pupils of Ledaig school were all present without a case of the disease apparent among them, while by Monday the children of 30 families were laid up. The attack was so sudden and so general as to appear to be almost atmospheric, just as the blight falls on the potato under certain climatic conditions. No doubt the disease has been in the surrounding districts for some time, but it is not supposed to be a class of disease whose germs can be conveyed except by contact.

APRIL, 1883.

When at the Black Island three weeks ago, our companion fired at a raven that was nesting on the usual raven's cliff. On finding itself an object of undue interest, the female set off with the utmost speed for her companion, and shortly afterwards made her appearance with her indignant lord. The result of his indiscreet valour was a rapid descent with a broken wing, after a most gallant struggle in mid air with his manifest destiny. He proved to be a noble specimen, with his glorious blue-black uniform and intelligent bearing, and we felt exceedingly sorry that his habits were really so extremely repugnant to our modern ultra humanitarianism that we could not plead for his life. We did not know in time that the female was sitting on eggs, else we should have made an effort to descend the cliff; so no doubt she will succeed in introducing her young family into an unsympathetic world. It is only three years since the same nest was turned into a tomb, the mother and family having been shot upon the top of it, and their bones left to bleach where they died. The following year no nest was built by any of these birds on the island, but now they have returned to this particular corner, which appeals to their intelligence or instinct (?) as more especially suited for them. Now that the male has been destroyed and removed, we do not doubt that after the manner of their kind the female will obtain another mate directly and without loss of time. This is another fact that to our mind is quite unaccountable! A place becomes noted as a resort of a particular pair of birds, and these birds are captured or destroyed; by another season at the furthest, another pair of the same species of birds has come and taken the vacant stance, just as a young medical in a busy town would pounce upon the dwelling of a removing or departing successful practitioner. Do they look upon the vicinity as supplying a constituency, and hasten to keep up the necessary calls? "Howsoe'er these things may be," they never permit a favourable position to remain long vacant. Then, let any one of a pair be shot, and within a few days it is supplied with a mate. Neither ravens nor peregrine falcons are plentiful birds now-a-days, and, indeed, we should call both very scarce in most places, and yet neither seem to have the least difficulty in obtaining a comrade and replacing a departed mate. Whence do they come, and where do they put up in the meantime? Perhaps some correspondent can suggest where there may be an "Ornithological Matrimonial Arrangement Agency," where sudden bereavement is promptly and suitably solaced.

These birds have got well on with their domestic arrangements, and are now sitting very closely. During the severe weather recently, when snow was but a prelude to bitterly cold winds, the rooks set about gathering moss with great energy, in order to line their nests and fill the crevices between the very open stick framework. This showed an intelligent appreciation of the increased necessity for comfortable quarters, and a series of severe springs might end in a marked improvement in the dwellings of this sapient bird. It was quite pathetic to look out upon the nests close to the windows of our friend's house, and note the male birds bring food to the sitting hens, and feed them so considerately. We observed the mouth of one lady open sympathetically, while she turned to her husband, as if she anticipated a similar attention to that bestowed on his dame by the gallant bird before us.

In complete antagonism to the above picture of Arcadian bliss is the story told us by the many-wintered keeper respecting the rook's congener, the jay. That it is a rapacious rascal we are well aware, and we are open to convict it of any reasonable atrocity; yet, but for the reliable source from whence it comes, we should view the tale with suspicion, as the result of a misunderstanding. A jay had built its nest in a low tree by a stream, and had deposited eggs therein, so the keeper determined upon shooting the old bird or birds upon the nest, and lay in wait accordingly. What was his amazement to see a jay make its appearance near the nest, and then coolly thrust its beak into each egg in succession and suck it dry! Whether it had discovered that its nest was watched, and so destroyed it; or whether it was a stranger bird simply exercising its prerogative of living upon bird's eggs, regardless of that embryonic or degenerate honesty, "honour among thieves," we could not learn. "Corbies will no' pike oot corbies' een," but their jay-plumaged relatives apparently have to answer a serious charge of devouring their own embryo families or those of their immediate connections.

The difficulty of discovering a duck's nest is proverbial, and the reason is that the bird always covers up the eggs before it leaves them, unless forced to do so in a desperate hurry. Strange to say, tame ducks retain this peculiarity, and will always throw straw or grass over their eggs after laying, if they have opportunity. But it is certain that our ducks are not far removed from the wild state, whereas our fowls are of Eastern origin and of an ancient civilisation: for the most part, they have forgotten this little trick, if they ever employed it.

Long ere we reach our destined goal at low water, the tangle fronds have emerged from the water, showing by the deep, rich fringe to the tide that the water is receding rapidly and far; while further along on the sandy stretch the *Zostera marina* is exposed for 20 yards, with its inhabitants. These, however, are few, except several fine specimens of the *Trochus magus*, or large whorled trochus, whose shell when exposed loses the common-looking outer coating, and appears resplendent in opalescent mother-of-pearl underskirt. The butterfish *(Gunnellus)* are many, and in most cases they encircle their ova, fast approaching maturity. Of late we have noted more especially that the spawn of this fish is scarcely ever found apart from the parent fish, which refuses to leave it. In two cases this week we picked up from them their masses of eyed ova, and placed them in a dish. The sun was warm, and the eggs were not long exposed to the heat ere they all commenced to wriggle into life, so that ere we had proceeded far the dish was alive with little gelatinous, huge-eyed fellows from both swarms; while before we reached home not half-a-dozen eggs remained out of the two lumps of spawn. Only two or three were nonfertilised or dead. This seemed the more remarkable to us, as the deposits were apparently of very different ages; at least, the one lot had separated widely apart, as the eggs gradually do before incubating, while the other had not apparently made any advance towards seeking greater elbow-room. There seems little question that warmth has a remarkable effect in facilitating the incubation of the ova of seafishes. The quaint cases of the dogfish are twined among the seaware along this boulder-clad spit of beach, and we note that several of them have already been penetrated and the contents devoured. The holes were neatly punctured, as we had previously observed in the case of the similarly-constituted tough skate eggs. Splashing across to the exposed boulders further seaward, we set down our various receptacles and look around. Our eyes are for a time distracted by here a rock oyster under the shadow of a stone, there one dragged from the farther deep by the tangle fronds that are clinging to it by their roots—now there is a big fellow skulking under the black ware, lying so flat that it looks like a splash of lime, while on turning over this heavy stone another is discovered firmly attached to the bottom thereof. Whew! you are too late, my friend, so you can wait till we return from this rich crimson object over here. The crimson object proves to be a mass of beautiful ova, presumably of the "lump sucker," or cock and hen paidle.

So we return to our chance acquaintance of a minute since, who has stuck his nose between two stones and remains otherwise uncovered, with the sunlight gleaming upon the rich bluish greys of the young conger's skin. This is the second we have met to-day about a foot in length, so we slip him into our bag, and on arrival at home foolishly toss him into a bucket full of razor-fish, *(Solen Siliqua)*. Scarcely had we turned our backs when the inevitable quack! quack! told of enemies nigh at hand, and we rush back only to find that the whole young conger had already passed down the gullet of one of the ducks. How it got on there, and how the host managed to arrange for the stranger, we cannot imagine.

Not a nest yet visible, we say. But we hear of a wren building in one corner, a sparrow carrying material in another, while all the woodland rings with melody this fine evening after the storm of these later days. On Wednesday week we drove up the glen on as fine a day as could be anticipated in the merry month of May, with nothing but the backward state of vegetation to speak of spring. The air was mild, the sun warm, the landscape bright and beaming, and we felt, like lotus-eaters, solely bent upon enjoying existence. This was followed next day by a sharp wind, and by the end of the week we had fresh snow down to the foot of the mountains, with a severe thunderstorm and howling hailstorms on the 14th, and violent gales all this week. The birds were so taken aback that they once more packed as if for winter, and seemed to have made up their minds to give up all "galavanting." To-day what a change! Have the pairs gone back to the same mates, we wonder, or have they taken advantage of the little interlude to reconsider the subject and exercise anew their right of selection! On the whole, we are inclined to believe in the steadfast character of a bird's affection so long as the same mate is procurable, although no doubt the most of them are readily reconciled to the inevitable.

MAY, 1883.

Our pen naturally indites the familiar name, although at present at a considerable distance from the familiar scenery. London beds are gay with many-coloured tulips, and the orchards of Merry England are rich with their heavy show of blossom; and yet on the whole the vegetation of Kent and Middlesex or Hereford and Gloucester is not further forward than that of Benderloch a fortnight ago. So we shrug our shoulders as we travel on the 9th of May through the richer counties of England to find ourselves in one of the combs running from the Cotswold, with a bitter chill in the air and a Scotch mist, followed by an English drizzle, and succeeded by a cosmopolitan rainfall, reminding us of the comparatively balmy Western Highlands.

We sit and look out on the land of flint chips, Roman remains, and modern manufactures, and wonder if the rest of those foxes have been captured in our isolated homeland. Our friend's lambs have been disappearing mysteriously, and three of reynard's cubs have paid the penalty, while the "old folks from home" have been waited for patiently. They have many foxes on the Muckairn side, and perhaps a score have been slain there in a year by one keeper, but with us they turn up rarely, and receive due attention on their arrival.

"Oh! foxes. We have lots of them here in this hunting country," says our host. There was a cow in that paddock with the high wall on the top, and one day the hounds in pursuit of the fox forced it to make for the wall through the field. No doubt the animal would have got over the wall had it had time, but the cow joined in the pursuit, and tossed the fox right over the wall on her horns. This strange incident was repeated some time afterwards, the cow a second time throwing the jaded fox over the wall, having evidently entered with the greatest excitement into the attack. "Was it not an effort to save the fox?" we ask; but are assured that the foxes are so numerous about, and the onslaughts made by them so serious, that the cow was quite in earnest in its enmity.

"Paid for!" says a voice, as the little dog sits patiently waiting for the expected word, with the lump of sugar on its nose. So long as it is placed there with the assurance that it is wholly "on trust," the little fellow will quietly await its release from the moral restraint thus imposed; but the moment the magic words "paid for" are repeated, that instant the poor fellow claims his due. You are no doubt of opinion that he merely knows the words mean "you are free to go ahead," and is afraid of getting no more unless he awaits them, and that an animal, after all, can really be taught no moral lesson. The tiger-barred cat with the white breast knows a great deal better, as she sits quietly with nothing but a wriggle of her sympathetic tail, on the fender stool. For that is the wonderful pussy that killed the chicken from the brood brought out in the yard. She was caught in the act, brought before the resident authority, and by alternately slowly showing her the result of her great impudence and thereafter applying the cane, she was brought to a thorough appreciation of the nature of her crime, and the heinous character thereof. "No more kill the chicken" will be the verdict, no doubt, as pussy has had her lesson, you say. Quite a mistake, however; she has learned a great deal more than this, for she soon returned with another chicken *alive in her mouth* from a distant quarter, not only returning it to the yard, but taking it to the very hen from which the other was removed.

It is seldom we see a lobster in the seas around us, and yet they must be by no means scarce in some quarters, more especially on the rocky Kingairloch coast. A friend informs us they are like many animals of terrestrial habit in their fondness for certain corners; just as a bird will keep year after year to the same nesting place, and if it is killed another takes its place—in all probability that having been the cradle of the newcomer. Again, every sportsman knows that year after year he may kill his bird or his hare about the same corner, and so it is with lobsters. Our informant assures us he has taken a lobster of large size at low spring tide year after year from the same snug rocky cleft; and this either means that the place appeals to the home instinct of the lobster kind, who will not permit it to remain unoccupied, or else that some of the progeny of the former occupants are about, waiting to slip into the home of their infancy. At anyrate, there must be a considerable number of these crustacea about the neighbouring waters, and our *alter ego* writes us that a goodly specimen of the cod kind brought news of a lobster-inhabited neighbourhood last week. For upon inquiring at the well-filled fish he was found to be as garrulous as Tennyson's Oak, and not only explained what he delighted to subsist upon, but displayed three fine specimens of the lobster kind that he had carefully sampled. Although the aggregate size was considerable, they were yet individually under the regulation dimensions; and as it was very necessary to make a severe example of those contravening the Act, it was relegated to the pot. Now, what can a fish preserver, interested in Acts of Parliament, do with incorrigible miscreants, without a regulation guage, that takes three lobsters at a gulp? This question lies at the bottom of all our fish legislation. We want many classes of fish that prey upon one another, and we have no definite notions of how we are to regulate their mutual interchange of incivilities. The simplest, most direct, and most intelligible mode of keeping up the supply of many comparatively antagonistic species, is to incubate them in quantities, and turn their fry into the sea in suitable quarters, either confined or free, as appears best. We have no doubt that in this way lochs deserted by the herring of recent years could be re-stocked, and many comparatively barren stretches of sea bottom be supplied with suitable varieties of fishes; but in such areas of water living *food* must be bred as well as fish.

In the court of our relative's farm-yard there is a trough supplied with water by means of a tap, requiring several revolutions to turn on the supply. It was found that the tap was being regularly turned and the yard overflowed with water. On watching the evil-doer, it turned out to be one of the horses that with its mouth turned the tap until the water flowed, as it thereby obtained a fresh supply, all horses being extremely particular as to the purity of the water they drink. This, to our imagining, was a highly intelligent horse; but we are assured its neighbour is far ahead of it, for not only does it regularly turn the tap and drink, but, when satisfied, *it turns the tap back again and shuts off the supply.* We are assured the household, in hiding, have witnessed this performance a considerable number of times!

We were sitting in a comfortable apartment lately, after luncheon, talking over the intelligence of jackdaws, two of which, belonging to our host, were in the habit of teasing a sickly pigeon that owed its weakness greatly to their satanic attention. Whether the idea originated directly and was then arranged between the two darkies, or whether it gradually dawned upon them from dragging each a wing of the persecuted bird, is not known; but they suddenly started off into the air with the pigeon, each supporting a wing and carrying the terrified bird into the empyrean, returning with it in safety, however, to the garden.

The door opens, and in bounces a beautiful dog. "Shut the door, sir!" and at once the door is closed. He can and does carry messages to and from stable or gardeners, and a spaniel is jealous of his responsibility and the confidence reposed in him. So it too is despatched with a note to the stable. It returns very rapidly with a piece torn off the paper—the usual voucher from the recipient; but such promptitude arouses suspicion. The letter is found to be undelivered, and the discovery is made that this sharp youngster, thinking the object was to obtain the piece of paper back, had really taken the letter just out of sight, *torn a piece off of the customary size,* and returned therewith! "Oh! that is nothing to what the large dog did the other day," when— But, really, although our informants are quite serious and most thoroughly reliable, we have just caught an incredulous smile creeping over the cheek of our reader; so we can only assure him that, although we have not seen what we state as having occurred, we cannot do other than believe it!

What a change the last month has made over the face of the country, and how much our relative position has changed during that time! Whereas five weeks ago we were really further advanced than they were in the South of England, to-day we are much behind in many departments of vegetation, although our braird is as vigorous as any. Three weeks ago the apple orchards of England were heavy with bloom; to-day the apple trees of our locality are only now at their best. The heavily-freighted standards under the shadow of the scaur are very dainty, but just see those three old veterans in the schoolhouse garden! In one the mass of pink and white bloom entirely conceals the wood and leaves, and Millais would have despaired of depicting one tithe of the brilliant bunches of blossom.

Still the craik or landrail must feel itself like a precocious genius creking before its time in a backward world; and as its harsh voice reaches us now from the more vigorous undergrowth of a young plantation, now from the longer grass of a protected bank, we feel inclined to stroll over and mention casually that we consider such precocity to be youthful folly unable to read the signs of the times. Why should you come before the vegetation is ready to hide you, as your gentle eye glints over the top of the braird above which you are peering on tiptoe? You little fool, keep to the heavily-clad ditches or the luscious south, and don't announce your unmelodious message until the world is ready to receive you and it!

We noted the destruction of a litter of cubs that had been discovered under the neighbouring scaur, after a large number of lambs had been found dead. The attempt to secure the parents did not prove successful, as the weather was bitterly cold, and those lying in wait did not keep to the highest point of the scaur. So the fox, as is customary with this wise animal, sought the point of vantage in order to scan the vicinity, and, peeping over, discovered its adversaries in time to make good its retreat. But what exercises the minds of those interested is, the *tails* of the lambs killed were alone taken to the young cubs, so far as could be seen. This is looked upon as an endeavour to provide playthings for the youngsters—for the young of foxes, dogs, and cats all play with the tails of themselves or their parents; and the supply of extraneous appendages are supposed to have been provided by the knowing Reynards for the purpose of withdrawing the youngsters' attention from their own brushes, or else amusing them when the old folks were from home.

JUNE, 1883.

Everything tending towards fruiting; and there is a row of stately cabbages running to seed! "Come and see this peculiar growth on the cabbage," we call to the partner of our wanderings, who loveth "all things, both great and small." Down the row until we come to one of the larger growths, and, looking down upon a knot on the stem apparently, there meets our gaze two upturned bills, with the mandibles stretched to the uttermost, as the little wretches rise on tiptoe full of the great expectations of hopeful ignorance. A chaffinch's nest upon a cabbage! Surely a most unusual occurrence. We do not credit them with sufficient intelligence to suppose that, when they saw these cabbages flowering, they anticipated their being left for seed, and can only conclude that they saw a snuggery apparently suitable and entered into possession. If success is to be the sole test of intelligence, we must give these birds the credit for wisdom; under ordinary circumstances, however, we would have considered them a pair of little fools! The constructive and secretive power of the chaffinch is yet so marked that we must acknowledge their superior abundance to be partly due to their superior dexterity in the breeding season.

We watch their progress down the rough piece of grazing ground with interest, the question "fun or earnest" formulating itself as they proceed. A young dog and a pig of the same size as itself. The dog is clearly in fun —its tail twirling, and its antics unmistakable. Verbal speech may be given to conceal our thoughts, but such natural language is not to be misunderstood. The pig is clearly more amused than annoyed, and soon enters fully into the spirit of the puppy, and with its tail twirling and its stiff little carcase attempting similar evolutions, the game is kept up between them. All this time the dog does not lose sight of the fact that he is driving this particular pig and its companions off the ground; while the pig equally understands this fact, but is determined to enjoy a romp on the way. Who that watches domesticated animals but must acknowledge to a far greater amount of sympathy between opposing species than is conceivable under natural conditions. Remove the bitterness and keenness of the struggle for food, and the hereditary feelings thereby generated, and all animals above the lowest display these touches of nature that show their physical kinship and their mental inter-sympathy.

A little pond on the slope of the hill suitable for a small fish-pond. So it is cleaned out, frogs in multitudes are removed, and the bottom thoroughly purified, and all prepared for the reception of the lately hatched youngsters. The umbilical sac is scarcely absorbed ere the pond begins to fill with fresh water algae, notwithstanding a constant run. The warders now have to remove vigorous young eels with a "penchant" for still younger trout; water newts in numbers have to be removed; and the deadly water beetles are still upon the ground. It is curious to note how rapidly these various foes of the fishculturist make their appearance in a carefully constructed reservoir, and how much life a little dribbling rill from the hillside can supply when a suitable store of nourishment entices it. Indeed, the first practical result of any effort to increase the supply of man's food is to instil into a multitude of wild creatures the belief in such supply being specially provided for them. It is both cruel and troublesome to disillusionise them; have mankind not frequently entertained similar peculiar fancies as to Providential provision?

Life is now rampant this "merry month of June," and as the weather is mild and the ground well moistened with genial showers, everything animate is revelling in the unaccustomed combination of plenteous warmth, and yet sufficiency of moisture. We are strolling along enjoying to the full the splendour of our woodland vegetation, when our attention is called to an object dangling in the air about a yard above the grass. At first it looks like a head of dried grass hanging on a gossamer thread, but we have seen similar gymnastics performed before by a caterpillar too frequently to be misled, and so we seek by tickling the little fellow to get him to wind himself up again, a very ingenious performance that we used to enjoy observing. But this one is determined to go down, and refuses to climb, and we petulantly sweep the long grass we are using across this rope, tossing the grass from us when we have done so. Cruelty, you will say, to destroy his rope ladder, and cast him friendless among the long grass! Wait a bit! Not only does he not come to grief, but, to our surprise, the slender gossamer line carries grass stem and caterpillar both, rudely as the former was added to its burden. The tenacity of this line, that is scarcely perceptible unless the light falls upon it in a certain direction, must be great, and the caterpillar must have prepared it against emergencies, when an additional weight, quite equal to the creature itself, driven violently against it, and hanging on to it, fails to destroy it. We left the double burden dangling and swinging in the breeze, the caterpillar still seeking to reach the grass by a steady descent.

Those fellows are making a most unconscionable row, and we always start them about the same place on the knoll. It is clear they must have a nest about, although by this time it is late for eggs. Thus we reason; and partly stimulated by pride as a nester, partly stirred to it by their continual iteration, we beat the ground steadily without result. We find what we would consider the empty cavity that had formed the simple nest of the birds, but they go on piping as vigorously as if we had robbed them of their treasure. Amused at their pertinacity, we follow them as they mislead us further and further, until a little knoll intervenes, when, leaving one to pipe and shout at us, the other drops quietly from the hilly point seawards, and with the peculiar sand-pipery flutter skims off in a wide circle to the old spot. We hurriedly mark it down, and again go over the ground without success—when!—the piping gets more tremulous and uncertain, halts altogether, and there we have the secret. Still as a mouse, and not unlike one as it squats on the rocky moor, nor making the slightest motion as we place our hand upon it; but the young piper has obeyed its parent's orders, and trusted to its moorland hue and diminutive size. A beautiful creature, as the young of all the class are always, with its light coloured breast and dark brown line down the back, the down rich and feathery, the eye bright, and the whole trim little figure most engaging. We lay it down on the grass field within reach of the parents' excited piping, and watch it as it hurries off with the nervous, dodgy-stagger of the genus.

A little further over on the hill are the nests of a rock pipit—our shore-frequenting lark—and a titlark. Both are representative nests, just where those birds are always in the habit of building. The pipit, on a rocky point over the shore, has coiled the dry grass in a knowing nook; while the titlark has chosen a little hole on a bankside on the summit of the point. The eggs of both birds are rich dark brown, and aid in effecting concealment on the moor. Whiff! Out goes from the very edge of the cliff, where a little heather and dried grass form a projecting eve, a little lintie, and we know that this is also a favourite nesting-place of the twite. The concealment of the nest is perfect, and we would scarcely have discovered it had we not caught sight of half a dozen delicately-speckled bluish-white eggs. Had the eggs been brown, like the others, we should scarcely have noticed the whereabouts of the nest. We are acquainted with no more dexterously-concealed nest than that of this little linnet; and it has been almost always through accident that we have found it. But why should the eggs be coloured as they are?

Scratching itself? No, it is too steadily persistent and exact in its movements. What is the little fellow about? He has on the muzzle with a row of iron spikes, so frequently placed on Highland calves to prevent them sucking their mothers. But this effort of man's is very often a vain one—a Highland cow's skin being tough, and a calf's ingenuity wonderful. We have even heard of cows that lay down and rolled over, so that the youngsters could obtain a drink without progging it. The muzzle is carried back and tied round the neck with a small rope in this case, and the calf has discovered a fallen tree with the stump of a small branch standing up at right angles. This it is endeavouring to insert between the cord and its neck, so as to tear the latter off, and during our somewhat lengthened observation of the fuzzy fellow it did not vary in its consistent and intelligent endeavour to release itself of the muzzle. It clearly understood that the neck cord, and not those about its head, was the main difficulty to be overcome; and, having found this suitable projecting stump, it would no doubt keep steadily at it until the cord gave way. We were much struck with the intelligence displayed in going direct to the heart of its grievance, and never wavering in its confidence in its own perspicuity. It is very difficult, indeed, to circumvent a Highland cow and calf.

We have come to look upon Meteorology so much as a matter of barometric and thermometric readings, that it is quite refreshing to come upon a more liberal rendering of the term. Thus we muttered to ourselves as we turned over the little eight-page pamphlet within whose modest bounds the Archæological and Physical Society of Bute has published the interesting observations of Mr. James Kay on the natural phenomena and seasonal changes noted by him at Rothesay. The importance of the booklet is infinitely beyond its unpretending appearance, and if every district in the country were to provide itself with an equally careful and intelligent observer, and an equally cheap and sensible abstract of observations, we should soon be in possession of a series of recorded notes on natural subjects within the reach of moderate purses and prepared for ready comparison. Not only have we wind and rainfall, thunder, auroras, halos, and rainbows, but the return of the seasons is indicated in the most interesting way by the date of flowering and leafing of trees and shrubs, and progress of vegetation generally; and the date of arrival of certain birds of passage. It is curious to note that the corncraik has only varied over seven years from the 4th May to the 15th; while the swallow has varied in its arrival from 14th April to 8th May, and the cuckoo from 22d April to 3d May. The corncraik and cuckoo thus varied in their arrival eleven days, while the less certain swallow varied twenty-four days. One can scarcely fancy a more useful work than this in connection with our latest and least advanced science, and a series from properly selected centres throughout the country would be invaluable to the student of more than one branch of natural phenomena.

If white-coloured petals are an evidence of retrogression and a sign of "dissipated energy," there are an exceptional number of such decking the country at present. One hillside is beautifully shaded by means of the white masses of May thorn, more than sprinkling the green foliage of the copsewood; the white clover is especially abundant. The rowan tree blossom has been also most luxuriant, and we are having a foretaste of that coming world of colourless blossoms we are threatened with. Will your eyes by that time be so cultivated as to distinguish such a multitude of gradations in the whites that the refinement of shades will quite compensate for the loss of the ruder and more primitive hues? It is scarcely possible to imagine an ugly natural world—the Black Country is not Nature's making as it is—or one from which a cultured eye could not draw nourishment for its artistic colour-sense.

It is most aggravating! There is shouting and wailing in front and behind, for the fine array of ducklings have been sadly weeded out. Every day finds a victim, and perhaps two, and the drove that lately followed their hen mothers has got "small by degrees, and beautifully less." At least one of them was seen to disappear in the maw of a heron that is a steady visitor to the stream in front; but the bulk of them have been pounced upon when in the upper course of the stream by one or other of a pair of blackbacked gulls. The hens on these occasions seem rather pleased than otherwise, and make no effort to beat off the marauders, but cluck the remainder together and drive them home before them, the little fellows getting a tremendous scare that lasts for an hour or two only. Hens fight so desperately for their chickens, and a gull is such a cowardly brute, that we could not account for the foster mother's calm acceptance of the situation, unless they were so aggravated at the determined partiality of the youngsters for the water, that they resolved to let them "take it." We do not believe a wild duck would have lost a bird under such circumstances, for we have seen a mother and fifteen youngsters frequent the bay in front, undiminished in numbers until all were quite large.

It was a superlatively fine day as we tumbled into our boat and prepared for a holiday to the Eilean Dhu—a day that comes once in a twelvemonth, with the tide just right and the sea peacefully calm, and only a whiff in our favour to cool the rowers and calm the exuberant spirits of the excited youngsters; for the boat is well filled with "a mixed lot" as to size, and an equally "mixed lot" as to provender.

It ought to be too late for the bird world, as we have delayed our visit too long; but the season all round is backward, and we are hopeful of showing to the rising generation at least a rising generation of seafowl if nothing else. In spite of the lesson they received during the gales and high tides, the sandmartens are busy on the sandbank at Shian, where they have perforated it afresh with their burrows, to take the place of those flung ruthlessly into the sea. A ring plover crosses with its sharp cry, and some one suggests a nest on the gravel spit. Far too late in the year we assert positively, as we have taken their nests in April: but our boatman has a nest with young birds, and another with eggs, close beside our home, so Sir Oracle is obliged to subside on this occasion. The late spring has thrown everything behind, and anything in the way of incubation is still possible. Three porpoises are disporting in our own loch ere we leave it, and as they have been there for some few weeks must be finding fish of some sort. Sea trout have been leaping occasionally of late, but very few on the whole, and they must be up at the head of the loch lying near the mouth of the rivers, which have been too low to admit of their ascent. A shoal of small fish dashed past our keel the other evening, which appeared to be the larger species of sand eels (*Ammodytes*); and skate are still falling to the spear as they come shoreward to spawn. A few razor-bills are swimming in Loch Linnhe, having evidently finished their labours of incubation, as we know no place in the neighbourhood where they breed.

What a shout! and wild with excitement the boys almost tumble headlong into the sea in their efforts to be first to play Robinson Crusoe on this desert isle, with the wild goats on the edge of the cliffs and the sea birds screaming at the invaders. What a disenchantment when an old she goat actually came up to inquire the meaning of the frantic rush at her kid by a youngster that had succeeded by superhuman exertions in getting hold of its tail. Alas for Robinson Crusoe, the pursuit of wild goats has to be exchanged for a butterfly net. We scramble round the shore to find the nests of the gulls mostly inhabited by a rotten egg, or a bundle of animated fluff. "Bring me a young gull" is the last request we heard ere our boat left the shore, and here are several of the little fellows, still as death, lying in crevices of the rock, which here is all on end in thin laminous strata. A halt is called again and again as we passed a gravel bank or rocky promontory. Look carefully. There are three little fuzzy balls among the stones. At last the eye rests upon them, and as the owner's hand follows his sight, and seeks to secure one of the little fellows, the creature sets off at a hard stagger. These are young oyster catchers, and are not unlike the young of the plover genus. Another companion calls to us as he stands at the edge of the gravel with a droll smile on his face. Beneath him three dead (!) gulls are lying, one in the nest just out of the egg, the other two having tumbled out of the nest into odd corners where their hue admirably aids in hiding them. Crossing another gravel strand we laugh outright at the spectacle presented. Two young gulls on the rampage had heard our advancing steps, and there they were some yards apart, with their heads thrust into hollows in the gravel, imagining themselves, or hoping that they were, concealed. Stupid wretches, you mutter! but how about the fact that they very nearly succeeded in eluding our sight, although they are but a day or two old, while you and I have played at hiding in a still more imbecile way at as many years of age. A child at a few years is like a young bird, and fancies that perfect stillness—freedom from movement and sound—is the main element in concealment; and both are right, as nothing catches the eye like the smallest movement, while a large dull immovable object will escape our observation.

Not a merganser, not a sheldrake to be seen; what is the meaning of this? First one egg, then another, then a group of eggs, followed by group after group all sucked empty as we proceed around the islet. What can be the cause of this? The grey crows have steadily robbed every nest of sheldrake, sawbill duck, and wild duck in the island, and these seem to have taken their departure in disgust. We regret this result sincerely, as these are about the only haunts of the sheldrake inside Mull that we know of, and this noble duck is becoming scarce. The grey crow's passion for eggs is excessive, and doubtless it is the only way it can obtain an easy and luxurious living at this time. We are surprised to see scarcely any terns about, as these birds claim a certain portion of the island as their nesting-place, and they should now be in full fling, seeing they succeed the gulls. We come upon one nest with eggs all cold, and begin to suspect that these rascally grey crows have driven away the dainty terns for fear of their nests being robbed like the ducks. We do not recollect of seeing anywhere such destruction of eggs, and two pair of crows are flying overhead to account for it.

First one skeleton, then a second and a third picked clean, tell of the presence of the peregrine in the isle, although we have only seen a kestrel dash away from the face of the cliff. On examination we find that the Blue Hawk has actually been living upon Razorbills for some time back, as at least half-a-dozen of these birds have been eaten by them. We did not think in the first place that a peregrine could readily capture a "dooker," nor in the second that he would condescend, except in extremity, to eat such fishy birds.

They are gathering round the potato pot, and all telling at once of the wonders they have seen. We don't recollect getting a butterfly in the island, but moths are plentiful and elegant. The large clouded buff with its beautiful marking and brilliant edging goes dancing over the brackens; the six-spotted burnet in black and crimson is poised in conscious splendour on the curled heads of these still unexpanded fronds ; while the emerald moths, like gems from the mine, are resplendent for a moment in the sunshine, to sink and lose themselves the next among the verdure. What a wonderful fund of beautiful life is around us, and the youth wax eloquent over the beauty of spiders and the surpassing voracity of young black-backed gulls. No wonder our ducklings disappear in the maws of the parents.

In vain the human chickens are clucked together. At the last moment the two youngest have levanted after some treasure at the far end of the Isle. Where can they be? is our anxious question. As if there could be any question. We go straight to those young black-backed gulls, and sure enough excited voices and flushed faces, and a carefully tended handfull, tell of another pet added to the household; and two boys, oblivious of time and distance, tide, and coming darkness, and of all except the pulses of the summer and a vigorous nature filling their hurrying veins, wonder mightily at an anxiety they cannot understand, in face of an untrimmed world akin to their unbroken spirits.

INDEX.

Abnormal growths on beech, 136	Cannibals, ... 198
Acorns, ... 96	Caprelli, ... 50
Adamsia, pallatia, ... 135, 161	Capturing specimens, ... 184
Angler, ... 107	Carnival of Mollusca, ... 232
Annelids, ... 180, 181	Cats, ... 114
— and Caterpillars, ... 237	Cat and dog, ... 112
— and Hydractina, ... 206	Cat and chicken, ... 301
Ants, ... 208	Caterpillar, (Hanging) ... 209
Apiculture, ... 62	Cattle in sea, ... 211
Apple trees in blossom, ... 305	Cattle and oak branches, ... 137
Ascidians, ... 5, 51, 67, 68, 196	Chaffinch's nest in cabbage, 306
Atherina, Sandsmelts, 181, 182	Cheepuc, ... 120
Atmospheric effect, ... 269	Cirl Bunting, ... 274
Aurora borealis, ... 246	Cockles, ... 188
Autumn Tints, ... 224	Coletits, ... 98, 150, 172, 254
	Collie, ... 167
Barnacles, ... 2, 44, 91, 192	Comet, ... 247
Bats, ... 120	Conger (young), ... 299
Bees, ... 70, 127, 214	Connel Falls, ... 84
Beech leaves, ... 7	Corkwing, ... 200
Birds flocking, ... 273	Cormorant, ...121, 213
Birds and flowers, ... 219	Cottus, ... 40
Birds and oats, ... 48	Cow, ... 10-12, 252
Birch, ... 96	Cowrie, ... 43, 227
Blackcock, ... 122	Crab and sponges, ... 6
Blackbird, ... 171	Crab apples, ... 59
Black sheep, ... 207	Crab with ova, ... 104
Blackberries, ... 26	Craik,... 305
Blight on alder, ... 11	Cregan, ... 249
Blind adder, ... 208	Crowberries, ... 26
Blossom, ... 7	Crows and mussels, ... 255
Blue-rock pigeon, ... 213	Crustacea spawning,... ... 263
Blue-tit nest, ... 8	— as scavengers (small), 230
Brittle star, ... 42, 162	Cryptogerms,... 100, 116, 146, 160,
Buck in bulb house, ... 249	170, 244
Butterfly, ... 26, 66, 232	Cuckoo, ... 13, 16, 167
Bullfinches, ... 151, 279	Cuttlefish, ... 198

INDEX.

Dandelion-downs,	9
Deer,	63, 83, 202, 274
Destruction of shore-life,	123
Dog, intelligence of,	304
Dog and gooseberries,	36
Dog-roses,	61
Doirlinn (stranded in the)	286
Dookers and gulls,	212
Douglas pine,	80
Dragonfly in Glasgow,	204, 207
Dredge in Loch Etive,	244
Duck,	39, 138, 275
Duck drinking,	12
Duck's nest,	297
Eagle and kestrels,	20-22
Echinus,	191-276
Eel,	239
Emarginula crassa,	245
Encrinites,	142
Esnagara,	32
Etive Loch,	288
— mollusca,	291
— squall,	289
— no oysters,	290
Fieldfare,	274
Fields reverting,	272
Fish food,	303
Fish fry,	179
Fish-pond,	308
Fissurella Graeca,	218, 267, 275, 288
Fisheries,	82
Floating gravel,	217
Flowers, late,	85
Foliage,	74
Food of skate,	4
Fox,	300, 306
Foxglove,	49, 147
Frogs,	61
Gale,	73, 91, 116, 130, 263
Gnats,	112, 127
Gobies,	178
Goldencrest,	197
Golden plover,	38, 47
Gooseberry in blossom,	85
Gossamers,	234
Grasshoppers,	26, 214, 232
Grebes,	70
Grey crows,	105, 316
Green crustacea,	243
Greenfinch,	196
Growth of seaware,	236
Gulf stream,	110
Gulls,	23, 26, 28, 29, 211, 272, 313, 316, 318
Gunnellus,	72, 179, 214, 226, 284, 297 (See *Transactions of Natural History Society of Glasgow, 1885, on "Domestic Habits of Butter-fish").*
Haddock young,	293
Halo round moon,	84
Hare or rabbit,	164
Hawk and pigeon eggs,	216
Hay crop,	202
Helcion pellucida—lævis and parasite,	88, 235, 236
Hen in wood—cackling,	221
Heron and ducklings,	37
Herring,	81, 86, 104, 131, 212
— blown inland—Lewis,	293
Hermit crabs,	52, 104, 126
Hermit and *Fissurella Græca*,	161
Highland calf,	311
Highland farmers,	166
High tide,	228
Hinge of pecten,	238
Holothuriæ,	191, 246, 291
Horse,	128, 283, 303
Horse chestnuts,	7, 58
Horse beech,	18
Ice and seats,	103
Ice tablets,	155
Incubators-patens,	28
Individual intelligence,	222
Iris,	160
Isocardia cor.	262
Jackdaws,	47, 148, 304
Jay eating Jay's eggs,	296
Kay's Meteorology of Bute,	312
Kestrel,	37, 317
Killing sparrows,	65

INDEX. 321

Laburnum, ... 59
Lapwings, ... 47
Lima, ... 163
Liver, The 9
Lobsters, ... 302
Low tide, ... 141
Lumpsucker, and ova, 226, 284, 298

Mackerel, ... 212
Measles, ... 294
Medusae pulsations, ... 193
Medusa in fresh water, ... 184
Mergansers, ... 176
Meteor, ... 84
Midges, ... 203
Mirage, ... 64
Mosel thrush, ... 274
— and chaffinch, ... 176
Modiolaria, ... 43
Mollusc in woodcock skull, 174
Mollusca, gregarious, ... 133
Montague sucker fish, 237, 284, 286
Mosses, ... 149
Moths, ... 35, 48, 317
Mussel, ... 90, 130, 191
Mussel and oyster, ... 2
Murex erinaceus, ... 236
Mya truncata, ... 139, 181, 186
Mysis, ... 45, 86, 131, 180, 184

Nesting, ... 299
Northern diver, ... 107
Northern lights, ... 223
Norwegian lobster, ... 191
Nudibranchs, ... 5, 72, 125

Oban games, ... 59
October colouring, ... 78
Oysters, ... 2, 126, 156
Oyster-catchers, 27, 47, 98, 112, 271
Owl, ... 148

Painted eggs, ... 216
Palaemonidae, ... 242
Palmipes membranaceus, ...50, 134, 227, 276
Partridges, ... 214
Parasites, ... 5-6
— on crab, ... 46

Parsley fern, ... 30
Peacrabs and parasites, ... 277
Pectens, 56, 67, 133, 142, 162, 229, 240, 245, 262, 275, 290
Peregrine, .. 11, 23, 65, 213, 317
Pes-pelicamis, ... 135
Phalarope, red-necked, ... 98
Pheasants, ... 98, 123
Phosphorescence, ... 180, 234
Pinus nobilis, ... 115
Pipe-fish, ... 72, 185
Pig-swimming, ... 75
Plaice with fingers, ... 187
Polynoe viridis, ... 292
Pontobdella, ... 42
Porcelain crabs, ... 191
Porpoise, ... 94, 315
Potatoes, ... 8, 80
Puppy and pig, ... 307
Pycnogonum littorale, ... 144

Queen of Benderloch, ... 115

Rabbits, ... 106
Rats eating rat, ... 197
Rats and shell-fish 102
Ravens, ... 294
Razorbills, ... 315
Razor fish, ... 56
Redbreast, 151, 171, 175, 180, 209
Redwing, ... 119
Returns from cereals, ... 60
Rhizostoma, ... 52
Ringplover, ... 314
Rockling, ... 284
Rockpipit, ... 119-210
Roe-deer, ... 147
Rooks, 6, 47, 57, 74, 82, 114, 144, 154, 168, 193, 231, 296
Rough Hound—egg, ... 3
Rotche, ... 271

Saccharina frond, ... 187
Saithe, ... 105, 176
Salmonidæ, ... 205, 259
(*See paper on Salmonidæ at Sea in Appendix to 1886 Report of "Scotch Fishery Board," and*

INDEX.

Report of "Scotch Fisheries Improvement Association)."
Sandeels, ... 245, 315
Sand-martins, ... 105, 314
Sand-smelt, ... 5, 53
Sandpiper, ... 7, 8, 310
Sap in plants, ... 201
Scotch thistle, ... 63
Seals, ... 21, 176
Sea anemones, ... 57
Sea fish in fresh water, ... 184
Sea grub, ... 88
Seamouse, ... 51, 134
Sea-swallows nesting, ... 16, 26
Sea trout, ... 196, 212
Sea water and pasture, ... 186
Sea-weed, ... 85, 157
Serpent-mound, ... 128
Serpulæ, ... 155
Serpulæ on hill, ... 272
Sertularia, ... 190
Sheep in water, ... 137
Sheep, ... 163
Sheldrakes, ... 21
Silver fir, ... 97
Skate, 1, 3, 67, 108, 139, 160, 172, 182, 194, 255, 315
Skua—Richardson's, ... 10
Sloes, ... 223, 224
Smokes (The Three), ... 248
Social gathering, ... 264
Solen pellucida, ... 290
Sparrow's nest, ... 144
Spawn, ... 158, 159
Sphagnum—abnormal growth, 258
Sponge and hermit, ... 210
Spider, ... 217, 239, 240
Squirrels, ... 95, 159, 251, 281
— and young birds, 280
Squall Roussette, ... 154
Starfish food, ... 228
— and tapes, ... 140
Sticklebacks, ... 72
Stoat, ... 143
Storm, ... 278, 281
Stormy petrel, ... 94
Sucker fish, ... 179, 276, 277, 286
Suicide of animals, ... 265
Sunstar, ... 143

Swallows, ... 38
Tangle, ... 125
Terebratulæ, ... 190
Thatch, ... 77
Thunderstorm, ... 87
Tits, ... 175, 209
Titlark, ... 210
Top-knot, ... 40
(See Transactions of Natural History Society of Glasgow, 1884, paper on "The Top-knots."
Trout, enemies of, ... 208
— in winter, ... 250
— ... 31, 121
Trochus magus, ... 297
— zizyphinus, ... 124
Turkey and ducks, ... 215
Turkeys on wire fence, ... 241
Twite, ... 310
Vegetation, ... 118, 233, 263, 283
Velutina laevigata, ... 50
Venus casina, ... 192
Wagtails, ... 231
Weather prophets, ... 270
Weever fish (Trachissus draco), 203
Whale, ... 25
Wheatear, ... 160
Whilk, ... 125
— spawn, ... 86, 111
Whinchat, ... 274
White butterflies, ... 210
White flowers, ... 313
White horse, ... 71
White throat (Curruca cinerea), 25
— lesser, ... 24
Whiting, young, ... 293
Winter scene, ... 253
Wind on water, ... 69
Woodbine, ... 149, 201
Worms drowned out, ... 93
Wrass, ... 199
Wrens, ... 171, 209
Yellow flowers, ... 209
Yew berries, ... 75
Young flat-fish, ... 177
Young frogs, ... 18

Crown 8vo, cloth, 6s.

BENDERLOCH.

By W. ANDERSON SMITH.

Opinions of the Press.

"TIMES."—While Mr. Anderson Smith does not neglect the scenic aspects of Nature, he devotes most of his space to sympathetic pictures of the life that abounds on land and in sea. He is evidently a well-informed naturalist.

"MORNING POST."—The lovers of natural history will be charmed with this interesting book. Mr. Smith is equally entertaining and instructive.

"SATURDAY REVIEW."—There can be no manner of doubt that these "unpretending notes," as Mr. Smith modestly designates them, were well worth reprinting; and we should have lost much had they been left buried out of memory.

"THE FIELD."—The interest is continuous to the close. His style is lively, without any affectation of fine writing.

"THE ACADEMY."—We cannot fancy a book which would prove more useful and interesting to every poet-naturalist who uses his eyes and ears. "Benderloch" is, in many respects, a charming book.

"GRAPHIC."—Had Gilbert White lived beside Benderloch, he would have given us something very like Mr. Anderson Smith's "Notes from the Western Highlands."

"DAILY REVIEW."—The "Notes" will be read by few people by whom they will not be enjoyed.

"GLASGOW HERALD."—Almost every page shows how much a loving, patient, and intelligent searcher can find worth noting in the commonest natural phenomena, and how much interest can be thrown round such researches, or even the most casual observations, by the manner in which they are described.

"QUIZ."—I admire Mr. Smith's style; you seldom see such pure English in a daily paper.

"EDINBURGH COURANT."—The papers are very attractive.

"DUNDEE ADVERTISER."—Mr. Smith thoroughly understands his matter, and he writes so freshly that the work will be found a pleasant guide to the Fauna of the West Highlands.

"BRECHIN ADVERTISER."—Hundreds who never had the opportunity of reading them before will join in expressing to Mr. Smith their obligations for putting within their reach such a series of sketches, hardly excelled in interest by anything of the same kind known to us at the present time.

"OBAN TIMES."—There is all the grace and attractiveness of a racy and full style wedded to a fund of information.

Uniform with "Benderloch." Crown 8vo, cloth, price 6s.

LOCH CRERAN:
NOTES FROM THE WEST HIGHLANDS.
By W. ANDERSON SMITH,
Author of "Benderloch," "Lewsiana," etc.

Oblong Imperial 8vo.

"ACCORDING TO COCKER:"
THE PROGRESS OF PENMANSHIP FROM THE EARLIEST TIMES.

With 26 Illustrative Examples from "Penna Volans," and other old works on the subject.

By W. ANDERSON SMITH.

Crown 8vo, price 6d.

SEA-SIDE ECONOMY.

By W. ANDERSON SMITH,

Corresponding Member of Natural History and Geological Societies of Glasgow.

PRIZE ESSAYIST.

Norwich, 1881.—1. Pisciculture as a Source of National Wealth.
2. Oyster Culture.

Edinburgh, 1882.—1. Various Methods of Oyster Culture.
2. Oyster Culture in Scotland.
3. The Utilisation of Fish Offal.
4. The Fish Supply of Great Cities.
5. Various Means of Curing and Preserving Fish at home and abroad.

London, 1883.—1. Best appliances for breaking the force of the sea at the entrance to Harbours and elsewhere.
2. On Salmon Disease.

Highland and Agricultural Society.
1. Oyster Culture.
2. Marine Highland Industries.

"Sea-side Economy" should be read by all who go to the coast.

Second Edition. Crown 8vo, cloth, with Illustrations, price 2s. 6d.

LEWSIANA.

By W. ANDERSON SMITH.

GLOBE.—"Lewsiana" is a very clever book. Mr Smith understands well the feeling of those brought up by the sea-shore in the neighbourhood of wild moors and desolate mountains, and in some introductory verses renders the feeling with considerable pathos and grace. His descriptions of the people, with their mingled simplicity and shrewdness, are quite as good as his remarks on the country.

WORLD.—We are satisfied that Mr Anderson Smith is a veracious chronicler, who has taken great pains thoroughly to master his subject; who writes in a light, agreeable, and graphic style, and, to judge from the illustrations which accompany his letter-press, has the gift of pencil as well as pen.

SPECTATOR.—It is true that Mr Anderson Smith's papers in the *Glasgow Herald* had the precedence in point of time of Mr Black's novel . . . he has therefore done wisely to reprint them, with many others, in a separate volume, one which is really of considerable interest, bringing, as it does, most distinctly before us the lives of the inhabitants of these little-known islands, and grouping together graphically, yet succinctly, much information concerning their flora, their fauna, and their ancient history.

INVERNESS COURIER.—Mr Smith writes in the spirit of one who appreciates the humble virtues and understands the peculiarities of these isolated islanders. He does not come, like so many strangers, merely to wonder and smile. We can commend the book.

STIRLING JOURNAL.—The author is always ready to do justice to the many good qualities of his Hebrideans, whom he likes well; and he is enthusiastic in his praises of the good points in the wild scenery, which he is never tired of exploring. His off-hand sketches are quaint, graphic, vivid, instinct with qualities which could not exist apart from truthfulness.

www.ingramcontent.com/pod-product-compliance
Lightning Source LLC
Chambersburg PA
CBHW021207230426
43667CB00006B/590